Note for Librarians: a cataloguing record for this book that includes Dewey Decimal Classification and US Library of Congress numbers is available from the Library and Archives of Canada. The complete cataloguing record can be obtained from their online database at:

www.collectionscanada.ca/amicus/index-e.html

ISBN 1-4120-5270-x

Printed in Victoria, BC, Canada

TRAFFORD

Offices in Canada, USA, Ireland, UK and Spain

This book was published *on-demand* in cooperation with Trafford Publishing. On-demand publishing is a unique process and service of making a book available for retail sale to the public taking advantage of on-demand manufacturing and Internet marketing. On-demand publishing includes promotions, retail sales, manufacturing, order fulfilment, accounting and collecting royalties on behalf of the author.

Book sales for North America and international:

Trafford Publishing, 6E–2333 Government St.,

Victoria, BC V8T 4P4 CANADA

phone 250 383 6864 (toll-free 1 888 232 4444)

fax 250 383 6804; email to orders@trafford.com

Book sales in Europe:

Trafford Publishing (UK) Ltd., Enterprise House, Wistaston Road Business Centre, Wistaston Road, Crewe, Cheshire CW2 7RP UNITED KINGDOM

phone 01270 251 396 (local rate 0845 230 9601)

facsimile 01270 254 983; orders.uk@trafford.com

Order online at:

www.trafford.com/robots/05-0165.html

10 9 8 7 6 5 4 3 2

TIME *photo, 4/1/93 – Kathleen Wood (mic) – Joie Cook's gig at Blue Monkey.*

Newspaper & magazine reviews
What the critics are saying about the Babarians:

MODERN MATURITY, Feb-Mar 1994 – "[Poets] meeting at Cafe Babar are the 'Babarians'. [These] new San Francisco poets love to attack the established social order, [they] are the incursion of poetry into popular culture."

SAN FRANCISCO CHRONICLE, 2/5/93 – "They [Babarians] join the ranks of Ginsberg, Ferlinghetti, Corso. **Nancy Depper** is "a showstopper."

S.F. BAY GUARDIAN, 11/4/92 – "**The best poets working in America today. The cradle of the American avant-garde tradition.** Formed in the crucible of real economic despair & political threat. Poets of lowered expectations & political rage. Cafe Babar is the symbolic crucible of the spoken-word scene where gather the keepers of the flame – the poets doing poetry before it caught the public eye."

DER SPEIGEL, 6/7/93
His [**Alan Kaufman's**] work is like mixing echoes of Angela Davis with subversive pop music."

S.F. WEEKLY, 7/31/91
Maura O'Connor – "The fragile spirit of William Butler Yeats with an ability to finesse great emotional rawness; impressive."

S.F. WEEKLY, 7/31/91 (cont)

"[Cafe Babar] is the spiritual center of the San Francisco spoken-word scene.

Bruce Isaacson – "Blends intellectual precision with intuitive grasp and the mysteries of emotion."

Mel C. Thompson – "Skews our fears and ruthlessly scrapes away at them to expose a layer of stark horror & keeps scraping."

Bucky Sinister – "Punkish ... mischief & unpretentiousness."

S.F. BAY GUARDIAN, 2/5/93

Julia Vinograd –- "Embodies the spirit & constancy of the poetic heart; contemplative & consistent, a solid spiritual conscience."

Daniel Higgs – "Drives language to the cliff of pure song – otherworldly lines that defy linguistic gravity."

Vampyre Mike Kassell – "Heavy metal magick & punk style; enormously entertaining."

Dominique Lowell – "The Janis Joplin of spoken-word."

Alan Kaufman – "Avatar of Lenny Bruce, Walt Whitman & Jackie Gleason."

S.F. EXAMINER, 2/9/93

Danielle Willis – "... as normal as the kid next door – if your neighbor happens to be a vampire-identified dominatrix lesbian Satanist stripper who loves transvestite men –[she] drips with venom."

POETRY FLASH, 4/90

Eli Coppola – "Tender; Fierce honesty; Intimate."

Laura Conway – "Prophetic"

Bana Witt – "Flamboyant"

David Lerner – "Clever-savage rap" & FACT SHEET 5, 4/89 — "Ezra Pound of the Babar scene"

New American

Underground Poetry

vol. 1: the babarians of san francisco – poets from hell

DAVID LERNER & JULIA VINOGRAD & ALAN ALLEN – EDITORS
SPECIAL THANKS TO MAURA O'CONNOR & ZOE ROSENFELD

<>

Unusual or unconventional spellings & punctuation when they occur reflect each poet's style. All poems are copywrited to their respective authors & to previous publishers (as credited) if appropriate according to prior arrangements made between individual poets and their previous publishers.

San Francisco Babarian Genre

Foreword by Alan Allen

Cafe Babar (named after the storybook elephant) is a little Cafe on 22nd & Guerrero behind the Mission District in San Francisco. From there on the West Coast from the mid-late '80s up through about 1994, a unique group of poets gathered on Thursday nights for a feature, followed by an open mike.

The poets performing or reading their work there became known across the United States and in Central and Eastern Europe as some of the best poets in the U.S. They valued emotional honesty and their poems captured it. They found academic writing boring. Regarded the bohemian beatnik poets of North Beach as 'puffed-up', has-been, even geriactric.

Counterparts in New York seemed somehow to make commercialized poetry, won grants, performed for money, and worst of all influenced the Madison Avenue slop shops who with second-rate hearts start caricaturing poetry in tv commercials. The babarian poets were broke. Won the west-coast slams but couldn't afford the tickets to go East to compete. Lived only to write, to perform, to read. Many were without jobs (with notable exceptions), or disabled, or addicted, or worked in the sex industry. Most struggled to pay the rent, or eat well, wore thrift-shop clothes. IQ's were the highest, hearts the biggest, poems what mattered most. Was all about feeling in their voices, their words, their lines, their lives.

Preface by Julia Vinograd

Throughout the early-to-mid '80s the *Spaghetti Factory* was a central collecting spot for North Beach 'beat' poets. Then it closed. We bounced uneasily from one place to another: *Banan Place, On Broadway; Peters' Pub,* etc. We were glared at suspiciously by everyone from elderly dart players to rock bands who thought we had no business wasting their warm-up time. Gradually the people changed. The poetry changed – we definitely weren't 'beats'.

The Babar poetry scene started when Joie was scheduled to do a feature one night at a coffee house called the *Meat Market.* We all got there, there was a fairly big crowd, and there was a 'closed' sign on the place. Joie demanded a reading *in the middle of the street* right there, she had all her stuff ready, and she was *going* to have a reading. QR Hand just laughed and said, "Follow me, there's a place we can do a reading that has beer" – that did it. We walked down about two blocks and there was the *Cafe Babar.* QR talked to Alvin (the owner) and Alvin let us read right then in the Babar.

The next thing we knew we had a weekly reading. It grew into a big event, complete with audiences of non-poets. Over the years it turned hot and cold. A batch of the women, (it was almost a contest thing, a spoof), would turn up in T-shirts and flip them up during the reading (topless). It was one of the high points of San Francisco cafe life.

A genre of new, impatient *Babarian* voices emerged: personal, vivid, very much in the modern world from tv to mtv to the sex clubs – a voice influenced by the LA slums of Bukowski and the NY slums of Jim Carroll – but undeniably San Francisco, the San Francisco tourists never see. The depth of this voice is surprising, almost dangerous, like a classical statue materializing in the middle of a busy highway; a voice that's sometimes out of order, in a world broken by hunger, madness and AIDS; a voice that is the *Zeitgeist,* the spirit of the times.

Introduction by Richard Silberg

Popping Poetry – excerpted from *Poetry Flash*, #205, 4/90

Babarian poetry swings all the way to the right of the applause meter towards a poetry of presence. As opposed to movements that have centered on magazines, a college, a writers' group, the Babarians have forged their work in a performing space, the backroom of the jazz spot Cafe Babar on Twenty-second and Guerrero in San Francisco. It's a small room, tiny for the crowds that have surged in there, the smoke and the commotion, furnished with wooden chairs, bleachers behind them, mirrors on the ceiling, and corrugated metal on the walls. Readers often use that metal to pound on, a shivered cracking sound, for emphasis or rhythm or just to get the crowd's attention. On a good Thursday evening, when Babar is going right, there's a feeling not unlike jazz or rock, the performative lightings, the whiff of meat and blood.

As a movement, Babarians focus on that performing voice. The Babarian voice goes for personhood, somewhat like the voice of Bob Dylan's lyrics, or a comedian's voice, or the voice of a TV newsman. Emphasis is shifted from the page to performance. The poem on the page is more like a script or a score.

And Babar isn't just a singular phenomenon; it networks with other poetries both in time and space. Open readings are heating up all across America. Poetry 'slams', head-to-head poetry competitions, surfaced in Chicago some years ago. For years poets have been 'fighting' in Taos for the "Heavyweight Champions", and there's serious slamming at Bob Holman's Nuyorican Poet's Cafe in New York. In recent years the San Francisco Bay Area has positively bloomed with open readings; New York has two open series, a poetry open and an open featuring 'performance'; Los Angeles has a number of open venues. Perhaps this open, participatory tendency means poetry is starting to be popular, to reach the people in America.

The feeling at many opens, certainly Babar, leans to the shamanistic, not simply 'literary' but a speaking in tongues, communion in a sacred practice. From time to time poetry has tried to purify itself, to cut through ornament, dead wood, and reconnect. Walt Whitman, with his "barbaric yawp", did that in America for some decades after the Civil War. Rimbaud, the adolescent shooting star, in France around 1870. [In the '50s and '60s] in America the Beats ... took on that purifying, recharging task. Some powerful stuff has been written at Babar, poems with an edge, poems that might matter to people besides professors, critics, other poets.

Babar is at least triply interesting. First, for itself, its raucous power and humor, for the talent it attracts and showcases, the movement that's grown up there. Second, Babar commands attention because it's a notable part of something larger that seems to be happening nation-wide – the proliferation of open readings, the sense of poetry as partici-patory, give and take – a sense diametrically opposite to most Americans' brief high school or college experience of poetry as some-thing hundreds of years old and quite dead.

Which brings us to a third Babarian focus of interest: its relation to the question of poetry and audience in America. Poetry has become a dis-tinctly minor art in our time. The audience has grown tiny; poets often seem to be writing for each other, for themselves, more people writing it than reading it, etc. We get the sense, true or not, of an art that's become effete, irrelevant. The last genuinely popular poetry in America was probably written by the Beats. Now here comes Babar, in certain respects, from the same direction. They're angry poets, shake-it-up poets; they want to grab the audience any way that they can, by the gonads, by the throat, to explode their way to relevance.

In fact, there's a certain possibility that they, or similar poets, will suc-ceed, win their way through to a much bigger audience and readership. What would happen then? Would they be able to go on swallowing pop [culture], digesting it, and coming back with genuine art, in the way that Dylan or the Beatles did that? Or would they become popular in the sense of the 'slam'; would they suck up to the applause meter and become just entertainment – impure and simple?

Richard Silberg's latest book of poems is The Fields. *He is currently teaching "Writing and Appreciating Contemporary Poetry" at the University of California Berkeley Extension. He is Associate Editor of* Poetry Flash.

Eli Coppola 1

David West 21

Laura Conway 38

Sparrow 13 LaughingWand   51

Julia Vinograd   68

Zoe Rosenfeld   84

Vampyre Mike Kassel

145

Maura O'Connor

161

Ken DiMaggio

178

Bucky Sinister

182

Eli Coppola b.1961

Eli has an intensely personal voice, is known for unsentimental love poems, and is highly respected in the San Francisco poetry community. She has received a *PEN Writers Fund Grant;* and an *Academy of American Poets* award while attending Connecticut College, and earned an MFA from San Francisco State University. She manages the Beatrice M. Bain Research Group on women and gender at U.C. Berkeley. Her poems have appeared in: *Ajax Anthology, Bullhorn, Citi-Voice, Dangerous Stew, For Art's Sake Gallery, The Harvard Women's Law Journal, Long Shot, Poems From Earth, Squirm, The Women's Action Coalition: Spoken Word Archive and Recording Project,* and *Worc's.* Has several poetry chapbooks, including: *The Animals We Keep In The City,* Zeitgeist Press, 1989; *Invisible Men's Voices,* Blue Beetle Books, 1992; *As Luck Would Have It,* Zeitgeist Press, 1993; *no straight lines between no two points,* Apathy Press Poets, 1993.

To My Child Who Is 52 Days Old

We don't have much time.
We visit
through a prison cage.
There are people watching.
We don't have much time,
but I don't have much
to say.

I wanted to let you known about the abortion;
I'm sure you've heard rumors.
Forgive me.
It is an unceremonious thing that we do
in cases like this, in a world
like this. The alternative is: both birds,
one stone. Some lure us on with a pledge
to the sanctity of life, but how quickly the self same
would swaddle us both
with the strong ropes
of poverty.
So much more effective to break a heart
year after year after year
than just this once.
So you see, in my memory
you will be safe.

My belly swells at your insistence,
filling with blood and mixing
voices, we each weeping for what we will never see,
while hand after hand pries into my fault
line, insinuations of metal, plastic, jelly, q-tips, needles, hoses
and the eyeballs not to mention the
opinions
of millions of americans
jammed up
in the bottleneck
slung between my hipbones.

There are so many who rule
what they do not care
to understand. And the ugly things
keep
coming —

watch over me

I will be hard pressed to find my way
out of the vacuum and the glare and the fifteen minute sentencing.
It is still unclear
whether it is you or me on trial,
but no one will be set free.
The whole country's busy
trying to differentiate us,
to trim our souls
to make for neater law.
As though we courted any courts
at all.
As though we had not worked this out between us
a long time ago.

Child, I will get you the peach
you want, if you will sing
me a lullaby, for you are much closer to sleep
than I.

A Couple

A couple of words.
Otherwise

ordinary words.
He said:

I'm
going.

One body moves across town in a churning sea of bodies
moving across town.

No one notices
the irregular constrictions of my throat.

Walking from one room to another can suddenly take
days.

I shower repeatedly
baptism after baptism

in hot sorrow.
With my eyes closed I remember

us kids taking turns being the blind one
on the walks home from

elementary school
and how it felt

how startling
to once again admit

the enormity of solitude.
To continue I will

have to be deliberate:
find food

move about
quietly quietly

listen for trains
a cool thief of daily life

provoking no shadows until I dance again
with lust in my hands.

Which doors shall I open and close
searching the faces of young men everywhere

to discover why they keep
such ferocious secrets

like ulcers burning
beneath their hearts

shedding love
like a contagion of unbearable possibilities.

My home is by the wild river,
in the house of sticks.

It's Not A House, It's A Woman

I can get used
to not having
you here.
I do have blankets.
I've been trying to forgive myself
for 27 years now
and the outcome is still
anybody's guess.
Forgiving you
will have to wait.
Until the moon's
too full of itself
to hold water.

I'll walk the dog every day.
Offer martinis to my nightmares.
Like you did, chuckling.
I'll invent new ways
to make fire, always trying to get
the body temperature right.
I will not take my clothes off
when I sleep.
I will not sleep
when I take my clothes off.

I will wait, patiently, for everything,
eating regularly,
which will probably
kill me.

If you're not here.

But I must say,
you'll need more than cabfare
to outdistance my love static
on your radio.
You'll need
gunpowder in your next drink
to blast me out of your bloodstream.
You'll need a hundred thousand tomorrows
just to get through today.

Lotsa coyotes out there
howling for the moon, baby,
but I never yet heard
the moon howl
back.

Jury Duty

I was told
　　to call this number follow the instructions for group code amber
　　report to room 303 at the appointed time give my name
　　and wait

　　for further instructions

I was told
　　to empty my bag
　　step through the metal detector
　　put my hands up
　　while the cop ran his hands down my

　　breasts

waist
hips

I was told
   to follow the crowd
I was told
   to step back line up take a seat and calm down

I was told
   not to raise my voice

I was told
   it was not my job to question the law
   but only to uphold it

I was asked if I'd ever been convicted of a felony
   and if so what and did I do time
   (when they asked the old chinese woman she giggled and said she
   was a christian then they re-phrased the question and she giggled
   and said she was a christian and then they gave up asking and she
   never did
   answer)

I was told
   not to discuss or repeat anything
   I would hear or see in the courtroom
   (the judge repeated that several times for the people who couldn't
   speak english and I figured I could tell what I didn't see and that
   would do
   well enough)

I was told
   to observe the accused
   (he was an old black man his shoes were untied his jacket was too
   small his pants were dirty his face was cut up bad one eye blind and
   he didn't seem to know what was going on swinging his head in wide
   wobbly arcs to see who was talking though
   no one was talking
   to him)

I was told
   to weigh the evidence carefully

(the cops said he did it and the cashier from the chicken place said he
did it and the grocer from next door to the chicken place said he did it
and the judge said he'd been arrested six times before and the DA
said he was drunk when they brought him in and the super at the
project said he ain't never paid his rent anyway and had about ten kids
all bad
too)

I was asked
   if I could remain impartial
   (which is when the woman in gold lamé from the marina got up
   and said well no She couldn't because once She'd had over FIFTY
   THOUSAND DOLLARS worth of jewelry stolen and She was still
   terribly upset about that and no She didn't think She very well could
   be impartial)

I was asked
   to decide
   given the testimony of my peers
   whether or not the dying man was guilty
   of holding up a Kentucky Fried Chicken
   with a jackknife

I was told
   the consequences of his conviction
   were none of my concern

I swore to tell the whole truth

so help me

god

Casual Hands, Brutal Stars, Past Things

I remember watching
dragonflies, noting with particular
curiosity the   casual
merger of things
like dragon and fly.
        And I remember wondering if
            anyone else
            cared   about this.
I remember the fever   and my mother's   hands.
I remember not drinking   coffee.
I remember when the word AIDS was always
preceded by a word like hearing.
                    Or Band.
            Back then it could
            help you hear   better.   Heal.

I remember the first night I slept   in the open.
There have been so few nights
under stars, in all these years,
a measure of longing in light   years.
I remember when crying was just crying
and you did it when
you did it.
I think I remember when beauty
was vast, less   brutal.
less true.

Christ, I remember
going to the Bronx Zoo on a train,   with my brother,
on a Saturday in October.

And here's a thing that never happened
        that I'll always remember:

        Death takes me on a date.
        I am shy.
        Death holds my hand and we walk
        the pagan-pressed paths
        of a carnival, around in circles for the humor
        of it, because what other route is there
        for mortality to take,

and the daylight gets doused
with spectacular shadows that gather
into shapes of wild
animals and machines
sideswiping gravity

and death points out
the dragonflies and the   stars,
undisturbed among the offspring of Zeus
in the freak show

and death recalls   each time   past
that I called something
love

and he questions me about these   things

and he wants to know
and he says   you know
        darkness comes and goes
and I hold his hand tighter and crying happens
        and it's just crying,
        and my ribcage rattles
        and my throat swells like the bullfrog

and I feel a savage, unsettling peace.

Worknights

Monday

I was sitting inside the parked car
when the man began slamming the
red bicycle into the car with a
surprising amount of force considering
how scrawny his arms were
and how drunk he was
in the theatrical halo of a streetlight
shining on his slamming.

Tuesday

I turned down the alley and realized a man was following me
and that the alley was about to end abruptly
in cinderblocks and shadows.
My senses swarmed like a twister of razor blades
as I began to turn on him
he slid by, soft as the cheek of a pond
saying quite clearly
Pardon me

Wednesday

I pulled up to the stoplight
a tangerine LeMans twice the size of my car
pulled up alongside
real real close
through my open window
comes a man's
hot breath
Baby... Mama... Corazón...

Thursday

A man asked me for a cigarette.
The babies, you know,
he said.
I work every day, you know,
he said, holding out his hands to me,
lumps of hissing hot cracked asphalt.
Then in the dark face a smile flashed
like a switchblade —

Friday

As I stumble through the intersection of Columbus & Broadway
trafficking with adam & eve in the garden of bright broken glass
clutching the concrete buttresses of Carl's Junior
screaming at him to leave me alone
suddenly there's a woman's face
close to mine

saying real low
Baby, what's wrong?

And I say goddamit goddamit nothing nothing nothing
I'm fine I just gotta get out of here really I'm fine
And she says
Sugar,
if you're so fine
what are you crying
for?

Black Water

They called him a troubled child
back in the south because he caused them
trouble. Refusing like he did.

He accepted whiskey to dull the pain
after that big hand first swung down on his head,
slicing off the overhead light like a sickle.
It was the only thing he accepted, after that.
The only sign of the head wound was the low burn
left in his eyes. He relied more on his hands.
They grew, in proportion to his need.
They grew, sheathed in callous so he could handle things
without touching them.
They built things for pay but the money
always tore them down again, one way or another.
The voices of old men fused the wet cement
young jackhammers shattered.
And then even hands meant nothing.

He turned his exhaustion over to outrage
at night as the city's dingy carnival swung its hips
under fluorescent high wire acts.
Blinking martini signs strung the nights together,
high above the tatter paper days.
The permanent impermanence of it all soothed him
sometimes. He'd sit on the same stool all night,
watch the going and coming pass each other in doorways.

He took on all games of chance, played hard
and for the whole pot, whenever remotely possible
and by whatever means available.
He drank until he sweat a flammable sweat.
Bottles gathered on all level surfaces,
tossing off beady cold reflections of everything,
delicate vessels for oblivion
that smashed in a spectacular way.

The many scars and their ill-fitting stories did not lie to him
even when they did. It was somehow unavoidable to lie to them,
even when he didn't. Words broke open the pink mouth
in his faultless face, round and round and round,
unbroken words, unbroken.
Little tops of anger spun faster and faster in his eyes.

In the streets black water began to rise,
and with his first step out the ever-swinging doors
mad currents caught him at the ankle and turning a corner rushed
his knees. He grabbed a pay phone
and held on.

What A Significant Amount Of Objectivity Can Do

There's no healing
some wounds, you just got to catch
some of the blood
in your hands
and feel it
falling.
In this world run by rabid men
wearing several wristwatches apiece,
the irony is that scar tissue supplies
one with a significant amount of objectivity
when it comes to pain. They didn't figure
on that. Or that
the ivory tower collapsed or otherwise
is worth nothing
to the blacksmith
with his iron
in a boot camp of fire.

Eat the damn apple
before the padlock on paradise begins to spin.
Luxury is leprosy in its last stages.
We can change our names
as many times as we have to, but
there will be no hostages —
I repeat:
there will be no hostages.

The swaying of woman's hips will go on in her sleep
even while dreams of her are scoured out of skulls
by the diligent diligent hands of those who know
there is no penalty whatsoever in this country
for driving someone to suicide.

The father's hand
is aimed at the child's head.
The child's eyes are unblinking.

The ghosts are scared
of us now.

Flying

Odd times, poems come: in the middle,
on the bus, in the half-
awake time, seventh lap
in the pool, looking
up, sometime in early morning
when I notice something
about you in a new light
and now,
in the cafe on Eddy Street, with music and talk and traffic
to accompany the small melody moving
                              from the heart
out.

Love is often the work
of art, half-fulfilled, half-sung on my way
to work, to sleep,
shy and flickering like the smell of a flower
in air I move too quickly through,
                         without seeing,   the one sweet
breath.
             I care for you: powerful, delicate words,
because now is a world where care is only possible
and   all we can do
is defy gravity and sense and climb
the sheer face of it all, speaking such words as we can
even as the air
thins, fitting flesh to stone,
scanning for appropriate holds until one accepts
the groping fingers, the grasping hand, the body's weight
and motion.

There's always a moment
when your trust asks more than physics
has promised,
a synapse you lean your whole life on.

Little time for relief
when you realized you haven't died, because you still hang
on a bluff
side, and the sky is clear

and unforgivingly infinite
all around you. Lizards and beetles and birds
fidget and flurry by, amazingly
fit for this crazy life.
It will be more than hard.

And, as much as I'd like, I can give you neither
boost nor break. If you look you'll see
I'm strung to some other cliff,
latitudinally your bride. Only this:
to fall is the closest
we'll ever come
to flying.

Enlightenment And Muscular Dystrophy

There are drums beating   somewhere
   and it means   something
and every day it   seems
      more things mean
                  something —
and the things weave into each other and the meanings
weave into each other,
and I've given in
      to writing   about places I've never been,
about things I discern with senses
I can't control
                  ALL THOSE DREAMS
set in coral reef and rain forest —   around my neck
I string the small planets
of plentiful water, round dreams of furious life
fed with the heat and moisture of
                              summers, throats, young
imagination

As regards my education in physical   law,   well,
the first miles were easy — all meadows and flowers

                              and that lot —
I took 16 years in giant strides,
a child flying   in a summer race —
but I have slowed down   since then,
gravity and I grown close, longer conversations
between   my legs
and the land, these days — and though my sight is
    every day unbound,   my body
    is growing   still, straining for a simple step, unravelling
    a new grace,   a   life   of   crime
    before my eyes
will see between the eyes of any god.

In this living, tangled mass
of congo-paced poems and
    my mission   to find monkeys in the jungle, I heave
broken legs   with arms back brain and a bursting
heart,   taking one step at one time in one motion of
my one strength,
while the vine-fingers of every thing I've ever known
reach and root and wrap,
branches crack mud sucks and   I scream
    my love   of this world as I pry
each foot loose from the ground and   give it back
    more water!   Feed on!   the universe
of a body bathed in salty splash —   such a great work
                              of translucent flesh —
of earth green and gritty and growing
                              and grinning
as I set fire   to my cells
        to move
                    slower and slo   we r
    a gai n   and   agai n
                    slow er   and   sl o w e r

Cross Walk

Man's trying to cross the street.
Man's blind.
Beat and bump at rush hour rush hour's blind
to get home to get back to get dinner to get on
with it.
Man's trying to cross.
What if he doesn't hear
the light change what if the light doesn't see
him what if he can't smell how close
the car is
what if the car is two feet
into the cross
walk
what if the car runs the red light
runs him down into red light
the car that doesn't see
him what if the curb comes up too fast
what if the crowd confuses him what if they move
the steps put new steps in take the old steps
away
what if he takes one
wrong turn
what if he spaces out for one goddamned second
what if he loses count
of the steps the streets the turns what if
the whole thing's off just one
one anything
what if it's getting darker and later and further
what if he panics what if he panics like this all the time and no one
sees and the blackness gets blacker gets dense as suffocation gets
enormous as terror what if he falls and no one sees what if he gets hurt
and no one sees
what if
no one sees
what
if

no one

April Fool's Day

I go to a bar at midnight on the first day of the fourth month
in a year of tears.
There are a lot of people in the bar.
They are all moving.
They are all talking.
It's unnecessary for me to talk.
I get a scotch on the rocks with a hand signal and a flash of my license
averting my eyes so the bartender will not be alarmed.
He studies me briefly
but I am only a swarm of shadows shed by Bic lighters.
He can't tell my heart stopped beating weeks ago.
There are heads haggling and braying
in every booth upholstered in red plastic
arms airborne and fists insistent
they rattle the gleaming formica, rattle fixtures, linoleum,
all seventy two kinds of glasses
suspended from the ceiling over my head.
I see nothing but fingernails and teeth.
My drink and I are in silent and seamless complicity.
I don't look at it
even when I bring it to my lips
but I know where it is
at all times.
I pull my cigarettes closer, wondering when I changed
brands exactly, and knowing it is the memory of your hands
I'm avoiding.
Once again, your hands.
I can't light the cigarette.
I'll have to go without, as I've learned to do.

The bartender only notices I've gone because I left no change
no shiny trail
of silver.
In fact
I left no trail,
No trail at all.

Mississippi Street

i've lived here a year and a half now
make an easy basket with the toilet paper roll
every time
no matter how intensely pre-occupied
no matter how wasted
no matter even if asleep
in it goes

i know which few weeks of the year
the sun comes in the window onto the bed
in the morning at just the right time
so i don't need the alarm
bliss to outwit a little bit of civilization
there are frogs on the landing
spiders weaving new webs all the time
after sirens the dogs in the kennel by the bay howl
a goofy, eerie music

for each of nineteen months i've traded my work
for one room on a rocky shelf under a war zone
none of the laws of man give me permission but i call it mine
my lair and my fort
camouflaged cottage cushy foxhole
it's true i stock it like a fallout shelter
but i leave all the doors and windows open
even when it's cold
i left the only dream i ever had to come here
but at least i got food, books and a bathtub

sure homes can be broken
but sturdy camps built of debris
are the places i like to play best
the dump and the quarry
the docks crumbling in the winter harbor
the graveyard where i walk
over the dug and dug and dug again earth
bursting with boxes and bones
whispering names carved in stone to the wind

David West   b.1954

He writes: West has been reading at the open mike reading scene in the Bay Area since 1978, and in the '90s has begun to perform in New York and other cities. He often reads to live or taped music (jazz, blues, rock), or accompanies himself on different kinds of banjos. West writes about secretaries, children, drag queens, waitresses, or about his years as a political organizer on the left. His poems often tell someone else's story; more often than not, they are sad stories that tend to be funny too. Like many other longtime residents of San Francisco, AIDS has left its mark on his work. A soft delivery of what are usually hard topics gives his poems a weird spin. He has several chapbooks: *Evil Spirits and Their Secretaries* and *BAR,* Zeitgeist, 1990; *Elegy for the Old Stud,* Manic D Press, 1993; *You Only Get This Lucky Once,* Apathy Press, 1993; *The Show Goes On,* Road Kill Press, 1994; and several recordings of his work accompanied with music. West does not think of himself as a 'Babarian' poet, as he reads in many different places, nor, strictly speaking, could he be called a Poet from Hell. West is from Ohio. That's worse.

Elegy For The Old Stud

I took a tour of the old Stud last night
    it's a straight bar now in '92
    they call it the Holy Cow
    when I walked in I saw '78
    like a video in the background

through couples doing the ancient
    boy meets girl dance, Coco
    the ghost of the old Stud swirled by
    snapping his gypsy castanets

I saw Bobby in his nylons and rhinestone best
    reciting his elegant, tacky regrets

I saw Ascension in his habit absolving us all
    after 8 years in a Mississippi pen
    for one blow job, our mother superior
    had no use for penance

I saw Wanda who always won the cleavage contests
    with his beard & his chest like a gorilla

I saw Freddy doing his fabulous Lauren Bacall
    popping reds, saying "pucker up and blow"

Gabe was there, bored- there was no one to shock
    Gabe who once sprayed pachoulli on his beard
    draped a purple dress on his pot belly
    threw a lace shawl over his enormous shoulders
    and nervous as a rabbit in high heels said
    I'm going to play tourist
    in a straight latino club- wanna come?

I wore a suit and a hat & a butch attitude
    we sailed by the unsuspecting doorman
    then the bouncer began to snarl, heads
    began to turn, the rumor of the maricon
    muttered through the crowd, the music stopped
    some men clenched their fists
    and Gabe was as happy as I'd ever seen him
    then the salsa struck up the dancers danced on
    as though we'd disappeared

last night Gabe got bored the horror got to him
    his ghost leapt on a chair and screamed:
    WHAT ARE YOU DOING IN OUR BAR?
    as the kids below followed
    such formal routines, the women waiting
    for the men to make a move, the men waiting
    for the courage to do it

in the old Stud lust was such a casual thing
    they took turns in the alley
    giving each other head and lethal diseases
    they'd bid me good night
    and go off to the baths
    still dishing the evening
    and they'd sigh the next morning
    about the tricks who got away

one time Bobby even got on his knees
    to pray for a sugar daddy
    8 years later the virus hit
    right after he found one

and Coco od'd on bad mexican junk
    the others are mostly dead

Ascensions's still runs a commune up north
        with his habit and his lover
        and a shotgun by the door

Gabe god knows where Gabe is now
        maybe doing Liberace's makeup in heaven
        Bobby's on a respirator it won't be long

I saw their ghosts
        in the old Stud last night
        as the straight kids
        kept pouring in the door

Let's Get Some Guns

I met Mr. Gutierrez at a Nicaragua thing
ten years ago before he had his stroke
he started chewing on me about democracy
elections in this country were shit, he said
chinga, it's like voting for twinkies

you should get guns, armed struggle, compa
en serio, stop fucking around
he was smiling but he was also very loud
Marta stood behind him and waved
please, don't get him excited

Mr. Gutierrez, I said, I don't like guns
big demonstrations are hard enough to handle
he asked, why don't you organize the beggars
why, in '79, in Managua — he looked at me again
& sighed. you're right. America. forget it.

I saw him last week. now he uses a walker
I said Don Ernesto how's the revolution
these days? he said: it broke my heart
and dragged himself down the street

I wanted to yell YOU'RE RIGHT!
LET'S GET SOME GUNS
but I still don't like them
and I bet he would have said
you and me? who we gonna shoot?

The Show Goes On

*After making movies, singing, acting, and countless drag extravaganzas,
Doris Fish died of AIDS on June 22, 1991. A benefit held before her
death was called "Who Does That Bitch Think She Is?"*

I've known men so terrified
of who they grew up to be
their bodies are worse than prisons
& I've seen my share of elegant victories
over the male bastille
all it takes is style & the courage to insist
Doris even made it look graceful
when her hair fell out she had wigs for days
love has never needed a license to exist
the show goes on. the tide will change
but it keeps taking the best we have with it
old men with your stone tablets
let the pecking order beware
Doris Fish is dead but her drag's still here

once upon a time, in California friends
when I was hired as the token queer
at a politically correct hippyshit grocery store
I found myself necking in the vegetable cooler
with a girl, thinking what will I say
if someone sees us? I didn't seem to fit in anywhere
and I wasn't sure I should
I just couldn't swing that 45 caliber
conception of men who are sexy
depending on how many holes
they can blow in their victims
Doris's sluts a-go-go were more fun
than Sylvester Stalone & I think a laugh
is more persuasive than a gun
Doris is dead but the show goes on

there's a difference
between the direction of the wind and a trend
between accidents and tragedies, attitudes and men
between going down on someone and coming back up again
it takes all kinds of grace to sustain us
Doris fell off a balcony in a show one time

and kept singing while she hung to the rail
I see her face on the moon and get mad again
she'll never even be on a postage stamp - hell,
the first man the U.S. put in orbit also launched
a political career that ended in a banking scam
he got a postage stamp
I'll vote for Doris she was my kind of man
she had demands but they were very modest

go down Moses, leave the commandments alone
the promised land is a safe place to sleep
it's the freedom to make your way home, unmolested
loaded, in heels and gold lamé, at 3 a.m.
lord have mercy on the extravagant of spirit
when boys drive by in muscle cars, not applauding
you haven't lived till you've seen her housefrau in curlers
her dumb blonde but I'm smarter than you routine
Doris made me happy her wit was so crisp
doing sexual jujitsu on those old holywood roles

I like to imagine Doris walking down main street
in small town USA at high noon, disturbing
what passes for the peace these days
and I think it's even harder to change people
than the law: I want Doris on prime time tv
I've met children 10 years old
who already learned how to whisper faggot
I've been so sick of it I saw myself
sprawled on the sidewalk with a cup and a sign
that says another sensitive soul who couldn't hack it
can you spare a quarter? I need a new dress

Doris is dead & I'm not depressed, I've had it
this is insane. she's on the front page
in all her former health & glory
right next to a budget cutback story
they keep the army in the closet
they keep playing with their guns, fighting the most
ridiculous wars you ever heard of and Doris is dead
couldn't a few missile silos disappear in her honor?
couldn't the president just admit on the news tonight
he doesn't know what he's doing and if we knew
what he was doing we'd shoot him? Doris died

we have a plague on our hands
goddamn it we have a problem

Doris you can't leave we need you now
Schwartzeneger has his eye on the senate
they spent more money on the fucking gulf war
than they spent on all medical research
in the world combined since the century began
I get up and go to work in the morning
& even the Marlboro man looks sad
she was the queen of Vegas in outerspace
a pro, one of the best in the biz
Doris died how dare she we needed her bad
who does that bitch think she is?

For Jane, Wherever She Is

Jane was queen of the hayride,
kissed the quarterback
and caught his baby

like a flu, a badly thrown bouquet
she didn't need. She stole a car,
split, and five cities later

was still running. Pain taught her
to survive but being pretty
didn't hurt, and then it did.

LA brought out the blade
in Jane. She was no angel.
She was a dangerous woman.

She carried one small town
and three abortions in her belly
and at forty, she carried

them well. But some nights, late,
she lost her cool. She crawled
into bed and felt wicked.

She'd call me up, we'd laugh
about the Baptists and the Elks
but they were real to us

we felt the old hometown
rectitude crawling up our backs
like spiders. One day she was gone.

Haven't seen her since.
She may be orbiting
a thorazine ward

she may be in prison or feeding
worms, but some friends like Jane
go all the way around the sun

and I see them on the corner
many years later looking meaner
and more beautiful than ever

wearing a million more miles
and I say… "Holy Shit
you're still alive?"

The Cleanest House In Delaware County

JR came to daycare 4 years old
glistening with Brylcream
Sunday school smile
something brittle in the way
he cocked his head

The first time I picked him up
he popped me on the nose.
I slapped him, he socked me,
then I grabbed his fist.
He laughed: "Big Chicken.
Why don't you hit hard?"
Then he seemed to relax. Soon,
we never knew when JR's scrawny arms
would wrap around our knees.

One day he gave a mama dog
the same embrace and threw a puppy
from her litter in the furnace.
When he patted a girl
who saw him kill the puppy
she kept crying
so he brained her with a dumptruck.
6 stitches later we asked:
What happened, JR?
He hid his eyes and whimpered:
"Debbil get me."

I said draw me the devil.
He drew black lumps with tails
and said: "Dem's the Debbils".
He drew red slashes
until the paper ripped
and said "Dem's the Debbil's spears."
When he cried himself to sleep
we found the welts on his back,
so we went to visit JR's home.

Rumor was his grandma
had been raped long ago.
She brought up a daughter
she didn't want
who ran away and left four kids
so Grandma reared them too.

She was the unofficial mayor
of a tiny town, a pillar
of the Pentecostal church,
and people said
she had the cleanest house
in Delaware County.

When she opened the door
we smelled lemon oil and ammonia.
The vacuum cleaner was on.
In the livingroom 3 kids
were tied up in chairs.
She said, "Please sit down,
I'm just tidying up, these children

like to drive me mad."
She had such a calm sweet smile.

We found JR leaning
through the basement door.
DON'T TOUCH ME DON'T TOUCH ME
DEBBIL GET ME! he screamed.
grandma made him stand there
while she told him that Jesus
was the only hope he had
but if he shivered
she knew the devil was in him again
so she'd kick him in the cellar
and lock the door.

I asked, where's the devil?
JR pointed downstairs.
When I turned on the lights
the black lumps he'd drawn
were rats and they scurried away;
the red spears were lightcords
she whipped him with.

Grandma said the devil
doesn't understand prayer
devil only understands pain.

We put the kids in a foster home
where none of them did too well
JR's going to kill somebody someday
he'll end up in prison
and nobody will give
two good shits why he did it.

You Only Get This Lucky Once

after 6 months of training in a cadre school
(where I learned that Stalin did make
a few mistakes; but give or take
a few million dead Russians
he did what a revolutionary had to do)

I was assigned to canvass Hunter's Point
where no doubt thousands
of working class blacks
were dying to hear
what a white boy from the burbs
had to say about class struggle
and the African-American question

so one warm Sunday afternoon
as fearless as only the young
white and stupid can be
I wandered down Palou toward Third
armed with petitions, volunteer cards
and the party newspaper
with a headline about Mao Tse Tung

I talked to the grandmas getting out of church
who said they'd read 'bout Mr. Tung
some other time, I hit laundromats
and grocery stores, I walked into bars
where one guy playing pool was so amused
he bought the only paper I sold that day
and offered to stand me a drink

the fact that I hadn't seen another white face
for miles didn't bother me. people said
you're crazy, but they wished me luck
though it never crossed my mind they meant
I'd be lucky if I made it to Third Street

I was thrilled as a triggerhappy marine
fresh out of bootcamp, rearing for action
this wasn't the three millionth meeting
in smoky rooms where earnest intellectuals
drafted one more leaflet nobody could read

this was the real thing
working class African-Americans
treating me like the comrade I wanted to be
or perhaps like many indian tribes
treated epileptics and the insane
the Great Spirit was with me
I was speaking in tongues
too devoted and dumb to fuck with

I didn't get into trouble
till I found another red
6 foot 3, in a dashiki
with a different set of positions
about class struggle
and the African-American question

he started shoving me
every time he made another point
like why didn't I go back
to Europe where I belonged
which suddenly sounded good to me
I would have settled for the Mission

in retreat I fell over
a baby in stroller
whose mamma pushed me off
the baby screamed
the dashiki guy lunged
I was lying on the sidewalk
stunned and scared

that's when my savior
waded through the crowd
six foot five maybe 300 pounds
he threw the dashiki guy
up against a wall
set me on my feet
and said this kid's ok

he'd never seen me before
turns out he was a janitor
at General Hospital where the party
led a strike once and saved his job
he recognized our newspaper

he walked me through the crowd
and whispered: son, you might wanna catch
that bus over there. you done enough
good work for one day, why don't you
take yourself a little vacation

How Was Your Day Dear?

at our peak, after work
I'd go to her place
she'd come to mine
and we'd start fucking

that was our
how-was-your-day-dear fuck

then there was
the late night
I'm terrified fuck

the wake up
it's morning
what might happen today
I feel fantastic fuck

the mid-afternoon
you are gorgeous fuck

the please pickmeup
I'm floundering fuck

the you're leaving town
I need to stock up fuck

or the wait till you taste
these tomatoes this fish
you're going to eat
like a queen tonight fuck

or the frank died
hold me & weeping fuck

or the I'm not sure
you love me anymore
prove it fuck

or the out of nowhere
for no reason fuck
that could kick out the stops
and roll for hours

the trapped fuck
the sad fuck
the fuck that never was

or the last fuck
the inevitable
last one

The Night Before The Art Went On

The night before the new bank opened I was sitting at the CEO's desk
on the 28th floor in my rentacop uniform (which didn't fit but the
company guy said the uniform was fine, I was just too small). I was
avoiding my appointed task of persecuting homeless drunks — try
saying "Excuse me, sir" to a 300 lb. walrus at 2 a.m. — I won't risk
annihilation for minimum wage, I only do things like that for free.

Anyhow this CEO hated me because at 7 a.m. one Sunday he
marched into the bank to find me reading with my feet up, and I
smiled, I was ready for him; I said Atashi-wa, Atoko-noku, which in a
dumbshit-American trying-to-talk Japanese way was supposed to
mean good morning sir, but the Japanese secretary who taught me
the phrase 'played a little joke'. It really meant baby I love you — Mr.
Samurai scowled and marched on, though later, my boss said don't try
anymore Japanese on that guy.

Then one Sunday, the building was done. Swingshift before opening
night, no buzz saws, no hammers no HEY JACK construction guys,
just deep carpet smelling new and lots of soft leather chairs. It was
dead as a Sunday bank can be. My boss called at the end of my shift
and said West, you have to guard the penthouse tonight, somebody
flaked on me. Your nuts are on the line. This is important.

I knew he was really saying, you get to work swingshift on top of day,
but I said fine. I needed the money and a little credit with Oliver
wouldn't hurt, I looked scruffy and didn't do my rounds. So, I rode to
penthouse, and lo & behold, this bank that already stank of marble
and parquet floors now had its own museum. Picassos and gold leaf
illuminated manuscripts, Alaskan statues, African masks, a
Polynesian canoe (WITH paddles), everything from Egypt to modern
Abstracts.

Oliver called at 10: he said the janitors come at midnight and graveyard didn't show – it's millions of bucks worth of art shit up there, West – you gotta stay till seven. I squawked. I'd been there since 7 that morning. Oliver began to plead. You can fuck off, read, smoke, I don't care. Just keep an eye on the cleaning crew, ok? I said, Doubletime? He agreed. I settled in at Mr. Samurai's desk and Oliver brought me coffee. Shit, that alone was worth it.

I could hear the janitors before the elevator opened, they were laughing and yelling, then wham tinkle boom, they were pushing out carts with dustpans & vacuums and buffing machines. A man in the lead with a showercap and curlers said hey Mr. rentacop how do you do, ok team are we ready? are we set? let's get mean, let's get clean, let's get the fuck out early!

They cleaned with all the reverence you'd give your boss's poodle. A Chinese lady stuck her feather duster in an ancient alligator's jaws and said TEE HEE HEE. A latin woman squirted pledge on the Polynesian paddles and muttered about how dirty they were. Another woman was dusting the Picasso. I said: "That's a million bucks you're dusting there." She said "million dolla piece of shit, you axe me." The guy in curlers squinted at a scary African mask, stuck out his tongue and said, "Aintchubaaad."

When they were done, they said – you got it easy guarding this crap man, nobody in they right mind ever touch it. Someone else whispered: that's why they don't pay him shit. For a moment they seemed to take pity on me & the strawboss said: two more floors then we party. You wanna get bent you come to floor 13 around 6. I was tempted, but I was also falling asleep. 24 hours in a bank were enough.

You're Not Alone

You're not alone.
that's why your chin's dry.
That's why you have a fresh diaper.
Sleep. I'll eat the meal you couldn't refuse.
It made the nurse so happy: you want peas?
You said sure. Potatoes? Great.
Steak? Ok. Then you puked.

I'll watch your face, as soft and composed
as a fugue, marching toward its tonic.
I'll watch sitcoms with the sound turned off.
Don't stay awake for me.

You were ready to die three weeks ago.
You said who wants to be a giant bedsore?
You had your seconal and booze,
but your lover wasn't ready to lose you.

Did you give him his death
so you felt you owed him yours?
Did you wait till you were too weak to choose?
I know you never stopped wanting to live.
You just got tired of dying.

Whatever the reason, your Calvary began.
You let him guard you from friends
who would have fed you death like tapioca.
he kept you alive till you were little more
than a smile with lesions.

Tonight you raved: you're here!
Let's get a cab! Let's ride down to the wharf!
I want to go the end of the pier!...
then you sank into the mercy of morphine,
& the gift I gave your jealous lover
was a night on the town
while I held your hand

and whispered: sleep tight.
You're not alone.

Diseases

some diseases grab you by the throat
overnight, you're a blob in a bedpan
you can't even say "PULL THE PLUG"
some diseases throw you on the floor
fill up your bladder and make the phone ring
mosquitos light on your hand like tiny birds
you learn to lie there and watch them drink

when that witty, sexy thing
you like to think you are
gets hits of pity from passersby
for a while you stop looking up anymore
you can't stand to see the gimp in their eyes
it takes two to do this tango
one to twitch one to hold up the mirror

all it takes is a few trips around the block
as a gyrating patient from a neuro ward
to make you face certain harsh sexual facts
like forget it. just jack off
some diseases won't even let you do that
the nurses strap down your hands

most diseases come with a complement of drugs
a mixture of malice and mercy- they may
cure the shakes, but they give you the runs
stop the pain but your mind is numb
you get so bummed out you consider suicide
then the doc says: you feel depressed?
I should have told you
this stuff can make you moody

that obsessive reading of medical literature
the way symptoms you don't even have yet
haunt you more than the ones you got used to
some diseases nibble a piece at a time
and you're never sure what they'll eat next

when you smell like death
even close friends flinch
they get a whiff of where they're going
and it stinks. hell doesn't smell like sulphur

it smells like piss you have to sleep with
the erosion of trust that your body
is even listening to you
let alone following orders

I remember wobbling to the grocery store
three blocks two intersections, on a cane
still digesting dilantrin for breakfast
and having been misdiagnosed, the drug
was only making things worse

falling twice, jerking through the parking lot
scaring three station wagons silly
but I made it to the grocery store
I paused to study the difficult doors
& leaned on the plastic rocking horse
the one that gets spastic for a quarter

thinking: if those idiots staring at me
don't appreciate that feat, fuck em
they'll miss my next act too
I'm going to buy a dozen eggs
and carry them home unbroken

Laura Conway b. 1953

When Laura reads she puts across pure poetic energy, hypnotizing audiences with the power and honesty of her poetic vision. With Bill Pollack, Laura used to put out a yearly anthology called *The Clay Drum*. At one time Laura and Bruce Isaacson and Dave Gollub together edited what was to become *Bullhorn*. Laura has been a frequent presence at the Cafe Babar, and has founded several open reading series in San Francisco. Laura grew up in New York and Oklahoma; and has since lived in San Francisco. She has traveled widely from Manhattan to Mexico, from Puerto Rico to the Ozarks. She has been a union organizer and passionate advocate of many causes of political and economic justice. She works as a teacher of young children. She has co-edited several small magazines, including the controversial CROW in the mid-'80s. She has chapbooks and books out, including, *To Knock Something Hard In The Dark,* Bench Press, 1980; and *My Mama Pinned A Rose On Me,* Red Flower Ink, 1986; and *The Cities Of Madame Curie,* Zeitgeist Press, 1989. Her current works in progress include a play titled, *Lot's Wife;* and a series of poems and stories called, *The Lost Gospels of Mary Magdalene.*

The House Itself

There was always a priest at those dinners
  and a housewife coquettishly attempting
Grace through sexual distance
This is the house where the gorilla's hands proudly serve soup
Where the father blows his trumpet
  to wake the children and the dead

There was always a surgeon at those suppers and a tongue-tied
  nurse handing him scalpel, sponging the wound
This is the house where the cats sleep balanced on the rafters,
  paws hanging down like jaguars in the jungle
Where the eldest daughter wanders the hallways like catacombs
  searching for her 2nd trimester babies
This is the house where rain lives in the attic

There was always a salesman at those liquid lunches and a
  woman wearing the distributor cap from his car so it wouldn't
  be stolen while he slept
This is the house where my breasts talk to each other
Where the three of us take the elevator all the way up to God,
  custodian for the Museum of Martyrs
Where he unlocks the Cupboard of Betrayal and reads the
  multiplying fish stories: How many times love,
  that fallen angel, will tempt and abandon us

There was always a bill collector at the breakfast table and an
  eager secretary transcribing obituary notices from shorthand
This is the house where the mother takes Thorazine and hides
  from the sun like a finger holding a place in a sock
She sings Danny Boy to the dinner dishes. She dresses up her
  eyes for the annual Christmas Ball at Holy Redeemer.

There was always a proper gentleman at High Tea and a Geisha
  girl waxing his floors, murmuring: Hai, Yasashi Hito,
  even when he contradicted himself
This is the house where fingernails served as canapes
This is the House of the Most Powerful Hand
This is the devotion of my sorrowful heart
This is the house where bees lose themselves

There was always a Christ boy balanced on a large wounded
    thumb at those dinners
And Blaze Starr in blue satin in Daddy's briefcase
This is the house of the Black Madonna
This is the house where the middle daughter sucked her thumb
    and loved being a boy
    and loved being a girl

There was always a veterinarian at those suppers, keeping the
    animals' heads above water; and a Stray Queen Cat in a
    gleaming palace behind the pines in the yard
She had many cats in attendance. They brought her kittens in
    silver bowls
She tore their little heads off
This is the house Lot's Wife let go of, let go on without her across
    the plain to Zoar
This is the house where Hearts were played with the neighbors
This is the house where the storm windows never came down
This is the house itself.
This is the house itself.

Two Who Fell Off

In the morning I realized I'd followed my father all night,
    calling to him, wandering through rooms ancient and blue
    as Minoa.
I worried about this. I worried about the sexual implications.
I thought of the man I let finger me on a bar stool while the cops
    broke up a knife fight. I thought of the man who had to
    relinquish his knife to the bartender before he could be
    served. I thought of the man in the waters of the Buffalo
    River.
I thought of the man with a mole on his ass, whose twin sister
    killed herself, leaving him unable to stomach mirrors.
I thought of the man who wanders the graveyards of America,
    searching out the tombs of old ball players.
Father, who are we? We are the two who fell off.
We are caught in the dreamtime.
I am the one. You are the other.
The air around us howls and churns with an extinct ocean.
Childhood seems as remote
as Pompeii; buried under lava and ash.
You are not there. I am over here. I have climbed this sky
    many times.
You only did it because you were a soldier. Inside your head a
    soldier waited to be told:
        You are to bring me the one bleak eye the Three Blind
        women pass among themselves.
        You are to cut yourself open with honor.
        You are to see if your breath makes fog on my mirror —
I will write my name in it.
I believed if I couldn't find you, I couldn't find
    love: there is no digging in that air.
We are like the old riddle: a pound of feathers, a pound of bricks.
We are falling at the same rate of speed.
When I dream like that, that I am calling you?
It is *you* calling *me*.
The blue rooms are everything but earth.

Don't Let Me Come Home A Stranger

Last night I couldn't rouse myself. A hand was turning me over in the bed. I said: What is this? Who is this? and couldn't rouse myself.

The night before we drove to the river. We stopped at a little park with a fake waterfall and a redwood bridge. I stood looking into the water. I pretended it was a hundred years ago. Another country. Deep woods. You said: I've had seven cars in my life. I remember them all like dogs who've died.

The silence burns holes in the darkness. This is how a star becomes, like love, growing denser, collapsing under its own weight. You were so beautiful when I loved you. When we lived where the leaves changed. And I changed. You called me Stranger.

Well let me tell you — everything's stra—nge. Gravity lets us drive upside down over bridges, over water they call Bodies. The heart is a four-door. Sometimes sorrow comes along for the ride. Let's just say timing is everything.

In the dream I thought: There's a stranger in bed with me and I can't wake up. I was terribly frightened. I couldn't move. There was no face. Just hands.

A wise woman buildeth her house. A foolish woman tears her house down. Call me Fool. When I looked up from the river the humpbacked moon was the skull of a child rocking itself to sleep in the sky. You were talking about a Mustang. How it had broken down outside Paradise and you had to leave it there. Uh-huh.

It was never meant to be Paradise. Ask the old: Pair O' Dice: a place for gamblers. Many men and many women burn memory here. I imagine cutting mine out with a knife but never do.

A dream is simply bridges where before there were no bridges. Finally, with great effort, I roused myself. I told the stranger Take back your hands, I don't need them.

And walked away. Left it there. When we were more than the sum of our parts. Yes. You were beautiful. Better than money. I won't forget. I am beautiful now. Don't let me come home a stranger.

Having Heard Of War She Tries To Make It Real

The world is as small as a radio.
Every day it broadcasts from the Office of the Dead,
piling up arguments as old and hard as stone.
    and the children play with it
    and the widows draw their veils against its light
    and the young women grow it in their wombs
    and the young men break their bones on it
    and the river carries it
    and the trees wither in its wind

My grandmother told me
You used to be able to tell who the murderer was right off.
    Whenever the murderer came near the body, the body broke
    out bleeding.
Now it's empty.
Now it's like the medieval test of chastity:
    We lie with violence like those two lovers naked in the bed,
    the sword between them. In the morning there's no blood.
    But you know something happened.

Having heard of war I
try to make it real.
The man and the woman at the next table debate the innate
    aggressiveness of the species. Getting angrier and angrier.
My father, my uncles, hunker down in the driveway at dusk. It
    is thirty years ago. I am the daughter leaning quietly against
    the dogwood. My left foot plays with the tire of the car they
    worked on all day. They rub the red wincing eyes of their
    cigarettes against asphalt. Tear the ends of the paper, scatter
    tobacco. They tell me: Soldiers do it. Light draws fire.

Having heard this, I
try to make it real. I imagine battlefields without any
knowledge of battlefields. It's like those nights when the moon is new.
It's there. I just can't see it.

Now the yellow bird sits high in the acacia tree shaking brittle
    pods for seeds.
Now the white cat hides among the purple flowers looking up.
Now the sun swings on its rope in the west.

Now the moon swings on its rope in the east.
        The ancients call this
        The confrontation of the gods.
        The radio is calling it: A remarkable event! ... in
            the square today a one man threw a cloud of
            white petals into the air. A symbol of grief; a
            clearly illegal act.

He was taken away.
It is taken in. Swallowed.
Something happens.
Soldiers do it

Fire a gun over any river.
When the moon is new the
bodies will surface:
   women floating on their backs, men with their faces down.
That is the way I sleep.
Come near a Map of the World, the
countries will break out bleeding.
That is the way I walk.
Scattered. Grief-stricken.
Having heard of war
I know nothing except this:
        The earth is tired of it.
        There are no cities of refuge left.

The Cities Of Madame Curie   *(excerpts from a book-length poem)*

There is a broken circle
and a circle getting smaller and smaller.

Marie! Your children wear such frightened clothes!
They shiver
arms crossed and clutching their shoulders
They throw more wood on the fire
They carry the light with them into the caves and
paint the walls with their lives

The rain, the earth : borders are irrelevant
When they dance for the dead
It is the future as well as the past

I too was dealt aces and eights —
the dead man's hand —
at birth

I live in the city of Madame Curie
Her hair grows long in the Parisian graveyard
Matted and sticky as sugar spun between wooden spoons
— Angel Hair! —
Her skin dissolving into chaos
A promise old as stone
Then the mouth dreaming equations
This confusion of physics
                    hovering and slain
                    cruel and idealized
            Marie is the perfect and terrible mother
            Goddess of the dog days of the twentieth century
            Brilliant and modern as Radium

                            •

My sister-in-law calls to say she is pregnant for the third time
and it will be a boy
        The egg slips and mates
        The migration begins with neurons, their
          impeccable placement
            Minute homing pigeons of sternum, spine

She says she knows it will be a boy because a woman held a
    string weighted with stones over her wrist

If it moves in a circle, it's a girl. But it swung back and forth so ...

The light of the world
illuminating the abdominal wall: and inside a small fish sleeps
    in its circular sea

Can you say that place is
free
of contamination?

Where they never chose to make their home
The family gathered
and sheared
staked to the horrified light at Ground Zero
The well water tasting of metal
The clouds shaped like animals

Test it
as the scientist tests the Shroud of Turin, the
flutes and skulls from a cave outside Beijing
Radiation reveals the age

Savannah is burning, Madame Curie. You may no longer stop
Along the road to Savannah. If your car breaks down,
don't get out.

•

Here is a box to soften the street.
Here is my wrist.
Remove my hand and drink.

The city glows tonight.
Seven bonfires.
Light and guns like
Goya's Execution.

Lessie next door plays the slowest piano.

What is this
GODGODGOD — — —?
The bells of Samoan Catholics, American Indian Baptists,
break their backs on the cold-blooded wind

All day the sun made plums from green stones.
Tang brought the entire family to my door to return my wallet
— with all the money in it!

She said The Blue Angels frightened the baby.

Crows fill the enormous fir. The lights of Geneva Towers come
    on. Lessie plays each note
like it's a tooth from someone living here.

Tang showed me a small square of cloth on a ribbon around her neck.

There's a saint inside, she said.

Sliver of bone wrapped in sheeting.
It suggests the entire body
sleeping and holy with trust.

The plum tree in the yard gathers the darkness into its fruit.
If I rubbed Tang's bone against the fruit
I'm certain the fruit would throw down its tree
and walk.

Blues For Daddy

I know that/Music but not
studied
Dancing down the
stairs at twelve, Daddy gets out

the trumpet   from the linen closet

I
bring my hand to my mouth the way he
gets the horn to
fade with the
white cup on the end of the instrument
Baby Bees fly off my tongue He puts
78's from Tokyo on the hi-fi
I tie my bathrobe sash to the
bedpost
Use it for a partner Now I'm
swinging Daddy's face red as his hair
His lips disappear into the
slim gold mouth I dance
away from the bathrobe sash Move back
in Daddy's doing
                'On the Good Ship Lollipop
                it's a sweet trip to the candy shop ...'

That's when Daddy
did it, that's when Daddy was young
and Cool
Down on one knee doing me a
miniature concert —

Deep in my throat I can
make a horn sound, too
To this day a reasonable Sentimental Journey:
       'Wah uhwah uwah uwahuwahwah
       Wahuwha Uhwah wahwahwah ...'
The old man only played if you
pleaded with him
The instrument so gold like a dream
Put away Worn to pewter where he blew
He'd gone blind wanting
Life another way
I took it out sometimes
Cased like fine silverware in stiff maroon velvet
Pieces you had to
Fit together   Or he
couldn't spare the breath at the
end of the day
Man-O-War playing Daddy at the Dinnertable
45's of Dale Carnegie talking into an
empty living room
The trumpet cold as an ax in the woodshed
While the
traveling salesman with his
new-car-every-year
drinks 5 foot Mai Tais in Memphis' finest hotel lobby
Goes upstairs drunk, does something
in the dark with his
fingers and the air

The tinny woman's voice comes on singing:
       'Isn't it a Pity? Isn't it a
          Crime ...'
Daddy knocks his pipe
against his chair then he's
playing for her in the
hall by the linen closet

I put on my Hawaiian MuMu my godmother Dot brought me
back from an island,
Pull a stocking from Mama's top drawer over
my head
Pretend I have
long hair
I'm twenty-one
Exotic
The cats get excited Their
tails flair back and forth
Daddy sticks his head out from the
hall, says Satchmo like it's one
syllable
I know it
broke his heart I know he's
blind and not telling I know he
tried to take us camping once
Out by lake Erie — He Can't get a fire going with coals —
I know he only played it
once in a blue moon and then only
for the kids I know he played
basketball in Korea and
Reveille at the
darkest hour
I know he let the water from the hose run into the
yard on the coldest nights
So we could
Skate
in the morning
I know he never got it out in winter
He played that trumpet in Oklahoma City
sitting in the heavy heat on the broad blue porch
Baby sister clapped her hands in the flower pot
I put
socks on my hands Pretended I was a
High Class Dancer in gloves

One time Daddy sucked a hornet in on a high note
Never came out the other end.
He says he swallowed it. I believe him. My Daddy always lied
   to me.
Sat there drinking Grasshoppers, Green Hornets

Said: Anything's possible. Said: I can do that, I can do that
Listening to these thick old records
long after all the horn blowers he'd known
gave way to Alpert and
Hirt
He'd stand up, work his
fingers in the air
Cause he'd given the trumpet away to a nephew
And jewels isn't the only thing we
pass on when we
Cross over

Sparrow 13 LaughingWand
b.1959

Sparrow is a street poet from West Virginia — with a street poet / gay / hillbilly voice, very competently done. The poetry itself goes right to you, a pure speaking voice — the best descriptive poet we've got on the scene. When Sparrow describes something it's right there in front of you. Sparrow is a member of a radical faerie group; and is into magic. Autobiographical notes from *The Queen Of Shade:* "I was born taurus w/pisces rising in the coal and corn bread heart of west virginia; left school to pursue a career in vagrancy, experimental mysticism and small villainies. I've been around the block and tackled; got a million miles on my right thumb and now I live in Oakland. I've written since kidhood off and on; the last few years have been instigated and abetted by my lover, jack (who got me to take creative writing at Vista) and the utterly hopping open reading! small press scene in the bay area. Thanks everyone. I love intense print media, hard rock music, poetry, getting high, deep weirdness and movies that leave scars on your brain. My life is rich in friends and awash with drama." Chapbooks include *Bums Eat Shit*, and *Seven Dollar Shoes,* Manic D Press, 1990 & 1991; and *The Queen Of Shade,* Zeitgeist Press, 1993.

The Queen Of Shade

one in the morning   as quiet as it gets
im twelve blocks from home with sunglasses on   lookin fatal
feral
wearin dominion   im really high   invisible   im
dressed
to rob houses or hug shadows   im the queen of shade
                              vanity and drugs

give me a country where ive got the street to myself
nighttime sidewalks
keep my secrets   as long as i look fatal
                                   animal swish and smile in place
ive got sunglasses on   darkness be my nation
im as safe as you get until the lights and the big loud
                                        stereo sound
swell up around me   theres a car full of strangers and the
jagged music of their glass and metal universe
comin up behind me real slow   i aint invisible   ive got
sunglasses on
im a white faggot in north murderville
im nine blocks from home   im alone
im unarmed   im out of shape
on drugs   drunk   with no money   frozen into
                        a moment of noise and light
with every nerve in my feet and head and
                                   rapescarred asshole exposed
twangin a prehistoric bass riff about lunchmeat walkin
murderville adrenalin bloodshed murderville bad timin
                        murderville bad luck murderville
louder faster murderville happens every night
                        psychokiller   nightstalker
rockhead with a shotgun   death by mistaken identity
local kids gone mean and tribal because this is the fuckin slums
at one in the morning
undercover pussy patrol cops or less privileged misogynists
lookin maybe for lonely nooky presumin on my long hair or
sharp eyed homophobes with hards on and two by fours
theyre out for my ass anyway
the beast in me is wide awake but hes a shithouse rat and
this is bobcat alley   i wonder if lookin fatal matters when
youre dead and if i'll piss my pants on impact   maybe theyll
just take my rings and beer
                                   like last time
the car makes a left and fades away
im wearing nighthuggers nine blocks from home
its one in the morning   as quiet as it gets
im the queen of shade after the revolution

im the queen of shade on my way to the blade
in the land of the young and fierce
where my shoes clatter come and get it to
every wild dog in town that can smell fear and my hearts
a leper bell   attitude melted to clingy black rags
im not dressed to run   theyd catch me anyway
lookin right is important
when its all youre sure about besides death and malt liquor
ive got sunglasses on to pass for my shadow   im wearin
black
because night belongs to fear
the way day belongs to work and anger
so i wear its color for camouflage by alchemy
im the queen of shade manifestin the velvet shrouded angel
who stands between me and my next breath and says
its a hungry world
by the time i get home   the revolutions put down   for
now
my throat still thinks
                    its about to get cut by that guy across the street
i get upstairs my keys paranoid guilty windchime jangle jangle
fumble pokin at the lock
scared embarrassed home with just my fatal glamor intact and
                                        a forty ouncer
maybe if i chug it i'll get to sleep before dawn

And Fuck The Bad Karma

i was thinkin about the new age comin on
 and how someone had better tell the cops about it
when i saw the 2 white guys at 9th and mission
they smelled like beer and trouble   one was 40 or so
the kid had on cop shades at midnight   i wasn't into
playin chicken   i walked by thinkin positive
                    i walked by thinkin invisible
it almost worked
                         "hey lady do you got a cigarette
                                   yo uh
                                scuse me

DUDE"
they yawhawhawed   i wanted to turn around and rip
their cocks off with my tongue   and fuck the bad
karma   but there was a graveyard thump
in their laughin   i got half across
the street   the one who could talk yelled
                    "hey you wanna
                        suck
                        our
                        dicks"
i started runnin   because the new age is on us
when coyotes will live longer than lions   i started runnin
like a dog   like a wolf   like a hounded
faggot into an alley   they ran right by   i was thinkin
about the new age breakin like dawn and hopin it came
in windows where hopeless men were cryin
in front of the steel door that opens
onto night   i heard em runnin   i was thinkin
about the new age fallin on us like rain   and
someone
had better tell that wet wino
how the germs in his chest and
he and god were one   movin together into numb
love   and
the universe was perfect   it was the dawnin of the age of
aquarius and i was hunchin behind a dumpster
                            my heart jerkin 8 times a second
i stuck my head out slow because the new age
was comin on like a hit and i wanted to see if it was
really bullshit   the noises down the street
weren't music   but it's all relative   i crossed
the street and headed home
            thinkin about the new age and how somebody had
better tell the president   when i saw 2 drag queens
laughin outside a bar   the black one dropped a piece of rebar
        with a bloody tibetan clangg

                    the fat one had on cop shades
at 12:15   i kept goin down the street
there was an ambulance
a blood stain shaped like someone's aura and 2

white guys on stretchers   the kid wasn't saying anything   the ugly one
was cryin
i guess the new age
          really is coming on

Sixpack

friday night   too hot to sleep
curse of the alligator people on channel 13   babys
cryin again   blacknwhite tv   sixpack of warm beer
got laid off today   pint o jacktheblack
                              west virginias all about coal
                              west virginias all about
shotguns   trailerpark three years neighbors fight all the time
kid and a baby   nellys gonna have another
                              nellys got no front teeth
gonna have it by halloween   west virginias all about
babies in a trailer   its so goddamn hot   past midnight
          one day well have color tv   one day well have
          air condition   well have another
baby   just got laid off   west virginias
all about coalmines   beat to shit pickup truck
                                        refrigerator
broke down   cough all mornin   laid off
                                        warm beer
its so goddamn hot   its so goddman hot
its all about the baby aint shut up for an hour   its all about
the shotgun   empty pint   warm beer baby screamin
laid off   nellys drunk again
ninety two degrees   three shots   then the tv
one for the icebox   one more shell
sheriff came by later
nellys mommy at all the funerals
cryin why why
mustve been drugs   it had to be
drugs   west virginias all about
it

Trollbusters

when the word first came it
sounded like a rumor   one of those stories like
christmichael gettin caught asleep by the cops
who beat him to death and threw him
in the san lorenzo river   then
the word became flesh and went among us
trollbusters
drove by scribner park throwin stuff   they called us
trolls
cunts or scrotes   theyd yell take a bath and hit
you with a bag of shit   nobody
thought of gettin the cops   we were
outsiders   acid heads and food stamp nomads
we were a winter plague of panhandlers   we
were meat that season
trollbusters
walked up and down the railroad tracks with flashlights
it was worst when the bars closed
buffalo john got beaten
to lumpy shit with a bat   i came
home to my campsite and found it all
cut to pieces   my sleepin bag and
five years of poems gone
trollbusters
paraded by daylight with canes
with sunglasses and bandanna faces
trollbusters
raped crazy brenda on the beach and
came tryin to buy acid
so they could rambo on the dealers   we
started campin together   goin home before midnight
in fours and fives
the story got around   .
that they were cops little brothers
the story got around
that the merchants association had
hired them to clean up the mall
stories got around

like truth wasnt bad enough
trollbusters
posted flyers sayin
"bums and hippies beware
ninja revenge is everywhere"
trollbusters
came to the free kitchen
shovin people around
trollbusters
were local boys   and so nobody
ever thought of gettin the cops   until the night three
trollbusters
went cruisin
with a bazooka made out of
model rocketry parts and pvc pipe
they shot the first longhair they saw
on the river street bridge with a binaca bottle full of carbide
he nearly lost an arm   he wasnt one of
us   he was a cabdriver   and so the cops and the
press got involved   the word
trollbusters
got into newsprint   the wheelman
turned himself in and named names
they were all buff mercenary wannabes   reporters
were all over the place for a week
buying us coffee   writin us down   the paper got
letters sayin dont ruin these young mens futures
over our sorry asses   they got suspended
sentences after their parents paid off
the victim   the story was over so
the press went away and left us with
trollbusters
all that wet scary winter

Cocaine Pantoum

She's praying to the Versateller machine
Eyes red as pills and psych ward bright.
God's cold copper guts pulse hot money.
Cars are staring at her. Tellers mutter.

Eyes red as pills and psych ward bright
her religion ticks in a glass vial.
Cars are staring at her. Tellers mutter;
"Somebody had better call the cops"

Her religion ticks in a glass vial,
Her shadow chills the machinery.
Somebody had better call the cops,
She's a 51/50 for sure.

Her shadow chilled the machinery.
They had to come and get her.
She's a 51/50 for sure,
Praying for an instant miracle.

They had to come and get her
before the manna dropped,
Praying for an instant miracle,
She got a Thorazine Bed.

Before the manna dropped
(she wanted another hour of grace
But got a Thorazine Bed)
She was on the hellbound bus

She wanted another hour of grace
But that's blasphemy.
She was on the hellbound bus
For asking God directly.

But that's blasphemy;
No One shall look at his face.
For asking God directly
She was bound in tight white hours.

No One shall look at his face
Cold pulse God of laws, not miracles.
She was bound in tight white hours.
She prayed to the Versateller machine.

Grannybones

little old ladies   whispery skin and smoky hair
bottomless eyes of grief and mystery
death and memory movin
slow on glass legs   rheumatic skinny ankles
ringed with antique dirt
little old ladies pick up cups and pizza crust
they drink brandy in souplines wearin ripped up sneakers
                                        and obsolete tomorrows
                              they cant get drunk enough to forget
little old ladies with graveyards full of children
fell into age like a kettle of shadow
                              and came out scarier than soldiers
they walk across market street talkin to ghosts or
bent under bundles of petrified firewood
bones of city in city of bones pushin carts full of secrets and
          yesterdays pleasure to the welfare hotel on the cheap side
                                                  of hell
where the heaters break down and the radio plays backward
little old ladies tangled and waitin
inevitable unrespected always cold celluloid gray driftin eatin dry
                                                  bread
little old ladies are the scariest
they won the game   it wasnt fun
theyre way ahead of you and you dont know where they
                                        came from
or their names but
little old ladies are countin your bones
they know everything and they wont tell you
you bore them to death
bones of cities in cities of bones with little buzzard hands
with misery tattooed on their faces
with unimagined histories of pain and beauty
little old ladies   dead on sidewalks and psych wards
                    dead in rooms full of cats and candles
                    dead in newspaper beds and storefront churches
powdery eyes and healed over calendars
little old ladies remember it all

On the Downtown Bus

they sounded happier than me   that was easy enough
i was hungover   wearin a suit   thinkin about
bugs and cancer   but
they were talkin
murder   somebodys sisters boyfriend
got stabbed outside a bar   they were talkin
murder like movies   on the 72 bus   you
couldnt not listen   so i looked   they
were my age or so   two women in nurse whites
talkin murder   it was everywhere   one of em
had a patient whose husband fed her drano
     the other one said
shed had that guy from the papers who shot
his family and lit himself on fire   she said
he grabbed her tits   then   hey theres that
deadmeat sally bitch inna park   i'll get off this bus n
go get teresa   yeah
the fat one   that is sally aint it   i looked again
they were still nurses   still laughin   the first one said
shes dodgin clarence too   she owes him fifty bucks
     they both fell out
i wanted to laugh myself   or cry   but it was their
show
i'll tell clarence then   teresa just got
outta jail   she don t need to go back and she ll
cut sally s throat for sure   bitch got her brothers neck broke
by two rockheads for a hundred dollars
then there was
a guy they knew   shot in his front yard
by mistake   but he died anyway
you couldnt not listen   an old guy
just ahead of me kept lookin back
youd think they were his daughters
he hated em so bad

Larry Said

Oh, the filthy chalice of his skull
blown apart in New York.
Oh, his razorback heart and his lead sugar mouth.
Larry said his mother died in a house fire
             while he was in the joint.
Larry said it was political.   Larry told
the dumbest arrest story I ever heard   how he
broke into a liquor store and got too drunk to escape.
The Nevada beauty of his tomcat ass could
                         scratch your eyes out.
Larry said he was an honest thief.
Larry said I wasn't queer   because he loved me.
          Thanksgiving we had lentils under my tarp
          in a storm at Davenport.
Larry said he wasn't a queer
because I wasn't really a man,
that night he got shitfaced and came onto me
like a rubber lizard.
The next day I told him about it.
Larry said, "You turned me dow-wn?" like I'd
                called him a narc.
Larry said it was okay to sell incense and coffeemate for 20 bucks
          if you stuck with servicemen and tourists. We ran together
eight or nine months   through mushroom season
         six fistfights   a visit to my parents.
Larry said they didn't like him.
Larry said he loved me like a man so he couldn't get
          it up for me.   I never saw him get it up at all.
He said   he said   he said   every word
he said was a cock that spurted out from his
lips and knocked up the air with
another goddamn lie.
Larry was as sexy as death.   He was
 a Gypsy looking longhair Italian with a scarred nose
he got in a six car wreck   he said.
I left him drunk asleep in an irrigation ditch.
Three weeks later we met at the Rainbow
Gathering.   He had a New York girlfriend and

religion.   They were going to follow the Dead
shows
he said.
Larry said he loved me and he'd send me a half sheet
to make up for the twenty bucks he took from my
bag before I left.
Larry said life was too much fun to die over money.
A year later in Tucson Doc told me that
Larry said it was okay to sell incense and coffeemate
          right up until someone put his beautiful rap
          all over the sidewalk.
Oh, the hell soup of blood banging past his brown eyes with drugs
          battering that cancer which served him for a brain.
Oh, the filthy grail of skull that served
communion for his rat god.   Oh,
the lies he told   that still wake me up
with a sleeping bag wind like Nevada in my bed.   The lies
lasted longer than
any truth he had in him.

Bums Eat Shit

(graffiti on Market Street between 7th & 8th, San Francisco)

They
          sleep and stink and scream on the street
They
          expect to be fed
They
          piss in doorways and shit between parked cars
They
          curl up on sidewalks crying
They
          call you motherfucker
They
          call you sir
They
          ask you for a quarter
They
          snub Jesus at the rescue mission reeking through

the sermon thinking only of the soup and doughnuts
They
ask you for a quarter and call you motherfucker
They
steal garbage from restaurants and stare in the windows
They
lean on disgraced walls and smile mysteriously at your shoes
                                                                and   then
They
ask you for a quarter, like
They
deserve to get paid for living.
They
worship garbage gods.
They
are scary, dirty and insane
They
breathe rotten candy breath in the faces that
They
ask for a quarter surely bound to wine and dope and pornopeep
shows, cigarettes and installments on early public graves
They
fuck in parks like drunk alleycats just
like the world needed more shopping cart babies
They
ask you for a quarter and then call you motherfucker
when you tell
Them
how it is.
                                    Bums eat shit.
They
ask you for a quarter and don't say please,
like
They
thought it came to you free, because
They
get everything free, clothes and food and cigarette butts,
free, and then ask you for a quarter, just like
They
could sell you
Their warts

Their canes, or the needles in
Their veins, and the garbled horror movies in
Their drive-in brains
They

    are scary, dirty and insane
They

    ask you for a quarter to buy fine wines
    to go with the foodstamp steaks and
    cocaine snorted through rolled up
    welfare checks in the back of a
    Lincoln Continental with velvet seats
    that smell like buttermilk
They

    sold their souls for cigarettes because
They

    wouldn't work if the job was rolling joints
    for ten dollars an hour in an air conditioned office
    when it's so much easier for
Them

    to ask you for a quarter fifty times a day
    seven days a week, Sundays and holidays,
    at three fourteen a.m. and at the bus stop.
                       Bums eat shit.
They

    are Mona whose stomach hurts all the time
    and Sue who writes poems on the sidewalk,
    RC and Pablo cast gay and teenaged from
    their homes, Wino Dave and Smiley,
    Daphne and her daughters, Otto
    who got fired and Otto who quit,
    lazy Mitch and crazy Swan and the other Otto,
    who slid from crime to carny to the street
    looking for Maisie who was saving up
    to become a woman and a dancer; she
    was good and you might have heard
    a lot about her but the spoon found her first, and
They

    are Louise whose husband would have killed
    her someday, and Dallas John who rode
    freight trains thirty years before
    he lost a leg, and Teresa who babbles

Bible and got gang banged by God and her
father before she was nine, and
They
are dying a million smelly deaths
on slow dirty asphalt.
They
are fighting old wars, space wars,
cold wars and germ wars inside
Their clamorous nitflected heads.
They
steal garbage, can you imagine stealing garbage?
They
have bruisy grabbing hands and American ancient
troubles living on
Their burlap faces.
                              Bums eat shit. And
They
ask you for a quarter because that's all the good
You
are to
Them.

Black As The Marrow Of My Hillbilly Bones

brown beans and cornbread
tater soup   deermeat
biscuits n gravy made of
bacon grease and flour
gun games in the holler
watchin out for copperheads
rattlesnakes and yellajackets
swingin on a grapevine
daddy worked underground
diggin up coal
and i was born with coal
in my bones   brown snuffspit and cigaret smoke
the greasy smoke from down inside
a gob piles black heart black as the marrow
of my hillbilly bones
i aint been back
this is a whole country over
this is fifty years away and
i aint even forty
i aint been back   it aint ever gone
the coal and the butternut trees
are in the way i talk and how i love jack daniels
my grannys needles in the jar   are memories cold silver threat
that theres a coaldust thumbprint on my health
it could happen next week   sugar could turn into poison
my daddys guns are the iron in me   blued or
               black like coal iron never less than beautiful
               black like black lung iron never innocent or
                 without a chill to look at
like grannys needles   never far from my dark holler mind
that understands blood feuds better than computers
however california i dance these days
im dancin in black bear boots
whichever library im borrowin stylins and cool from
whatever theyd call me back there
if i ever went back there
back theres back home   to the coal dust marrow
of my hillbilly bones
my roots are ramps and mayapple
my roots are yellaroot and poke
my roots are the ginseng that all got dug up

in the last 20 years and sold to the chinese   because
back theres where poor turns whiter than anyones bones
i got orneriness in church
instead of religion and even though ive developed
talents and proclivities   the god of that church
would hate me for it if he was real
still it aint church if they dont sing about blood
blood   my hillbilly blood that flowed from somewhere celtic to
back home
and all the way to high magickal high faggotry in california
blood my hillbilly blood that took to drugs like moonshine
                    that keeps me bein polite to old folks and
                    talkin to every dog i meet
the blood from my coal dusted marrow still likes it big
yeah
hillbilly bones love big american iron
                smith and wesson
                harley davidson
                cadillacs gmcs
                rock n roll
                coup de villes and   stratocasters
yeah man   hillbillies
dig big american iron   they feed it coal and their underpaid
workin lives
and im still   there   it came west with me
hung out in hippieland and a dozen cheap wine queer bars
it read my poetry in a back home voice that never once
choked on what i fed it
sometimes i love my hillbilly bones and blood
they remember the taste of oven roasted squirrel brains
                        served in their little skulls
sometimes they start in again about
                you white trash faggot
                you dopehead ass rip off
your poetry aint shit and youre goin to hell
but they keep me alive hillbillies don't opt out easy
if i don't die drunk or if
the sugar or my daddys cancer don't get me
i'll live a hundred years and turn to leather and grapevine
tough like grandma
smokin her pipe   rockin and spittin snuff off her front porch
buried a country and a century away
where they grow hillbilly bones

Julia Vinograd   b.1943

Julia came on the scene long before the Spaghetti Factory. She's a Berkeley *living legend* and a fixture on Telegraph Avenue for twenty-five years. Julia's work is that of a sophisticated voice rejecting sophistication in favor of writing poetry for everyday-people to read. Accessibility and directness are well-springs of her work. The ease with which she can be understood and the humanity of her vision have won her a large devoted poetry audience (many of whom after listening to Julia's readings discovered for the first time that they *did like poetry*). Her work finds its way into the local political debate (a People's Park poem was read into the record by a fan at a City Council meeting; her work appeared in a front page article of the Oakland Tribune). Julia's *Book Of Jerusalem* poems received an American Book Award from the Before Columbus Foundation in 1985. Julia Vinograd was raised in Pasadena, California, and moved early to Berkeley, the city she's become so identified with. Her mother was an English professor at UC Berkeley, and her father a biochemistry expert at CalTech. Born with a severe epilepsy, as a child Julia contracted polio and almost died. Julia attended UC Berkeley, then received an MFA from the Iowa Writer's Workshop. Julia has published thirty-six poetry books through small press; and has settled into doing two books per year. Julia is a freelance editor for Zeitgeist Press.

For The Berkeley Inn,
Where I Lived For 15 Years Being Torn Down

The wrecking ball swinging against the bricks
is big as crazy George's shaved head
when she took a heavy stick on full moon nights,
banged on all the doors
and bellowed for quiet like a charging refrigerator.
The cops always came when George had a quiet attack,
heavy shoulders, muscled neck,
it took three of them to haul her off,
and she was back the next morning.
As the bricks tumble she roars from the ruins
"Quiet, I said, quiet, you assholes!"
It's going down, the watching crowd gasps
with each blow, it can't be fixed anymore,
not even Charlie can fix it.
Charlie, the desk clerk mechanic
whose wife ran off with a cop, so he became a stalinist
and the landlady fired him each time he got drunk
but she always hired him back
because the elevator was in love with him
and wouldn't work for anyone else.
He had a dozen t.v. sets in his room
that he took happily apart and put reluctantly
back together. And he was kind to me.
I look at the plaster dust.
There should be records of that kindness
set in plaster like fossil leaves
but it's all gone now.
And Florence, the first landlady;
skinny, tough, always furious.
We said she'd run a whorehouse in Texas
which is the highest compliment
tenants can give a landlady.
She told me if I went out into some riot
She wasn't letting me back in,
so I stalked out nobly, collapsed from the tear gas
and Florence ran after me and dragged me back
more or less by my ear.
I once saw her threaten to call the cops on a cop.

As long as these walls stood they knew her name
but one wall is down and the second is going.
Now I have to write her name
and she never did think much of poetry.
And Guy, one of the oldest desk clerks
much too deaf to work but he wouldn't believe it.
Someone would come and ask for a room
and Guy would turn purple and yell
"You can't call me that!"
and reach for a nightstick under the desk
and whoever was backing him
would take it gently away.
Were we all crazy? Mainly we were friends,
and with friends it's not a pertinent question.
And there was the building itself.
There'd been a banquet room once,
closed before I moved in.
There was a t.v. room where we all came
and tried to spot ourselves on the news.
There were 5 floors of hotplates, potplants,
parties, people overnight
and never enough toilet paper.
There were cockroaches of course,
but very clean cockroaches.
I had a room with 5 walls and a view of the hills
I thought I would live there forever,
and I thought I would live forever.
A pile of rubble with pigeons circling,
but when I close my eyes I still see
that rug in the lobby: red, maroon, blue-looped
swirling, everyone swore it was the first rug on acid
and I see the switchboard behind the desk,
a tangle of beeping lines
as the desk clerk snaps,
"hold on a sec, just hold on."
And I'm holding
but it's hard.

November, 1990

Listening To The Radio

I am listening to the radio.
I am not listening to the radio.
I am listening to the silence in my room
behind the radio.
I am the radio. Listen.
I can hear the night sucking its burnt fingers
that touched the quarreling lovers.
I can hear the big trucks going out,
the white line whipping at their windshields.
I can hear the old women selling terrible roses
in the chlorine-lit subway.
I can hear the young hustlers, their tight jeans
glowing in the greedy dark.
I can hear the ghosts mowing their own graves.
It's very late.
Everyone else is asleep
with commercials pulled over their heads
dreaming of sex and cigarettes and money and work.
No, I don't know what they're dreaming,
I don't even know
if there's anyone else left.
The radio talks to itself like a bag lady
in an empty room.
Not to me.
I fell asleep an hour ago and didn't notice.
I am the radio.
I am the bag lady.
I am the night.
Listen.

Kaddish For Martin Horowitz

It's rained since you died
and I hated being out in the rain
more than I hated your being dead
because I was getting wet.
Everything continues as always,
I continue as always, dammit,
when something's funny I laugh,
and I'm not sure whether to be relieved
or outraged or both.
And I feel selfish, I want you back
for my sake, not yours.
You were someone to talk to
who could empathize without listening,
and always say the right thing in emergencies
and the wrong thing the rest of the time
so I could be right and bright and silly;
who could look like a cartoon of a N.Y. Jewish mad scientist,
and then be a N.Y. Jewish mad scientist:
who collected pythons and used to collect guns
till some nut acquired one from you to shoot his girl
and you got life except they let you out
because you were going to die within the year
and then you didn't,
and they were no end irritated,
and some professor wrote a letter
recommending you as an original researcher and said the girl
had been in his class and she was so dumb
he would've shot her himself if only he'd thought of it first;
who went around the world 4 times
to let the snakes loose in the rice paddies to catch rats
and explain yourself to the customs officials;
who was born blind and kept night-blindness and could read
only by taking off your bottlerim glasses
and touching the print on your nose;
who survived 2 plane crashes,
1 car crash, assorted fires
and 7 years of marriage;
who was on a guilt trip that meant opening all conversations
by informing your helpless listeners you'd worked on the Manhattan Project

and what about it?
who was a snob in all directions,
despising street people
and detesting academia
and lecturing yourself
and wearing a give away suit but never a tie;
who wanted your neutrinos back from the sun,
you took such things personally,
a neutrino has only spin and travels at the speed of light
passing thru walls with the greatest of ease and so do you now;
who had an affair with a witch
without a navel,
and a dike who could beat you up,
and a red haired smack freak you tried to cure
and get supplies for, more or less at once,
she's dead now too;
who was disastrous and irreplaceable.
It's been a month by now
and I still have to tell unexpected people
and watch their faces fall off
and see what their masks will look like in 20 years.
Who will always like my war poems best
and argue I'm not a pacifist
and tell me the hard boiled egg I just bought is raw
and I throw it at you to prove it isn't
and it is because you palmed it
and you're all over egg yolk but so pleased you proved your point
and won't let me forget it,
and I still go on being a pacifist
but who will slip me raw eggs now?
I'm not used to being emotional
and/or dead all over the stage,
but there is a hole in the air where once there was a man,
and Marty, what the hell,
is this your idea of a joke?

Childhood

Nobody beat me. Nobody hated me.
I was always a little in the way
but I wasn't blamed for it.
Everybody was very nice.
We had a Christmas tree for years
because I liked the decorations:
the frosted glass balls, the tinsel icicles,
the flashing lights
even though we were Jewish.
I had piano lessons because I asked for them
because a girl at school boasted about them
and I didn't have to stop
till I noticed I couldn't stand the piano.
I was sick a lot.
Maybe not going to live.
Father was polite to me
like an inconvenient guest.
Mother told me marvelous stories,
like messages to whatever came after death.
I'd never had enough friends
to know I was lonely.
I read a lot.
I wanted to marry either Bela Lugosi
or Basil Rathbone:
they both had such marvelous long fingers.
I remember squinting at dust motes
between the sun and the pale linen curtains,
trying to turn them into angels.
I remember my grandmother
telling my fortune every day:
all happy, all different, all lies.
There were plenty of toys and layer cake
with pink frosting.
I remember the pattern of the carpet in the hall
had more rights in that house than me.
It was a nice childhood,
but it wasn't mine.
It wasn't mine at all.

In The Bookstore

I went down to the bookstore this evening
and found myself in the poetry section.
But for every thin book of poems
there was a thick biography of the poet
and an even thicker book
by someone who's supposed to know
explaining what the poet
is supposed to've said and why he didn't.
So you don't have to waste your time
on the best the writer could do,
the words he fought the darkness and himself for,
the unequal battle with beauty.
Instead you can read comfortably
about the worst the writer could do:
the mess he made of his life,
how he fought with his family,
cheated on his lovers, didn't pay his debts
and not only drank too much
but all the stupid things
he ever said to the bartender
just before getting 86'd will be printed for you
and they're just as stupid
as the things everyone says just before getting 86'd.
The books explaining the poet
are themselves inexplicable.
The students who *have* to read them
cheat.
I left the poetry section
thinking about burning the bookstore down.
Some of a poet's work comes from his life, o.k.
But most of a poet's work comes
in spite of his life, in spite of everything,
even in spite of bookstores.
So I went to the next section
and bought a murder mystery but I haven't read it yet.
I find I don't want to know who done it
and why;
       I want to do it myself.

For My Tree In Israel

There is blood on my tree,
on the tree with my name in Israel.
The tears of tear-gassed crowds water the roots,
and the tears of rage
and the tears of grief for the dead.
Is this the tree I planted to bring forth life from the desert?
The broken bones of hands throwing rocks
and the rocks they threw pile around my tree,
the tree with my name in Israel.
It did not begin like this.
Everyone in my class planted a tree in Israel,
filled out a form and sent a letter
with our names.
I could've had pictures sent me of the tree
growing as I grew
but I didn't want to know what it looked like.
The tree didn't know what I looked like.
We shared a name, it was my name,
it was enough.
And now there is blood on my name
on my tree in Israel.
Do not speak to me of self-defense,
of necessity and nations and history.
There is no water in such words
and I need a glass of water before I sleep.
Do not explain, it may be true but it doesn't help,
it is not in the same language
in which my tree talks to the wind.
There must always be an Israel
because my tree is there
and they shall never come with axes
and cut down my name.
But there is blood on my tree
and the smell of blood
and I want my name to be good again.
I want my good name to grow in Israel
and put out damp new leaves every spring,
as soft as kisses.

The Sparechangers Came From Outer Space

The sparechangers came from outer space.
Underneath the grime of the "No Public Restrooms"
those weatherworn skins are green.
The sparechangers sleep in flying saucers at night.
The cops have been enforcing force fields
to fight the panhandling peril
from other planets.
The sparechangers have unfair superior technology:
they just look at you
and it's too late.
Their eyes are like that.
Strange constellations burn
where your conscience used to be.
Their blood is made of the tears
you locked away,
but they haven't been locked away yet
and it's certainly a plot.
Those shapeless freebox raincoats
are patched with rain
and hid as many extra arms
as a tentacled monster,
all empty-handed and spoiling the view.
Alien, unnatural invaders
shambling and shuddering in mudstained shoes
from the bottom of a Martian canal.
The space warp shifts behind their faces
like a 4-dimensional stutter.
The sparechangers are incomplete Lazaruses
with laser-gun glares
whose galaxy exploded behind them;
there's a black hole in their hearts
where everything went away.
Lost. All lost.
The sparechangers came from outer space.
      After all,
        we'd never let humans
        live like this.

For The Young Men Who Died Of Aids

The dead lovers are almost as beautiful
as razor-edged spaces in the air where they used to walk.
Do you remember his hand lazily playing
with the rim of a glass, making the ghost of a bell sound
for his own ghost, and the talk didn't even pause?
That glass is whole. Break it; break it now.
Break everything.
How can people go on buying toothpaste
and planning their summer vacations?
Vegetables would care more.
The potato has a thousand eyes all mourning for the lovers
who lived in their deaths like a country
foreign to everywhere for a long time before dying.
A long time watching people look away.
The potato only met them under the earth
after their deaths and still it wept. And we do not.
The ghost bell makes barely a sound forever.
The dead lovers are still in love, but no one else is.
He took his hand with him, a grave is as good
as a briefcase to keep the essentials in:
a smile, bones, a way of biting at his lip
just before looking into your eyes.
Shoulder blades cutting into summer like butter.
All the commuters in a rush hour traffic jam
are cursing because the lovers are dying
faster than their cars.
The child sent to bed without dinner cries
for the lovers, also sent to bed early and without.
Unfair. Throw the dishes against the wall. Break them.
The dead lovers are almost as beautiful
as when they were alive.
You can hear the rim of a glass
tolling for the ghosts to come home.
Break the glass, break the ghosts. Pull down the sky.
Break everything.
Dance on the fragments. Scream their names.
Get splinters of ghosts under your skin
torn and bleeding because it hurts,
                    because it hurts so bad.

Ginsberg

No blame. Anyone who wrote *Howl* and *Kaddish*
earned the right to make any possible mistake
for the rest of his life.
I just wish I hadn't make this mistake with him.
It was during the Vietnam war
and he was giving a great protest reading
in Washington Square Park
and nobody wanted to leave.
So Ginsberg got the idea, "I'm going to shout
'the war is over' as loud as I can," he said
"and all of you run over the city
in different directions
yelling the war is over, shout it in offices
shops, everywhere and when enough people
believe the war is over,
why, not even the politicians
will be able to keep it going."
I thought it was a great idea at the time,
a truly poetic idea.
So when Ginsberg yelled I ran down the street
and leaned in the doorway
of the sort of respectable down on its luck cafeteria
where librarians and minor clerks have lunch
and I yelled "the war is over".
And a little old lady looked up
from her cottage cheese and fruit salad.
She was so ordinary she would have been invisible
except for the terrible light
filling her face as she whispered
"My son. My son is coming home."
I got myself out of there and was sick in some bushes.
That was the first time *I* believed there was a war.

Halloween Poem For My Mother

This is your first All Hallows among the dead, Mother.
You shall wear the veil between the worlds
like a bride or a nun.
For this halloween and for no other
you are the virgin mother of death,
not just your children.
Later, like the rest of the dead
you will ride the buses of memory
with a dutifully expired transfer
and commute to your grave like an office.
All skeletons look alike,
all ghosts look alike
and sooner or later
all the dead look alike to the living.
But not yet.
I can see you trying on ectoplasm
before a nonreflecting mirror
trying to remember your face.
I can see you trying to pretend
it's not your first time,
embarrassed and shy among the experienced dead,
not knowing which of their ghost stories to believe,
do bones blush, Mother?
They used to hang bedsheets outside the window
to prove the bride was a virgin,
will your winding sheets hang there, Mother?
When you trick or treat the living
you don't have to be careful
of tylenol spiked tears
or razor blades in shadow apples.
Nothing can hurt you anymore,
not even this last of first times.
If your bones are still shakey
with memories of flesh, don't worry:
the dead won't laugh at you,
the dead aren't watching you,
the dead have no eyes, Mother,
but I do.

Scarecrow

An old scarecrow, black coat torn at the elbows,
old black tophat
stuck in a field of corn
not even the crows believed him.
They tweaked straw from his neck
to line their nests
and the green corn grew and grew.

One night in the dark of the moon
that scarecrow, he climbed down,
walked to the edge of the field
where a limousine waited,
a long black limousine.
He got in, spit one straw into black gloves
and said "Drive". The chauffeur drove
and the green corn grew and grew.

They said bullets wouldn't kill him.
There were stories of men
who emptied machine guns into him
and he just looked bored,
later what was left of them
was thrown to the crows.
They said it wasn't safe
to look at him too close
'cause what you see, it don't make sense.
They said nothing got to him,
no drugs, no women,
he wouldn't even bother to get a new coat,
why should he,
everyone knew who he was
and the green corn grew and grew.

People died.
Money changed hands.
People killed.
Money changed hands.
They were so used to it everyone believed him,
except the crows who sat on his windowsill
cawing all night. Cawing all night.
He stayed up all night to listen.

One night in the dark of the moon
he got back in his limousine,
his long black limousine,
and rode to the field of corn,
walked to the center
and climbed back on his cross.
An old scarecrow, black coat torn at the elbows,
not even the crows believed him.
They pecked out his eyes
and the blood flowed down
and the red corn grew and grew.

My Own Epitaph, Which I Better Write Because I Know Too Many Poets

When I am dead,
please don't say nice things about me.
I wasn't tall and thin and friendly.
I was short and fat
and I stuttered between silences.
I was me, please don't remember
someone you would rather've known.
Don't just remember the poems I wrote
remember the inconvenient rides I begged
and I always seemed to have a cold
and I was me.
Every one of my toes were mine,
please don't remember someone else's toes.
I often went to the flea market
and bought things that reminded me of me.
I liked mangoes, roast beef and science fiction.
Don't just say I was a good listener,
add that you sometimes wondered why.
Don't make me a one dimensional nice
with a tragic story or two
like everyone else.
I wasn't everyone else, I was me.
I carried a me black purse
and wore a me black dress
and I had a bad leg so I was usually looking

for a place to sit down.
I didn't smoke or drink or sleep around
and I was too shy
to be a fascinating conversationalist,
but I was very me.
Remember my ringed fingers,
my dirty fingernails,
my mouth playing tennis on the telephone,
the way my leg brace squeaked
when I went up to the microphone
to read a poem.
It was me the sun shone on.
It was me who escaped the suburb
and blew soap bubbles on the street.
It was me whose parents died
(in this poem no one else's parents died
because this is my poem).
I loved filling up my room with me.
I always read by naked lightbulbs.
I read late, very late,
not just for the books
but so not to lose the time I was me in.
I was the nightwatchman
and I knew the night was long.
Even when I was alive.
Please don't say nice things about me
when I'm dead.
Don't treat me with respect
as if I were a stranger.
If I'm lucky the poems will live.
This isn't for the poems,
this is for me.
From God's dubious blessing
to the buttons on my cap
to the godawful cough in the back of my throat
I was a me.
With my eyes.
Remember.

Zoe Rosenfeld   b.1969

Zoe came on the scene in the late Babar years. Her poems are layered, sensual and rich. She writes: "Zoe Rosenfeld grew up in Washington, D.C. in an insular family of four, rambling around a big, run-down townhouse. She was kicked out of college in Ohio and came to San Francisco on the bus a year later, where she studied writing at SF State. She has spent a little time in New Orleans, traveled around Southeast Asia and Mexico, and now lives in New York." Has a chapbook out, *A Swarm Of Flies*, Blue Beetle, 1993.

Scapegoat

> *"If only we could also <u>milk</u> the scapegoat!"* — Stanislaw J. Lec

When you rolled in like a Mississippi showboat,
tripledecker weddingcake boat, big magenta wheel,
I sidled up to you and swigged your gin.
By the time someone pulled me aside to say,
"Watch out — watch out for him — he's greedy, greedy
and not what he seems,"
we were already kneedeep in flirtation,
and the goat in me smirked
and rammed its head against the warnings.

And the devil took my goat's legs as his own —
now wears them bent and woolly,
pulled up to his hips like wading boots,
hobbles pagan and slovenly on them, cursing.
And the devil took my goat's horns,
those toy roots, and wears them
like a pair of circus pegs nailed to his head,
swaggering, mincing, glittering and glittering
in his trashy jewelry.

And they were right, of course. You *were* greedy.
You delved into me like an oil rig tapping for the hit,
delved until you struck heart.
Poured into me like junk mail through the slot.
You made me wait for three hours in the public park
full of smokers, liars, liquordrunks,
while I kicked my heels against a statue of Poseidon
and fumed.

And I found out about the others —
how you've learned to call them honey, call them baby
so you never slip, knowing
Romeo never whispered the wrong name
in Juliet's pale and waiting ear.
When you lied, red ants marched out of your mouth,
clanking in their tiny armor.
You're not the king of anything anymore.
Your crown was foil all along,
your robe, paper.

Me? My revenge nerve's twanged by everything, everything.
I've kissed a swarm of flies in the form of a man,
my hands gone black with that infection.

I blame the stubborn goat in me —
the goat that is small as a grandmother,
with its misshapen face and eyes shied apart like magnets.
I blame the goat in me that will not listen to good advice.
I blame the goat that kicks the fence
and chews trash all day.

Story

⌣ ⌣gain.

That same story,
in which she is lava and gold shoes, honey, electric.
The way she tells it, the Geiger counter ticked
with the sheer plutonium of her,
her atom-splitting, radioactive glow.
How she danced with every boy,
her dance card full of names,
the spiderweb pages wrinkled and moist.
How she knew every step, swept through the Lindy
smooth and grand as a big American car,
kicked her shoes aside, danced in stocking feet
in the volcano-red dress.
And boys leaned against the dance hall walls
waiting their turn, their dates powdering their noses
a third time, far beyond envy.
Watching the red dress open like a tulip
as she turned.

But he's heard the story
a thousand times before.
She tells it at the laundromat,
tells it at the zoo to the apehouse janitor.
Every year there are more boys waiting for her,
every year their waiting dates grow more lovely.
But he was there, too; danced with her,
months before they married.
And what he remembers is not the stars
falling from the sky, the walls closing in to touch her,
but the ordinary way the sweat stood out on her lip,
like a woman might sweat pulling water from a well,
hoisting up the weight of it,
heaving the same bucket up year after year.

All-Night Drive

Your funny proof — this? This living forever?
You swearing, "I'm awake,"
"I'm awake"
at every mile,
shuddering, shaking off sleep.

At the last gas station, there was
a nickel in the toilet that wouldn't go down,
listing corroded in the filthy bowl.
A tiny spider dreaming in the sink.

Rigo, while you drive,
I doze, I dream we are sailing off a cliff.

We are wide awake
and the night is enormous.

The coffee flies up from the dashboard cup
like a tiny brown rug, hovers.

The gloves resting
palm to palm
rise up together like hands in prayer.

Rigo, we are spinning our wheels, suspended over a gulch;
we are wide awake in the same car, falling at the same speed.

Two bottles in the backseat roll, collide.

Rigo, though we're going down together
I feel so alone:

my love flying inwards
like a hawk
to the glove.

Motel

When you pull in out of a night
ragged with insects and sticky snacks from a Texaco,
always you are struck by
the way the room sits just-so.

What a mum-mouthed room it is,
how sworn to secrecy, how coyly implying
that it only just exploded into existence
when you opened the door.
The pleated lampshade prim in the corner,
the plastic-covered mattress anonymous, slack,
the soap square in the dish.
Whoever just shuffled out —
murderer, lover, bedwetter —
has left no trace — not one curled hair.
Whoever lay watching late-night TV,
whoever stood pissing
and missing,
whoever tossed in a squalid bed
dreaming of a creature that was
half Isabella, half sea-monster
has pulled out clean.

No sign of the terrible things done
to a spider found in the empty shower.
No sign of a father and a daughter
in the same bed
hunched at opposite edges of the mattress —
both too taut to sleep,
both having read *Lolita,* after all.

Nothing of any of this. Secret as a dumbwaiter.
All the clues pulled in
like a snail will pull in its eyes
and slide blind.

Or the maid — heavylagging behind her cart,
pushing slow past the gold doors —
has sanitized it all with her bottles and bottles.

Fortune Teller

Up the red psychic's stairs,
in a cave of cards and curtains,
she sits like a rotting head.
She reminds him of a whore,
with her gaudy get-up, inch of make-up,
and the smell of money on her hands.
"Ask me one question," she breathes. Hisses, really.

Long ago, the hot overripe South —
peeing by the side of the road in Alabama —
insects in the headlights
and cicadas sawing down the trees.

"Well?" — cigarettes, incense deep in the musk of her,
the noxious, giant smell of cooking
and sweat — "Well? Well?"

Bourbon Street was sick and hot
and he threw up in an alley
while barkers drummed up business
on the strip, "Step in!"
and all the women, gussied up and sweet
in their flowered dresses,
gone soft as pond sediment with sin, step in.

Three fat blue flies stagger in the hot room,
past the beads, past the drapes.

The dead dogs by the side of the road in headlong Juarez.
Flies washing behind their ears with their filthy feet
and meat left out for hours.

Even through her cunning, the old woman knows his fortune.
She knows the future, how it rounds like a fruit,
becomes great, becomes overblown, sinks into decay.

Through the curtains, the rooms of her house buzz on.
In the kitchen, her young daughter kicks her heels
against the greasy kitchen stool
and chews watermelon bubblegum.

The End

There you stand,
glowing, stupid and useless,
a dead star
still throwing down light.
I'm bored of your stories.
I know the frat boy story,
how he punched you in the vest
with his big class ring.
I know the city dump story,
how on acid it seemed
to spread its many white wings
and take to the air.
Your hat and your pillowcase
smell like your hair,
which is dirty and combless,
I know this.
I've burned my hands on the anarchy
of that hair,
and I'm left with the grassy mark of it
on my palm.
I know the story of the women from Texas,
twice your age,
with charm bracelets and big white teeth
who laughed and shook their silver-blond hair
and tried to get you into bed.
I know your box of bugs
and your fear of dwarves.
I know your tacky paper kitty
that forecasts the weather
by the fur on its belly.
I know your trip across the country
in the bus that smelled of
vomit, smoke, and dogs in front
and diapers and whiskey in back.
I know you hate the word 'mutton'.
Being with you is the perpetual feeling
of being in a bar by day.
Your dog Dinty Moore has pissed
on my things too many times.
Did I call you 'dead star'?
It's not enough to just say dead.
I want the head and feet to prove it.

Danielle Willis b.1967

Danielle Willis suffered a nervous breakdown at Barnard College in 1986 and was asked to leave until such time as she could provide written statements from two different psychiatrists that she was stable enough to continue her studies. Since then she has worked as a nanny, a poodle groomer, a dominatrix, and stripper, has published two books of poetry: *Corpse Delectable,* Hydraulic Press, 1990; and *Dogs In Lingerie,* Zeitgeist Press, 1990; and had a hit show 'Breakfast in the Flesh District" and recently sold her first screenplay. Danielle lives and works in San Francisco with her dog, Julian.

I'm No Good At Getting Rid Of People

this chick looked like Marianne Faithful only
she had a glass eye she'd pop out for you and
she kept rambling about dysentery and herpes of the face
she thought I had herpes of the face because
I had a bruise on my forehead from
banging into a wall at four in the morning two days ago
and I couldn't set her straight because I was
sprawled out on the kitchen counter on my fifth margarita
fascinated by my shoes and all I could do was
cackle in appreciation and bury my head in
Sharon's lap while
the chick that looked like Marianne Faithful with a glass eye
insisted I go see her very sympathetic gynecologist
about my facial herpes or dysentery or
whatever it was she thought I had
I told her it was just a bruise but she said
no it's not there's something wrong with your blood
I'm psychic I can tell and anyway you should
go see my doctor I see him once a week for
my gonorrhea I'm serious
then she went into the bathroom and started
fondling the bras drying on the towel rack and
singing an aria
Sharon and Whitney were cracking up and I was
pissed off because
she'd seemed interesting in the bar and she'd
turned out to be an asshole and I was too drunk
to get rid of her and Stéban was going to
have to do it for me and
I'm no good at getting rid of people
assholes or otherwise
the chain I'm wearing around my neck
is the present of this chick who was in love with me
and decided to quit her job at Church Street Station
and move in with me
she'd been living in the stockroom and had
nowhere else to go and anyway she was in love with me and
I really liked her even though she
made me uneasy sometimes
talking about fights she'd been in and what kinds of
weapons she knew how to use
she was a damn good fuck but I'd want to

throttle her afterward
because she'd cough all night and hog the covers and it was
all her fault because she was a chain smoker even if
she did have bronchitis
I was getting claustrophobic and I wanted my bed back but
I never said anything because I'm
no good at getting rid of people and besides
her parents had kicked her out at the age of 14 for
being a dyke and she'd been on the road ever since and
anyway she told me some great stories about
being a skinhead in LA like the time
she dressed up like Freddy Krueger and snuck up on this guy
who was tripping on acid and totally freaked him out
she also told me how she got a homosexual discharge from
the Marines and how there was a
warrant out for her arrest in
Florida for writing bad checks and how she couldn't stop
drinking and drifting and how her father had
raped her when she was 13
she said she wanted someone to share her life with or
maybe she didn't want anyone to share her life with but
she wanted something and she wasn't sure
what it was yet and she
wanted me to tell her what it was one night and
of course I couldn't and she put it down to
my not having done enough drugs
to be on her wavelength
I think she was close to tears but
I had begun to despise her too much to
be of any comfort and
she disappeared the next morning and
I don't know if she's dead or alive and
I'm no good at getting rid of people.

Pigbaby

They say they found a ten month old baby
in back of the ruined barn being
suckled by a half-starved piebald sow
and that the baby had the snout of a pig
and the sow had the eyes of a woman
and that inside the barn

old Farmer MacPhearson was
hanging from the rafters
They say there's a drowned girl
at the bottom of the well
who gets lonely in the summertime and
likes to teach passing children how to swim
face down
I used to throw rocks in our well to see
if she'd come up to play but
she never did
They say a woman in town
got so disgusted with her fat husband that
one night while he was sleeping she
chained him to their bed and
didn't feed him for a month – just
gave him water and stuffed cotton in her ears
so she couldn't hear him plead
until one day he
got loose and ate her up
bones and all
They say if you turn the lights off
in the bathroom and
look in the mirror and
say Bloody Mary 100 times she'll
appear in your reflection and
kill you
I knew a kid who tried it once
but chickened out at 98
They say beware the crossroads at midnight,
the old dark house at the end of the street with
the lights in the window
beware black cats and men whose eyebrows
meet in the middle and smell of dog
They say
They say
They say
They say I'm strange and I wish I were
but every time I've gone to the cemetery and
laid my head on the earth
listened for muffled breathing and
the stirring of limbs
I've heard nothing
but beetles

The Killer

the killer drove south over
the crushed head of a jackrabbit
in a pale green Chevrolet with the
radio crackling the
thin ghost of a mariachi band and
a suppository melting like a
sharp pebble in his rectum
around 2AM he came to a
small coastal town ravaged by meningitis
the local broadcast said
ten or twelve were dead already,
spinal cords shorted out like
telephone cables in the rain
there was no news of pursuit,
only a distant farm report and
miles of indecipherable static
the killer smiled, dangled
his arm out the window
the air settled on his skin
warm as gasoline and he
wondered if a brain could
become so engorged with fever
the skull would crack open
he still had traces of the
migraine he'd developed
three states ago and every time
he shifted his weight gum wrappers
popped like cellophane bottle rockets
in the lining of his coat
the last time he washed his clothes
was at some deserted laundromat on
the outskirts of Philadelphia
it was four in the morning and
someone had drowned a cat in
one of the washing machines
its fur was pressed flat and orange
against the glass and the
killer stared at it until
his clothes were done, then
got back in his car and
drove away wondering

what kind of asshole would
do something like that –
probably some jackoff who
still lived with his parents and
kept a collection of dead animals
hidden away in the basement under
a pile of ancient tabloids and
crude pencil sketches of his sister
fucking the family German shepherd
the incident irritated him
all the way to Atlanta where he
got himself a gun and a hotel room that
smelled of rainwater and chipped plaster
and sat up all night playing Russian Roulette
until he calmed down and fell asleep dreaming
of highways and stomachs split open
brilliant as pinatas at a child's birthday party
the killer hated amateurs –
they made the artists look stupid
in the morning he headed west toward
Hollywood and Spahn ranch but
lost interest a few days later
somewhere in Texas and pulled into
an all night diner for a cup of coffee
and a slice of lemon meringue pie
the waitress had puffy white arms that
jiggled when she took his order
she told him her name was Amber and
she was getting off work in half an hour
if he wanted to go home with her
the killer hadn't had sex in
almost three months –
sometimes when he'd been driving
for a few days straight the road blurred
into a black and white pornographic
film loop where everyone dressed like
it was the 1930s and the celluloid
jumped and sputtered whenever anything
remotely graphic began to happen
the waitress took him back to her apartment
and led him into the bathroom where she
showed him a dime-sized hole she'd
drilled next to the medicine cabinet

the killer pressed his eye to it and
stared in at a naked fat man sitting
cross-legged on the floor holding
an enormous iguana in his arms
he was feeding it crickets from a mason jar
and saying Pretty Girl, Pretty Girl
over and over again
the waitress said she could
hear him through the walls all night
she told the killer to
stay where he was and got down
on her knees and unzipped his pants
he came in her mouth staring into
the green and gold eyes of the iguana
just as the fat man gave it a
sloppy kiss on the top of its head
the waitress brushed her teeth and
sent the killer down to the corner store
for some beer and groceries
the cashier was a skinny albino with
a huge Adam's Apple that jumped up and down
like a pale frog in his throat
the killer only had seventy-eight cents
and a condom his father had given
him back in 1955 so he bought a
stale candy bar and a few pieces of bubblegum
and got back on the interstate heading south
until his car ran out of gas
somewhere in the desert
he pushed it off the road and
climbed into the back to sleep
there were wire springs like fingerbones
pushing up through the worn seat covers
and the killer dreamed he was trapped in the
final panel of a comic book horror story
where the dead rise from the grave
to punish their murderer
in the morning he drank the chalky dregs
of a bottle of Kaopectate he found in
the glove compartment and wondered
if he was developing a conscience.

Breakfast In The Flesh District

the ghosts are rising over
the faded marquee of a
boarded up strip club on
Turk Street: ancient girls
with chipped blonde faces
and voices clattering like
pigeons over the heads of
naugahyde-skinned men
sucking coffee through
flat brown donkey's teeth
while exhausted Vietnamese
housewives trundle past
with their shopping carts
and the early morning hookers
pace back and forth in
front of cafes hoping
the johns won't mind the
stubble pushing up through
their ruined makeup
no one in this neighborhood
gives a shit about ghosts –
they're as common as lunatics
and half as obtrusive, hanging
in the air thin and yellow
as nicotine while dogs bark
on top of piles of garbage
and fat women in clown suits
juggle bottles of Night Train
and spit teeth at anyone
who stops to watch
here, ectoplasm is just
another thing you
cough out of your lungs
at eight in the morning
Emily and I are having
breakfast at the Bon Ami
wearing 24 hours of makeup
and still seeing tracers out
of the corners of our eyes
we're the only ones paying
attention to the ghosts
pressed against the
flyspecked windows while

the waitress who can't
speak English calls us
Sweetheart and brings us
the wrong food
we're talking in the
vivid half sentences of
the recently brain damaged,
brilliant chemical insights
oxidizing in the greasy Formica sunlight
I pick at my bacon and stare at an
old man with a medium-sized goiter
eating a pastry that looks like
a shellacked pile of dog shit
there are other pastries in a
variety of realistic colors
glittering under a
cracked plastic cover guarded
by a black man with
eyes like shattered marbles
raving about how the
Strand Theatre used to be
the fucking Fillmore West and
now all there is goddamn
faggots giving each other
handjobs in the balcony
he blows his nose in his
hand and pokes the guy
sitting next to him and says
Hendrix used to play there,
fucking Jimi Hendrix
I laugh and the ghosts
filter through my synapses
like ozone
Emily is staring into
her teacup, she says she's
not ready to crash yet
I say me neither, I'll
probably run on adrenaline
until six or so
the Hendrix fan tries to
steal a pastry and the
waitress screams at him in
Vietnamese and he tells her
God is on his side and the
fluorescent lights start

whining like bullet-sized
mosquitoes at the base
of my skull and Emily is
saying she needs to
get the fuck out this
neighborhood – all the
guys are scumbags and all
the other queens are bitches
or stupid or both and any
one them would sell you out
for ten dollars
the Hendrix fan refuses to
relinquish his pastry and
the waitress goes to
get the manager
Emily asks me if I can
still feel the acid and
I say yeah and she says
her too, her ears are
ringing, she needs to
get home and shave her face
she says I'm lucky I'm real
and don't have to shave
my face and I tell her
she's lucky she doesn't
have her period
my stomach feels like
a throbbing blood clot
and I'm hoping my
tampon string doesn't
come out on stage
I notice that the
guy sitting at the
next table is reading
a glossy seven dollar
stroke book entitled
Dominated and Diapered
there's a guy on the cover
with a rattle and a potbelly
the manager and the
amputee cook are pushing
the Hendrix fan out the door
and I say check it out,
Emily, this is the
K-Mart of existence.

The Methedrine Dollhouse

we sit in your
methedrine dollhouse
with the black walls
and the velveteen sofas
and the crack dealers
hanging out in the lobby
scaring your tricks away
while you scribble your
memoirs on legal pads you
buy at the corner store
where the little boy
hookers call you dude
and pull your wig off
just to fuck with you
and you take a drag off
one of your Dunhills
and tell the guy on the
phone you're much too
exhausted to tie him up
so he'll just have to
content himself with
sucking you off instead
your spine is showing like
a ridge of fingertips
through your nightgown
and last night I dreamed
we rode on the backs
of manta rays through
gardens of the drowned
where ghosts with eyes
like comb jellies murmur
over the bones of pirates
and we breathed salt
water through frilled
slits behind our ears
and you're telling me
stories about the '70s
when everything was much
cooler and more decadent
and the phone rings again
and you tell whoever
it is that no, you're

not into that and
the radio is moaning
Don Giovanni and the
doorways are whispering
with black fabric and
we're rehearsing scenes
from 19th century vampire
novels and I want to
sink my teeth into
the blue veins above
your left breast and
feel your cock harden
through your panties
but I know you could
never get it up for
a girl so I just sit
across the room and
stare at you and
entertain ludicrous
notions that you're
the reincarnation of
Anne Bonney the
female pirate and
you cough into your
hand and tell me the
last time you were
at my apartment you
had this sick thought
that you were floating
upside down in my aquarium
and I tell you not to
think like that because
if you just write your
autobiography you'll blow
The Basketball Diaries
out of the water and
you say you suppose so
but you get embarrassed
by all the sleazy stuff
you'd rather write poetry
about evil transsexual
ballerinas living in
haunted Austrian castles
poisoning each other over

the affections of beautiful
Prussian soldier boys who
look like wax dolls and
you ask me if I want
any tea only we can't
use the China tea set
because that bitch Emily
kicked it against the
wall yesterday, well
actually Ernesto kicked
it against the wall,
Emily would never do
anything like that but
Ernesto is a vicious
little faggot and you get
up to put the water on
clutching your robe
around you walking slightly
stooped over like those
girls in junior high school
who were taller than
all the boys and I
try to find something
in my dance bag but
I'm too stoned and
you come back with
the tea and the sugar
bowl full of mouse turds
and tell me this girl
took pictures of you
last week and you're
pissed off because she
kept trying to make you
stand in the harsh sunlight
with no makeup and you're
really sick of artists and
their fucking Diane Arbus trips
always trying to make you look
like horrible street trash
because it's just not artsy
enough if you look pretty
and you realize you forgot
to shut the burner off
and last Tuesday you nearly

burnt the house down because
you left a waffle in the
oven while you went down
the street to get some
cigarettes and the fire
department broke one of the
windows and Emily is still
mad about it and you think
maybe all the speed
you've done in your lifetime
is finally causing your
brain to atrophy and the
doorbell rings and its
your trick so I get
my things together and
kiss you goodbye your
skin tasting like
pressed powder just
for a second before you
go answer the door and
on my way out the trick
says I don't have to
leave if I don't want to
and I'm so fucking
jealous.

Job Hunting

Kathleen and I walked over to Show World
on 41st and 8th partly because we wanted to
check out the strip clubs in New York for
future employment opportunities and partly
because I wanted to check out their
pre-operative transsexual peep booths
when we got there the desk guy said no
unescorted women allowed and I said well
I'm escorting her and she's escorting me
and he said no, it doesn't work like that
so I turned to this dude walking in and
asked if he'd be our escort and he
said sure so we paid his admission and
asked the desk guy which way was the

Queensland Theatre and the dude whose
ticket we bought said oh, you wanna see dick
and started to fumble with his zipper and
I said yeah, but we wanna see GIRL dick
downstairs the queens were all hanging out
by the private booths and this one tall
black queen in a purple bra and panties set
grabbed us and ushered us into her booth
and asked us if we had a nice tip for her
so I gave her five dollars and she whipped
her dick out said now you show me those
pussies so we pulled up our skirts and
I started eating Kathleen out and the
queen said that's right and demanded another
tip so I gave her more money and a minute
or so later she wanted more so me and Kathleen
decided to go check out the rest of the club
on our way back upstairs this short Jewish
queen who looked like all the girls I went
to high school with on Long Island stopped us
and asked where we were from and Kathleen said
we were strippers from San Francisco and we were
maybe interested in working here, did they
still do live lesbian sex shows?
the queen said they used to but now it was
illegal and I said that was too bad and we
continued upstairs for two floors to the
real girl peep booths where all these fat
bleached blonde women in polyester lingerie
were wandering around the hallway looking
pissed off and bored and Kathleen said we were
much better looking than any of them and
could probably make a lot of money if we
could stand the disco music and I said yeah,
these girls are cows, let's go to the magazine
section so we went and they didn't have any
cool fetish stuff so we bought a copy of Screw
to break a traveler's check and walked up
41st toward 6th Avenue keeping our eyes on
the sidewalk for needles while these guys
followed us saying check it out ladies,
coke is it, coke IS it and Kathleen said the
neighborhood was really annoying and if we
wanted to work in the sex industry in New York

we should probably just work out of an apartment
as dominatrixes which was one of her fantasies
anyway and I said the fantasy is cool but the
reality is more along the lines of ordering
naked old men to fuck themselves up the ass with
12 inch dildoes and waiting all day for your
appointments to show up and we ducked into a
little souvenir shop that sold Halloween masks,
I Love New York ashtrays and Tarot cards but
they didn't have the Crowley deck so we went to
Nathan's because that was Kathleen's favorite
even though I was more in the mood for pizza
and we drank several huge styrofoam cups of
coffee and I started chattering about how insane
I was the last time I was in New York –
my girlfriend had just dumped me and I was
convinced the Empire State Building was an
evil tower intent on my destruction and I was
on all this psychological medication and this
lady dosed me with Angel Dust at a showing of
"Tommy" at the Thalia and I started tripping
halfway through the credits and ended up
puking my brains out on a cot at St. Lukes and
the week after that they kicked me out
of Barnard for being suicidal but it's fun
being in New York and not being crazy,
New York is a bad place to be crazy and
Kathleen said the last time she was
in New York she was 15 and got picked up
for being a runaway when she asked a cop
which way was Greenwich Village and
the only thing she really remembered was
juvenile hall and how tough all the
little kids were, much tougher than the
runaways in California and I said that's
because they have winter here and people
freeze to death so they're a lot more
desperate and Kathleen said that made sense
and went to get more coffee and when she
came back I said another thing was
New York was very haunted and if you're
weak the ghosts will prey on you and Kathleen
said she used to live in this hotel in the
Tenderloin and she was doing a lot of speed

and she would have dreams where these
old Chinese men were sitting around a
table playing cards and there was a pile of
money on the table and a dead body under
the table and she must have seen this every
third night she slept there and I said
yeah, the Tenderloin is definitely haunted,
sometimes when I'm alone in the dressing room
at the Cinema I see movement out of the
corner of my eye and she said her too, one time
she was down in the basement waiting to
talk to James and on one of the old chairs
there were three paper stars with girls'
names on them: Silver who committed suicide
back in '86, Sassy whose boyfriend shot her
in the stomach and Sparkle who just died
of a heart attack, it was really freaky seeing
all those names together and I said I still
miss Sparkle, sometimes I think I hear her
voice and I turn around and it's somebody else,
the other day I was getting on the bus and
there was this black girl I thought was her
and Kathleen said maybe it WAS her but
only for a minute and it sucked that Sparkle
was dead because she was the buffer between
the girls and the management and she was
the only one who was halfway competent and
now that she's gone everything is going
down the tubes, they're hiring all these
white trash girls who let the customers
finger fuck them in the audience and the
toilet's always overflowing and it takes
them forever to fix it because Sparkle's
not there to hassle them and anyway
Sparkle was my friend and I said yeah,
I'm glad we got hired at Mitchell Brothers
because the Cinema was getting really
depressing and you make three times as
much money at Mitchell's and your feet
don't stick to the floor and they have
a microwave in the dressing room and
Kathleen said that if she drank any more coffee
she was going to have an accident so we
went downstairs to the bathroom where this

ancient junkie in a halter top started
screaming at us because we didn't have
any cigarettes and the pay toilets were
jammed and the only way to get into the
stalls would have been to slide on our
bellies under the doors so we decided to
hold it til we got back to our hotel room
and took off down Broadway staring at the
lights glad we weren't old yet.

Kicking Omewenne

The murderer Gilles de Rais
would sometimes cut down
a boy he was hanging
and cradle the half-strangled child
in his arms begging forgiveness
until it occurred to him
to finish the job
then he'd fuck the body and eat it
but I really think he meant it
when he said he was sorry because
monsters always cry over their dinners
and don't pretend you don't know
what I'm talking about, Spiderbaby,
you who told me you'd like to
perch on the chests
of handsome young men
and sing them lullabies while
slicing their eyes open with razorblades
and don't pretend you don't know that
you are as revolting and pathetic to them
as I am to you
with an asshole for a cunt
and me with a length of black rubber for a cock
I told you I wanted to be your boyfriend
that stupid night we did Ecstacy in Bob's bedroom
with *Highway to Hell* and *Houses of the Holy*
on endless repeat on the CD player,
candles shuddering in the greasy remains of dinner
and your tongue nervous in my mouth,
stupid because those four hours I spent
pawing your hatchling tits

and playing with your hair
were the best time I've had in my entire life
and don't pretend you didn't know
I wanted to drink your pain like blood
because you got me strung on it
like the opiate your name just happens to rhyme with
calling me up at four in the morning
to weep over dead cats and cab drivers
who might have looked at you five years ago,
calling me up because you knew
how hungry I was to listen,
saw how I stared at you
with the taste of Bedlam welling
like tears in the back of my throat
while you droned on about men
who didn't love you and the high price
of transsexual surgery
and how you were never
going to get a record label
because your music was too slow and morbid
for a generation that just wanted
to rub crotches and hip hop
and I'd murmur words of comfort while
sneaking strands of hair from your brush
and scraping flakes of semen from your bedsheets
for spells I was too much of gentleman to cast
and don't pretend you didn't know what I was
because you use vampires
the way medieval doctors used leeches
and don't you dare bitch about feeling drained
because there's enough poison in you
to swell a thousand of us to bursting, but then,
monsters are supposed to cry over their dinners
and you and I want so desperately to be monsters
and not just a couple of ex-Catholic suburban kids
with the right kind of hair and bone structure
to carry off the clothes and the ghoul makeup

The Awful Truth

I never told you
how many times I
freebased cocaine
with Bruce, I
never told you
I sometimes let
tricks eat my
pussy at the
torture chamber,
I never told you
that I let this
one New Age twit
who reeked of
patchouli oil
fuck me with
a dildo for
200 dollars and
I never told you
I came twice
I never told
you I tongue-
kissed Barbara
(the world's most
boring transsexual) in
her brown
Volvo and
felt so
guilty
about it
I invited
her down to
Santa Cruz
so we could
have a threesome
and her idea
of dominatrix
clothing was
a black stretch
top over flare
leg blue jeans
and she never
even took her

glasses off
I was so
embarrassed
I never told
you I was
in love with
Bambi shivering
in her Woolworth's
nightgowns that
always fall
open to reveal
her silicone tits and
balls nestled
between smooth
thighs coughing
her lungs out
between grandiose
reminiscences
of David Bowie and
Berlin in the '70s
and how any day now
she's going to
make a comeback,
one in a
long line of
snuff friendships:
Miranda who
looked like
Julie Andrews at
Buchenwald
junk sick in
my lap on
the dressing
room stairs,
me stroking her
hair close
to tears thinking
please die so
I can write you
a beautiful obituary,
Stephan who
is positive
for the AIDS virus
and welcome

to commit suicide
in my arms
anytime
people mistake
this for a
mother complex
I never told you
I was jealous
that you actually
killed people
in Vietnam
and that
sometimes I cruise
the transvestite
hooker bars for
some queen who
looks like you
did in 1972,
some freckled
blunt-lipped boy
with long red hair
and go-go boots
who strode down
Hollywood Boulevard
in hot pants and
see through blouses
and whose presence
I hallucinate
when we're
fucking on acid
I never told
you I cry over
your old photo
albums at night
because you are
nineteen years
older than me
and in ten more
years I probably
won't be attracted
to you anymore
and will never
have the heart
to leave you.

Dave Rubin b.1947

Dave Rubin's spoken-word CD, *Psychedelic Steppenwolves*, accompanied by the music of A Thousand Tiny Fingers, was recently released by Hands On records. He now teaches public high school in Brooklyn, New York.

He Said She Said

They call my block Vietnam, so many niggahs be
     gettin' shot round here

Dwayne say jail be fun cause we be stealin' niggahs
     sneakers and shit — white niggahs, Puerto Rican niggahs,
     Italian niggahs, all kinda motherfuckin' niggahs

Reggie say if Ronald Reagan ever come to mah neighborhood
     I'd fuck dat niggah's ass up. Word to the Mother!

Yolanda looked at Vincent's sneakers and say, "Dem niggahs
     be slammin'."

Teach say "If two times two is four, two is the square
     root of four. What's the square root of nine?"
     Sidney say — "Your face motherfucker."

Teach say "Today we'll watch *Waiting For Godot*",
     James say "Fuck dat niggah — I ain't waitin' for nobody."

"If you saw that the accident victim was still breathing
     what would you do?" Kim say "I'd loosen the niggah's
     collar — then I'd rob the motherfucker's wallet."

Tristan say "Yo Teach! we call this niggah Idi ... Aint this
     de blackest motherfuckin' niggah you ever seen? —
     When this niggah be lookin' at the blackboard
     he be lookin' in a motherfuckin' mirror — I'm a haf
     to dump that niggah's ass in a bucket'a white paint."

Vaughn say "I ain't never gonna vote for no Jesse Jackson ...
     You know niggahs got bad tempers and shit ... somebody
     liable to say some shit about da niggah's moms and shit ...
     and you know the motherfucker would go on an'
     blow up the whole goddam world."

Courtney opened a soda can with a nine inch blade ...

Ronald got jumped by 17 kids at the bus stop ... stabbed
     in the back ... and transferred to a white school ...

One kid shot another kid — Rodger say "Panama can't
    fuck wit' Jamaica ... "

Marcus say "Much niggahs in this school be havin' guns —
    Word! ...You know a gun is like an American Express Card —
    You don't leave home without it!"

Danielle poured lighter fluid on Kenyetta's sheepskin coat ...
    Burned it up in front of the Dean's Office ...
    "Because the bitch dissed me."

Keesha say "When my moms be too tired to fuck all dem
    Johns dat be comin' to da house an' shit —
    she make me go in there — an' give dem niggahs pussy
    den she gonna go on — an' take the money ...
    for her own nasty ass self."

Jamel say "Raphael got killed cause his moms was a crackhead —
    She be owin' money to dem drug dealers an' shit —
    So they runned Raphael over in the street —
    Right in front'a her face — Just to teach da bitch a lesson —
    Tires cold crushed his little assed head —
    An' then they backed up an' did that shit again —
    His moms be screamin' an' shit —
    Dat shit sad man — Dat niggah was my frien'."

Ron say "I only smoked it once — & when I got home...
    I started to feel like da kitchen be spinnin' around...
    & doan know why... but I felt like I was gonna
    kill my own moms — I ain't never gonna fuck wit' dat
    shit again."

Lee say "All you be hearin' is 'black history dis black history dat,'
    When they gonna give the white people a chance? —
    Word! These white motherfuckers really be on our
    dicks an' shit."

Dwight say "I'm tired'a hearin' about Martin Luther King.
    Dat niggah's dead. — Martin Luther King. Martin Luther King —
    Dat niggah can suck my dick — Why he always dreamin'?
    When da fuck that niggah gonna wake up?
    "Ah have a dream — Ah have a dream" —
    Ah dreams too motherfucker —
    Ah dreams about pussy."

Calvin say "Yo teach! Yaw shit is weak. I'm breakin' out."

Alyse say "Lawd have mercy!"

Willie say, "Aw, Fuck dat niggah, he aint even real."

David Lerner   b. 1951

He writes: Born in Brooklyn, 1951. Parents Reds in '50s in Underground. Grew up middle-class and twisted in Queens, NY, took to drug culture with vengeance in the mid-late '60s. Once met Timothy Leary backstage at the Fillmore East, but he was a total drag. Dropped out of high school. Joined a communal family. Moved to California at 21. Wrote poetry, worked construction, moved furniture, freeloaded. Became a journalist in the '80s, wrote articles about geek 6-year-old athletic stars and dying rock musicians for *Us Magazine, San Francisco Chronicle, California, Mother Jones,* etc. Got paid fairly well. Burned out at 35 and began to write poetry again, with new zest. Was discovered and wildly acclaimed by dozens. Has four books: *I Want A New Gun,* Zeitgeist Press, 1988; *Why Rimbaud Went To Africa,* Zeitgeist Press, 1989; *The American Book Of The Dead,* Grace St. Press, 1990; *Pray Like The Hunted,* Zeitgeist Press, 1990. Is 42, lives in Oakland with poet Maura O'Connor and 2 cats whose names will mean nothing to you.

The Crucifixion Of Johnny Carson

he smiled once too often
he cracked one too many
lame jokes
about Ronald Reagan
I got tired of watching the sequined backdrop
sway behind him as he
played air golf
while the commercial kicked in

the band was just too expertly bland
Doc's outfits hurt my eyes
he got married one too many times
to a Joan

so we decided to nail him up
we used a big old nail gun
and a stainless-steel cross
times have changed
but the song remains the same

he screamed bloody murder
it was pretty cool
and I felt a little bad
after all, he'd given me
hours of viewing pleasure

but I just got tired of that
pretty little smirk
that perfect gray hair
those retired-Lieutenant-Colonel suits
the headlines in the *Enquirer*

I got tired of Ed McMahon's
booming, desperate laugh
got bored with his belly too
and the cracks about his boozing

I got tired of all that intensely false
show biz camaraderie jive
the guests were always
throwing around

I even got tired of Johnny's
smooth silver touch with
old ladies and children

so we crashed the party
way past midnight
slammed him up against the wall
and popped the steel home

you should have heard him scream
it was really tasty
stripped down to his underwear
he cried too
it was fantastic

at first he hung tough
said things like
"What's the meaning of this"
and "Don't you know who I am?"
and "You'll never work in this town
again"

but when we
told him we never worked in this town
anyway
and yes, we knew who he was
and we couldn't tell him the meaning
for all the cunt in Malibu

his smile turned hard
and his hard face faded
and a blank look came over those features
that gleam so well

and the blankness started to shake
and the shaking shuddered
and then he began to cry

it was really special
when he cried
and suddenly I felt a little
bad for him
he breaks just like anybody else
I thought

it was nice to see him cry
and that was really all
we wanted
to see something that made sense
on that jewel of a mask

he wept like blazes
he screamed for his life

and I thought
shit, let's yank those things out
and give him another chance

but it was too late
the red light was fading
they were folding the set
he was
going off the air

and the look that crossed over his eyes
just before he
leaned over into The Next World

he sort of looked like Jesus

I know he forgave me for my sins

all in all,
I felt pretty good
about the whole thing

18th And Broadway

I remember him,
a tall, skinny black dude
on the Gladman Hospital psych unit
2 years ago

trying to look fly but
pushing shabby

eyes way too big in his head
talking too fast
trying to
style the dragon down

"When I was crossing the street at the
corner of 18th and Broadway," he said,
"I ran out of everything ..."

I howled with laughter. He smiled.
"See," his smile said,
"you're keeping up with me ..."

he was gone 2 days later
before I got to know his name
with a brown girl even
skinnier than he was

clutching her to his side

"She can't make it without me"
he said

when I was crossing the street
at the corner of
18th and Broadway

the other day
it seemed real wide

it was a sunny afternoon
but there was something wrong
with the light

I looked at people and
saw the bone and meat
beneath the fabric
twitching with nerves

the eyes like 2 fried eggs in the
middle

when I showed them pictures the next day

they smiled and
said I must be kidding

when I was crossing the street
at the corner of
18th and Broadway

I was astonished at how
alone I was

I knew there was someone I should
call, but I
couldn't remember the
telephone number

I felt so much it made me sick
and there was
nothing I could do about it

an alien asked me for my middle name
a cop wanted to borrow my glasses
a four year old girl asked me
how to get to hell

she said she had some business there with her
mother

when I was crossing the street
at the corner of 18th and Broadway

beauty was still the same
but she wouldn't
talk to me anymore

when I took my foot
off the curb

I got hit by 4 taxis
2 poisonous glances
half a dozen silences

only the silences
were real

when I crossed the street at
the corner of 18th and Broadway
I realized I wasn't so tough

fear was the only friend I had
and we weren't talking

it seemed like no one was casting shadows
and they didn't care

always smiling at some point
just outside my line of vision
and assuring me that
everything was fine

I knew they were lying

when I crossed the street at
the corner of
18th and Broadway

I was so alone the wind in my hair
was enough to make me weep

a leaf getting crushed
could ruin my day
I was so soft
it was frightening

when I crossed the street
at the corner of
18 and Broadway

I had no urgent intentions
no fond regrets or
contingency plans

the light said "Walk"
and I followed orders

a hole opened up at my feet
it said:
"you're home now"

it was too late to argue
I was already falling

I saw my poetry going by:

ornament to history

a bracelet on the wrist of Death

flowers on a grave

when I was crossing the street
at the corner of
18th and Broadway

I screamed and screamed

a bird said, "Hush now,
you'll only wake the demons
and they need their rest"

a doctor told me that I
read the wrong magazines and
should use butter instead of
margarine

the sea wind coming off the Bay said that
if I knew what was good for me
I'd catch the first thing smoking
north

and hide among the roses
till the fire comes

Five Dildos, Not Six

a friend of mine recently informed me
that in Arizona it's against the law to
own more than 5 dildos

5 is OK, 6 are illegal

with 5 you can walk down the street
waving them around like flags
but 6 gets you busted

can you image
appearing in court
charged with possession of
more than 5 dildos?

can you imagine *doing time*
for possession of
more than 5 dildos

I'd rather be a child molester
in jail
you'd make more friends

strolling through downtown Berkeley
the other day
I noticed a sign that said:

"Drug Free Zone"

put up a sign
and it happens

form a committee to
study the problem

settle on something
that looks good in the press

and let 'er rip

take pictures of the Mayor
standing beside
the Drug Free Zone sign

while he explains to reporters
how much he cares about
junkies

I understand the neighborhood kids
keep defacing the signs
by scratching out 'Free' so they read
"Drug Zone"

the city comes over
and takes down the signs
and puts new ones up

that the kids then deface
that the city then pulls
then the kids come back and ...

you get the picture

I wonder how much money
those fucking signs cost

between the well-paid committees
and the Mayor's time
and the poor bastards who
have to unscrew the goddamn things
and cart them away

money that could go for
hospital beds where people could kick
and recovery houses
where they could get straight

or M-16s and
telephone taps
and payoffs for rats

anything's cooler than a stupid fucking sign

this country's completely insane
public relations's what
truth used to be

a good Q rating's
what fame once was

the balance of power
where hatred once sang

and cretinous scum
in their leather thrones
making laws that are lies

for people so numb with defeat
they can't even howl

well I'll howl when I want to
and scream when I please
I'll rip off my clothes
and race naked down Broadway

with 1 dildo up my ass
and 1 in each hand
and 2 up my nose
and 1 in my mouth

I'll flip out when I have to
come back if I can
and if I don't make it
some other crazed loser

can kick my dead ass
all over the street
steal my 6 dildos
and run

The Heart

These days the heart is just another
piece of meat

a 5-letter word, whose image is
marketed in the patterns of dresses
distributed exclusively in the Midwest

found on charm bracelets and greeting cards
and targets

but I used to know the heart
when he was a big deal
modest and unassuming, don't get me wrong
but no shrinking violet

I'd run into him
crawling out of a dingy bar
in a crummy part of town

too drunk to blink
but looking for the moon anyway

I spotted him once
in Seattle
at the space needle
eyes up

he told me was was looking for God
I said, "I don't blame you."

once I woke up next to the heart
in the shotgun seat
of a shit-colored Buick

it was 5 a.m. and we were
somewhere outside Reno
coasting downhill to save gas

looking for a dope dealer
who'd done us wrong

we never found him

but I remember the sun crashing
through the driver's-side window
pushing everyone around
like it always does

and the heart was driving
I'd swear it
shone right through him

I remember when that
son of a bitch
lay down in the rain
in Texas

as wind burned the water
into your face

and he told me a poem
about what I don't remember

but the feeling of it
shook with
something bigger than beauty

had more Heaven than any sky

Used to be, a
long time ago
he'd
come downtown and
cut it up for us

turn up way past midnight
6 feet tall and
10 miles high, and

run it down
till it caught you

he'd tell, in a
voice as soft as
decent regrets and
harder than one last chance

how to live without water
survive your thirst
and learn how to sing it

how to find water in the
desert of your own desires

how to kindle an army of desire
with only two dry sticks
and a memory

The heart's eyes
weren't as nice as you
might think

especially as the years
went by
and it got harder and harder
for him to get a gig

I mean, he had a
friendly, slightly dumb expression
he'd put on for tourists

but you'd get up close
and they'd glisten quietly
with fury
a wild and happy fury

even when he was sore to breaking

he called it his
'pure and joyful hatred'

"Love," he once explained
"isn't some melting thing
that looks good
under dim lights

"it's more like
something on fire
that sings as it
burns . . ."

I saw him in St. Louis
turning wine into blood

I caught him in Jersey City
on a muggy August afternoon
reading a book of poems about
suicide and
laughing at the good parts

I clocked him by water
swimming in the sand
as the gulls above
screamed in a forgotten language

You know roses,
how some open looking like
the first girl you
ever thought you'd
die without?

and some
just barely make it
petals crumpled
perfume weak and sad

but they all do their best

that was the heart

"The heart," he said recently,
"is tired. It wants to
go lay down now. You

gotta have something to
break for. I'm going north,
I've got some cousins in B.C.
who'll put me up for the winter."

he always talked some long shit
the heart
but it always went somewhere
if you could follow it
into where it got dark and cold.

So he doesn't come around much
anymore
the heart

oh, I still see him
from time to time

on late nights
when I've had
too much to drink
he'll come and
walk with me for a while

but I miss the nights
so deadly rare these days

when he'd step out in public
an angel on each arm

looking mild, as always

and get up to blow

he might just step onto the stage
and stand there
watching the dust
float across the air

everybody getting pissed off

or he might be laughing
for hours
and you caught every word

or maybe he'd just
sit there
eyes down
rubbing his shoe
into the boards

and you felt like you'd been
crying for years

burning with a sweetness
never said its name

and traveled like
heat late for fire

bodies stilled, chatter flattened,
everything lifted up

so you could see the
moon in the sky
ever during harsh daylight

or the sun in a room
at night
burning every face

Hold On Tight — *for Joie*

sometimes the only way you can
stop yourself from shaking
is to
grab a hold of someone else

sometimes the only way you can
keep up your pride is by
burying it alive

sometimes you forget
where you planted it
and have to call out your friends and family
to help you work out
where it's hiding

and they may be
more pissed off than sad

sometimes you have to
wield your pain like a sword
because it's the
only weapon you can reach,

and every time you cut someone in half
you cut yourself in quarters
cause that's how it's played

sometimes it seems like all the world's teeth
are lunging at your throat
they don't want to drink your blood
just spill it

everyone knows this is true

sometimes panic like boiling water
slams through your belly
and eventually it chills down to a
simmer, but

you'll ache forever
where it scalded you

no matter what surgery
you bring to bear

sometimes loneliness grips you like rage
and all you can see is
everything you've lost and
everything you've sold

sometimes you walk through hell
like a candy store
picking out chocolates and comic books
while the Devil whistles a Broadway show tune
leaning on the register
grinning at your pleasure, and

sometimes you feel so good
you're puzzled

sometimes you ace the hangman
slip the noose while they're
busy taking bets
on how fast you'll drop

sometimes you wake up for a moment
in the middle of the night
and a breeze from an open window
brushes against you like a
girl you always wanted, and
gratitude leaves fingerprints
all over your dreams

sometimes mercy slaps against your door
like the morning paper
and friendship gets you drunker
than any drug you know, and

sometimes everything gets quiet
and prayer is as simple as sleep,
you're

talking to God as if He was
someone you used to shoot pool with, and
though you
can't quite understand what He's saying
it sounds like something
you can't do without

one of these days, when
the static dies down
you may know exactly what time it is
but until then you

just have to

fiddle with the dials
bang your heart like a gong
and hold on tight

For C.B.

I didn't love her, but
that was OK
she didn't want me to

we comforted each other for a while
and moved on

she drank too much
and played Brahms on the piano
and read lots of trashy novels
she could be very sweet

but she got mean when she drank
and it got old

she lived on the water
in a small California town
near San Francisco

she bought a new bed
because I had a bad back
and I'd lay in it at night
while she slept

listening to the buoys
tinkling in the fog

life had beat on her
pretty good
and sometimes she'd remind you
for no good reason

but there was a softness about her
she hid religiously

it would mostly surface during love
or when she
thought you weren't looking

and for a moment I'd
have trouble breathing

hope cutting a razor-thin line
down the middle of my skin

there was very little blood

I couldn't take her drinking
she pretended not to care
we broke it off over the phone
one afternoon

for 3 days I felt
like I'd been let out of prison

and then everything
was the same

it's been years
I can't say that I miss her
but I remember her
and she's gone

The Long Walk *– for Maura*

I'll walk with you
to the last stop on my line
I'll walk with you
down highways boiling with menace and
cheap advice
along the steel wire that
leads to the crypt of religion
across the final prairie of justice
to a land where music is coin of the realm
and everyone's heart must break
at least once a day

I'll walk with you
in stealth and suicide
in tombstone truth and blue panic
through the deaf winter and the busted spring
across a nation of broken carnival rides
down past a graveyard set aside exclusively for angels
over an ocean of charred teeth
beyond the ditch where God died

I'll walk with you
down a street you can only find
with your eyes smashed shut
past suspicion and revenge
beyond the stunned cries of a newborn
beyond the iron grip of sorrow
into the mind of a bullet
past cardboard trees and steel churches
to a valley that never ends
as far as we know

I'll walk with you
till my feathers burn up in the atmosphere
until all the names of God are
tattooed on my throat
till the sky sucks us up through a straw
until we're as dead as
any prehistoric code of honor
to the butcher shop at the end of the rainbow
to the source of crime

to the bland eyes of a serial killer
to a prison for people who can
no longer weep
to the anger of a butterfly
the anguish of a stone
a murderer's joy
the sorrow of a knife

I'll walk with you
as the days and nights flick by
like cards in a deck
I never really learned to deal
as we count our lives down
in dreadful slow motion
to the moment where it all disappears
and all that's left is
memory and meat

I'll walk with you because we're
heading in the
same general direction
and some company along the way
would be nice
because every once in a while
I feel like talking
and though I like being alone
when the wind slips its razor
beneath your skin
it's good to have a
fallback position

so take my hand now
cause it's getting kind of cold
and as the lights go out
I'll tell you a story
about how to walk in darkness
and carry your fear like a flag
and listen to no one who would
tell you to set it down

I'll tell you how to
keep your laughter cocked
like a gun in your pocket

how nothing will ever be wasted in heaven
how to travel to planets so small
you can hold them in your hand
to a theory of revenge so advanced
it might be admired by saints

to a clock that ticks backwards forever
and keeps perfect time
to a kiss that ends the world
as the sky takes a final sip
and we're done
everything goes white at once

America Is

the only industrialized nation in the world without
socialized medicine
yeah, he had a heart attack,
they brought him to
3 different emergency rooms before one would take him
because he didn't have
the only industrialized nation in the world without
she had to sell her house and
have the dog gassed because she was
paralyzed on one side after the stroke and
it was the only way she could get
the only industrialized nation in the world that
doesn't have
get people around her
who would
make sure she ate and slept and was
able to shit and piss without getting
too much of it on herself
they'll only let you live if you've
lost everything else in the
only industrialized nation in the world without
I remember when I was a kid and I'd read in
storybooks that in ancient times there were
beggars lying on the sidewalk and
people would just step over them like it was

nothing, and it seemed
exotic
the only industrialized
try laying in bed for 2 years with a
ruined back, and the
insurance company is looking up your asshole
and there's nothing wrong with your
asshole
and the insurance was paid for by deductions from your
wages as a moving man, and
you start dreaming about
buying guns and visiting offices and
emptying them into people who are only
voices on the phone
the only industrialized nation in the
there are hearings, and conferences,
and lawyers make money
and doctors make money
and clerks make money
and the pain gets worse
and they argue with you about whether it
hurts or not in the
only industrialized country in the world without
giant machines you must have flawless credit to
rent for
several seconds a day
drugs only God could afford
only the Devil could invent
only capitalism could market
in the only industrialized nation without socialized medical
care on the face of the

oh, yeah, there's another one
it's South Africa

Mein Kampf

"Gary Snyder lives in the country. He wakes up in the morning and listens to birds. We live in the city."
– Kathleen Wood

all I want to do
is make poetry famous

all I want to do is
burn my initials into the sun

all I want to do is
read poetry from the middle of a
burning building
standing in the fast lane of the
freeway
falling from the top of the
Empire State Building

the literary world
sucks dead dog dick

I'd rather be Richard Speck
than Gary Snyder
I'd rather ride a rocketship to hell
than a Volvo to Bolinas

I'd rather
sell arms to the Martians
than wait sullenly for a
letter from some diseased clown with a
three-piece mind
telling me that I've won a
bullet-proof pair of rose-colored glasses
for my poem "Autumn in the Spring"

I want to be
hated
by everyone who teaches for a living

I want people to hear my poetry and
get headaches
I want people to hear my poetry and
vomit

I want people to hear my poetry and
weep, scream, disappear, start bleeding,
eat their television sets, beat each other to death with
swords and

go out and get riotously drunk on
someone else's money

this ain't no party
this ain't no disco
this ain't foolin' a

grab-bag of
clever wordplay and sensitive thoughts and
gracious theories about

how many ambiguities can dance on the head of a
machine gun

this ain't no
genteel evening over
cappuccino and bullshit

this ain't no life-affirming
our days have meaning
as we watch the flowers breathe through our souls and
fall desperately in love

this ain't no letter-press, hand-me-down,
wimpy beatnik festival of bitching about
the broken rainbow

it is a carnival of dread

it is a savage sideshow
about to move to the main arena

it is terror and wild beauty
walking hand in hand down a bombed-out road
as missiles scream, while a
sky the color of arterial blood
blinks on and off
like the lights on Broadway
after the last junkie's dead of AIDS

I come not to bury poetry
but to blow it up
not to dangle it on my knee
like a retarded child with
beautiful eyes
but

throw it off a cliff into
icy seas and
see if the motherfucker can
swim for its life

because love is an excellent thing
surely we need it

but, my friends . . .

there is so much to hate These Days

that hatred is just love with a chip on its shoulder
a chip as big as the Ritz
and heavier than
all the bills I'll never pay

because they're after us

they're selling radioactive charm bracelets
and breakfast cereals that
lower your IQ by 50 points per mouthful
we got politicians who think
starting World War III
would be a good career move
we got beautiful women
with eyes like wet stones
peering out at us from the pages of
glossy magazine
promising that they'll
fuck us till we shoot blood

if we'll just buy one of these beautiful switchblade knives

I've got mine

Gia Hansbury b.1971

Gia Hansbury read at the Babar for a short time. Her work is vivid. She now lives in New York.

Magic

the other night I dreamed
I was in San Francisco again
heading down Valencia
sidewalk sun shining down
when I heard music
I heard Sarah Vaughan
calling from around a corner
a giant jukebox
a Seeburg Consolette like
an old-fashioned radio
gleaming cherry wood red
dials glowing gold

a tall blonde walked up to me
and I stuffed the machine
with nickels
so we could dance
right there on the sidewalk
under the sign for Oso Negro
we danced
the way you dance
to Sarah
slow
the rest of the street silent
empty
except for me and the blonde
and I knew she had been a dancer
once
in the city
with her yellow hair twisting
up around her head
her long calves sharp
in a pair of red heels
and I knew her name must've been
something like Dolly
or Dolores or May

because she knew how
to dance to Sarah
and she knew how to kiss
and that dream ended long before
the music did
Sarah went right on singing
the last thing I knew
I had handfuls and handfuls
of thick yellow hair
and the taste of lipstick
on my teeth like magic

When The Traffic Gets You, Remember The Fog

– (graffitied on the wall at Cafe Babar)

san francisco
sitting in the car
rush hour
over heating
on the golden gate
waiting for the big one
to pull us into the deep
and then the fog
fell down from the hills
hugged the little car
until nothing
but cool white
to see

in new york
it's the smell of fruitstands
in february
canary melons
singing
and bins full
of sparkling oranges
then tulips
bending towards you
a yellow cat
at the ankle

every town

has its pretty things
in the middle
of all that bullshit
jesus
what else is there
to love
but this kind
of loveliness
the girl
in the bar
fishing the cherry
from the bottom
of her drink
the quiet man
on the street
chanting *this buddha*
walks alone
with all the shop windows
shining behind him

the sun grabbing
a handful of grapes
here
a neat stack of apples
there
and then a gold dress
hanging
ropes and ropes
of sweet sausages
strung like garland
the sun
on a girl swearing
as she steps
into a slushy puddle
even this
goddamn
is beautiful
because her hair
is loose on her shoulders
and smells clean

Vampyre Mike Kassel b.1953

On the scene early-Babar, originally from Boston, Vampyre Mike Kassel comes to poetry via rock'n'roll. Vampyre Mike is a strong poet and comic genius, and tends towards the macabre. Mike wrote the book and music for a play called *Bat Soup*, about Dracula and the Marx Brothers, with Mike playing Groucho playing Dracula. It ran many months at the Hotel Utah in San Francisco. He writes songs and has recorded a 45 single; and played on and co-produced the album, "Pasha And The Pagans". He is a very popular performer with San Francisco poetry audiences. Horror poems are among his best. His images are usually quite precise and sharp, and audiences appreciate his direct low brow appeal. Chapbooks include *Going For the Low Blow, I Want To Kill Everything,* and *Wild Kingdom,* Zeitgeist Press, 1989, 1990, & 1992; *Graveyard Golf,* Manic D Press, 1991; and *Just Say No To Despair,* Cyborg Press, 1991.

Going For The Low Blow

You chide me for frivolity.
For my inability to resist going for the cheap laugh,
the low blow,
the greasepaint moustache.
You say it diminishes my "art"
and, when I say Art is man with no arms or legs
who hangs on a wall,
you say that's just what you're talking about:
going for the low blow.
I fear I have low tastes.
You were suckled on Rimbaud and Baudelaire
and that's cool,
but, I was raised on *Mad* magazine
and the Holy Trinity of Larry, Moe, and Curly,
blessed be their pies,
and, when you talk of Kaufman,
I think: George S.
Now, don't get me wrong,
I think Bob was as good as they come,
but anyone who tells me "Animal Crackers"
isn't a poem
is gonna get an elephant in his pajamas
and a genuine phony Beaugard oil painting
plastered to his ugly kisser
and let him explain *that*
to the boys at the Museum of Modern Art.

You tell me Jim Morrison
was a pretentious, prancing clown
and I say
any man who is willing to risk a Florida penitentiary
to see how his dick looked under a green spotlight
is worth ten language poets
any April Fool's Day in the Calendar of Saints.
You want warm, candle-lit love in an incense-laden bower.
I want triple X slam fucking
with sex toys made by Tonka,
guaranteed not to break
at the moment of supreme absurdity.
You think I should be writing about Nicaragua and AIDS

and I wonder how long
you would have lasted on the Orpheum circuit,
playing five shows a day following "Swayne's Rats and Cats".

Is there an argument here
or merely more kinds of art than were ever dreamed
in our philosophies?
I don't know or really care
but I *do* know
that anyone who thinks that a laugh is worth less than a sigh
and that there is no Zen to the art of pie throwing
is operating on half a battery pack
and I pray
that the ghost of Julius Henry Marx
comes to you some suicide-tainted night
to pry you out of your whalebone corset,
steal your wig,
sell you some useless Florida real estate,
and teach you how to dance
before the dogs of reason
turn off the footlights,
tear down the theater
and leave you alone in the dark
forever.

I Was A Teenage Godzilla

When I was ten
I was hit by a very small nuclear warhead
which slipped out of a torpedo tube
while my cubscout pack was visiting
the Navy submarine U.S.S. Caligula
on a field trip.
The incident was hushed up.
The other cubs perished
but I mutated into a Teenage Godzilla
just like in the movies.
Only I was still only five feet ten inches tall.
Just a friendly li'l two legged radioactive Komodo dragon
with glow in the dark halitosis.
It wasn't so bad.

My parents were pissed
but the government paid them off
and they just had to kind of live with it.
In high school, it had its ups and downs.
True, no girl wanted to kiss a lizard.
But, on the other hand,
the hoods left me alone after I melted their '54 Chevy
into modern art with my nuclear breath.
The only problem was that I used to hibernate all winter
until the science class rigged me up a special suit
out of solar batteries and electric blankets.

After graduation I moved to San Francisco
where they're used to dealing with the exotic.
I ended up starring in porno movies
like "Lizard Lust", "Claws of Desire",
and "Debbi Does Tokyo".
Once the girls found out the tricks I could do with my tail
and elongated forked tongue,
I never lacked for female companionship.
I'd be there still
but the head honcho used to like to show off
by having me light his cigars with my nuclear breath
and one night, I was a little drunk
and accidentally torched his head.
From there, I drifted.
I lost self-respect. I had no goal in my life.
And that's when I started eating cities.
At first it was just a few broken down one horse towns
just to keep body and soul together, you understand.
But from there, it grew.
Whistlestops, cow towns, bedroom communities.
It became an obsession.

And, as my appetite grew,
I grew:
25 feet high, 100 feet high, 500 feet and growing.
Soon, it took a fair sized metropolis to satisfy my craving.
I'd eat the power lines first for a jolt.
Then the elevated trains. Then I'd get down to business:
trucks, houses, skyscrapers, the city dump for pity's sake.
I knew I was out of control but I couldn't stop.
I was fighting the Army, the Marines, the National Guard.

But I didn't care; I was too far gone to care.
I took everything they could throw at me:
tanks, cannons, lasers, chemical weapons, small nukes.
They hit me with a Poseidon missile
and it just made me hungry.
I ate Seattle, Vegas, Salt Lake City.
It got so bad that I needed to crunch a suburb
just to get out of bed in the morning.

My social life was totally shot.
Every burg I hit was evacuated before I hit the city limits.
I didn't care, I was totally crazed.
Des Moines, Akron, Chi Town, Pittsburgh, PA.
I don't even remember eating Philadelphia.
I'd just black out and when I came to –
instant urban renewal.
All I cared for was where my next
skyscraper was coming from.
I was totally unstoppable.
And then I hit rock bottom.
I ate my home town and everybody in it
and didn't even get a buzz.
My parents, my friends,
Boris Badenov Memorial High School
gone in a crunch of molars
and all I could think about was scarfing the shopping mall.
That's when I looked myself straight in the eye
and admitted that I had a problem.

I wanted to stop but didn't know how.
Thank God I had good supportive friends though.
It was Mothra who told me about your program.
I knew I couldn't kick it alone, so here I am.
This is my first Monsters Anonymous meeting.
My name is Godzilla and I'm a cityholic.
I know it won't be easy,
it'll be a struggle every step of the way.
But, as I look around the room, I see I'm not alone.
All of you, Mothra, Rodan, Ghidra, the Smog Monster,
you've all been there. You know what it's like.
I know you'll be there for me.
The clinic's got me on maintenance.
I'm eating old Hollywood movie sets while I kick.

I've started your twelve stomp program.
But I know that's not enough.
The strength has to come from deep within me.
I've embraced a higher power.
You call it God,
I call it Tyrannosaurus Rex Mundi.
And I pray to the Lizard King that,
with your help and His,
I'll beat this thing
one crunch at a time.

Blues Walking Like A Man

I met an old blues man named Blind Voodoo Eisenhower
in a bar in Oakland called the Radium Pit.
He was talking about the good old days,
'way down south, playing fish fries in Georgia
for 5 dollars a night
and all the catfish he could stuff in his pockets.
About playing cathouses in N'Orleans
and getting catscratch fever with Jelly Roll Morton.
He pulled out a mojo hand, made out of a real hand,
and filed its fingernails, all casual-like
right there at the bar.

Said he'd gone down to the crossroads at midnight
and got run down by a feed truck.
He was drinking hellhounds straight up
and smoking Unlucky Strikes.
He was wearing a suit made of whiskey stains
all sewn together like patches.
He was sporting a barbecued pork pie hat,
a glass eye, and a gold tooth.
He had a .69 caliber pistol
and was packing a shiv in his back.
"That's the one place the cops never look," he told me.

Said he'd come to Chicago in a suitcase
ridin' the baggage racks on them long, lonely trains
up from Mississippi, where he'd sharecropped
on Dockery's plantation,

and drank straight from the cotton gin.
Said he'd had to leave the southland
after snitching Robert Johnson off to the Devil
for a bottle of demon liniment and a Mexican divorce.
Said he'd hit Chi town and it never got up again.
Put a silver bullet into Howlin' Wolf
and drank Muddy Waters from a hollow log.
Had him five wives back in Tennessee,
each one uglier than all the others,
and just itching to put an ice pick between his ears.
He'd be there still, but he'd run out of ice.
Said he'd left Chicago the night he saw Little Walter
get sucked up into his own mouth harp.

He put the harp on the bar, a Hohner Chromatic,
and asked me if I cared to take my chances.
I told him the only musical instrument I played was the jukebox
and bought him another drink.
He drained it, put that harp to this lips,
and sucked the bartender right up into that harp.
He cut loose with a lick,
and sucked the whole bar up into that thing,
just me and him, sittin' on bar stools in a vacant lot.

Said he had five fine women workin' them Oakland streets
and he had to check up on 'em.
He let loose with one last wail, and I was sittin' in the dirt,
lookin' up at the full moon,
a fifth of alligator wine by my side,
and a black cat bone to stir it up with.
"Dogs begin to bark, hounds begin to howl,
watch out, strange kin people,
little red rooster's on the prowl."

Why I Don't Buy *Hustler*

No, it's not because *Hustler* is a horrible sexist publication that exploits women. You could say the same thing about *Cosmo*. No, it's not because of the stupid racist cartoons. It's not even because I ordered an inflatable sheep doll from one of the ads in the back and the vibrating vagina broke down in a week, seriously injuring my dog Shep.

The reason I don't buy *Hustler* is the same reason I don't buy *Club* or *Genesis* or *High Society*. In their middle core pictorials, it's always the same: these randy sex-crazed dudes and dudettes are always about to commit conjunction, always just on the verge of committing carnality, always slavering over and above each other's pink parts but, somehow, it just never happens.

The penis is always nanoseconds away from parting those pink panting pussy lips. The girl's glistening tongue lusts down towards the quivering clitoris of her clamoring concubine. The full red lips form a perfect O over the tiny pearl-like drop of pre-cum that glistens from the glans. The greased dildo hovers vulture-like over the puckered portal of Gomorrah but, somehow, some way it just ...... never happens.

These models must be some of the most frustrated people on earth. One can visualize the photographer getting the final shot, pulling out a whip, and laying about him yelling, "Alright! That's it! Back off! Can't have you smearing her body makeup and messing her hairdo! We've still gotta get the beaver shot for the centerfold! Everyone else, hit the showers!"

Sometimes I imagine that the pictorials are actually photographs from Hell where rakes, sensualists, and sluts of all stripes are being punished by being perpetually placed in hot sexual situations with attractive and willing partners only to find an invisible barrier between them at the penultimate moment of penetration, stopped cold by an invisible force which, for lack of a better word, we must refer to as God. The same God who gave us all this sexual equipment and the nigh-irresistible urge to employ it and makes us buy these stupid magazines where sexual congress if forever frustrated. These are not pornographic magazines, they're religious texts. They're nothing but sanctimonious sermons preaching perdition! It would seem that we're to be punished by eternal frustration in the afterlife for the lusts that compel us to buy stroke mags in this life! We're already being punished and it costs us five bucks to boot. So who's getting exploited here anyway?

I suppose I'm just a sentimentalist at heart. I wanna see that penis slip between those cunt lips the same way you always want to see Lassie make it home safely in the last reel. I want to know that everyone got fucked happily ever after. I don't need Calvinist religious tracts slipped into my pornography so I say fight the right-wing bigots who publish this anti-sex propaganda! We want pink on pink! We want connection and consummation! We say to hell with this touch football jive – we demand a full contact sport! We don't allow prayer in our public schools, I'll be damned if I can see why we must endure it in our pornography! It's a clear-cut case of Christ versus cum shots. And I know which side I'm on.

So stand straight and proud. I mean tall and proud and the next time you go down to your local magazine dealer, look that sucker dead in the eye and say, "I take my pornography the same way I take my music ... hardcore."

Fuck The Homeless

I don't see the homeless anymore.
I just step over them like dogshit on the street.
I don't notice the bleeders, the shoeless, or the cripples.
They just blend in with the rest of the trash in the gutter.
I don't even hear the screamers anymore.
It's just more audio riz
like car alarms and sirens.
They've all turned into fixtures
like lamp posts or pigeons.
That's what they are –
human pigeons
cluttering up the sidewalks
looking for crumbs.
Scram!

Somewhere along the line
I accepted the notion
of disposable human trash.
It no longer seems
reprehensible, pitiable, or even Republican.
It's just there.
Somewhere along the line,
I crossed the line
and somewhere on the other side
was Michael Skilling.

Michael Skilling is an old friend of mine,
poet, ex-band mate, SSI most valuable player.
He washed up on the shores here recently
broke.
I couldn't put him up in my hotel
because, when he lived here,
he pissed the manager off so badly and so consistently
that he's ready to kill Michael on sight.

We couldn't ship Michael back home
because the buses were on strike
and I suddenly saw
how easy it is to become
human excrement in this town.
He was a street person suddenly,
sleeping in the bushes at the Palace of Fine Art,
wandering the streets talking out of his head,
his rotting shoes ripping his feet into steak tartar.
I'd slip him some bucks
and he'd turn them into white port
and get even sicker.
I'd try and put food in him
and he couldn't force it down.
We'd let him crash on my girlfriend's floor
and he'd fidget and mumble and pace
all night long so that nobody could get any sleep
and we wanted to put him back out on the street
and we didn't want him back on the street
and we didn't know what to do with him.
And then, finally, praise the gods,
Greyhound settled its affairs long enough
for us to send him back home on a scab bus
(where he found that his old lady had split for Arizona
with the same guy who had driven him down here
in the first place, but that's another story).
But the point is
that, in two weeks,
one of my best friends was reduced
to street sludge
and there was nothing I could do about it
because I'm only one short paycheck away
from being there myself.
And they want me to know it.
and they want me that way,
and I'm sick, sick, sick
of thinking about the homeless.

Death Warmed Over

I've been haunting the hospitals again
watching Death work his sleazy cabaret act
working out of another borrowed emaciated form
that used to be one of my friends.
This time, it was Jim's glazed eyes
from which he winked.
Death wore his wasted face like a saggy mask.
He could make it talk and spit.
But even Death couldn't make that
stick and skin puppet dance.
I'll give it a 65.
I mean
if that wormy old bugger is going to give me
yet another ghost to take care of,
he should at least cap the swan song
with a saucy jig.

I'm accumulating ghosts at an alarming rate.
On new and full moon nights,
my room resembles a danse macabre version of
the stateroom scene from "Night At the Opera".
There's
Cybele with the infection eating her up from inside,
Irene pouring brandy onto her corroded liver,
Johnny Muddy swinging from my ceiling on his noose,
Vinnie and Reb grinning at each other
with the moonlight shining
through the matching bullet holes in their heads,
Tom dripping river water all over the rug,
Barbara's severed head chattering on my bed,
her face covered with cigarette burns, blood, and semen.
I must belong to the Sloppy Death Club.
Not one of those suckers left a pretty corpse.
I'm weary of propitiating their spirits
and tending the walking wounded they left behind.

It's dusk now.
The shadows are starting to move around my room.
I set up the candles (one for each spectre)
and arrange my little offerings.
I wonder if I'm being too cold-blooded,
already planning how I can

make room for one more.
The wind is rising. The fog rolls in.
I hear the first groans and whispers.
I light the candles, pour the drinks,
and burn the special incense
to make the scented smoke
from which they fashion their forms.
They're closer now.
"Where's Jim?" they whisper, "Where's Jim?"
"Not quite yet, my pretty ones," I croon,
stroking their smoky sides,
"He'll be here soon enough,
don't begrudge him his last look at the light."
After all,
as the skull grinning beneath my skin
keeps reminding me,
Death is king of this world.
Mortals are born with the meter already running,
and it's always been
later than you think.

Cable From The Bunker Of The Last Unrepentant Rocker To The Ghost Of Jim Morrison

Jim,
you were right to take that header in the bathtub.
If you had lived, they would have made you
better.
They would have
tossed you into Betty Ford,
force fed you Antabuse,
bathed you in healthy thoughts,
made you jog.

They would have dressed you in a
three piece black leather business suit
and taught you about real estate.

They would have made you
crawl across the pages of *People* magazine,

write autobiographies,
hug Phil Donahue.

They would have made you
suck big Jesus dick,
do benefits for the Cirrhosis Foundation,
kiss the patent leather hooves
of Madd Mothers
and Parents' Music Resource Harpies.

They would have made you
eat wheat germ and shit,
judge poetry contests,
talk at high schools.

They would have made you
live in a better house and garden,
save a rain forest,
sing a duet with Linda Ronstadt.
They would have made you write
three thousand times on the blackboard of your soul:
      "I WAS A BAD LIZARD".
They're beating on the walls of my bunker, Jim,
shouting:
      "Ecstasy can be cured!"
      "You're not living up to your end
      of the social contract!"
         "Do you know what that cigarette is doing to
your lungs?"
There's cracks in the walls.
The Good Health Police
and Citizens for a Sane and Sober Society
have broken out the stun guns.
They're shouting something about safe sex and crack babies.
      They want to help me, Jim.
           Splash over to one side, there,
           I'm climbing in.
           This bath tub has
           a familiar ring.

Dead Girl

There is a dead four year old girl
who lives in my hotel.
The story is that she died in the basement
and the bloodstains won't come off the floor,
not even with Bon Ami.
Late at night, or on sultry afternoons,
she taps timidly on my door;
when the answer, the corridor is vacant.
Perhaps this used to be her room
but, because of the magick wards I erected,
she can't pass over the threshold.
I'm sorry about that.
I had no idea of her existence
when I erected them
and feel bad
                about dispossessing
a four year old ghost,
but there are other things out there
that I definitely do *not* want in my room
and, besides, the one time she did get in,
she threw my books all over the place
and I hate having to spank dead children.

Sometimes, in the horror hours,
I hear the bounce of a ball down the corridor
and the patter of little feet.
The folklore is that the building is owned
by her grieving aunt who refuses to sell
for the sake of her ghost waif.
I, therefore, owe my continued tenancy
to the little ghost girl
and feel sorry when I hear her
at her solitary play.
I'd like to do something to make her happy.
        Perhaps I'll kill her a little boy
        to keep her company
        in the gray playgrounds of the night.

Poetically Incorrect

You come up to me after the reading
and say the piece I wrote was tasteless, hateful,
grossly unfair to your special interest group,
and definitely
NOT FUNNY.
Now you stand there blocking my path to the bar
with an attentive and earnest look on your face
and an underlying current of smoldering menace.
What can I say?
My dear, dear friend,
I have been writing for a long time now
and have found out
that you can't write anything without pissing someone off
SO IT MIGHT AS WELL BE YOU.
I mean
if it wasn't you up here,
quoting the party line at my face and keeping me from my
next beer,
it'd be an earnest and attentive representative from:

The Lizzie Borden Battered Children Revenge Squad.
Chinese-Americans Against Fu Manchu Books.
Christians for Repressive Toilet Training.
Concerned Stalinists Against Irradiated Food.
The United League of American Paranoids
Who *Have* Found Communists Under the Bed.
Deep Ecologists In Favor of Universal Suffrage for Trees.
The Berkeley Mothers In Favor of Castration
For All Convicted Smokers.
Jews for Hitler.
The Let's Put Pants On the Zoo Animals Committee.
The Crack Dealers' Benevolent Fund.
The Child Molester's Scoutmaster Guild.
Rastafarians Against Drug Abuse.
Trekkies for U.N. Recognition for the Planet Vulcan.
The United Feminist Let's Take the Dick
Out of Dictionary Writers' Collective.

Fundamentalist Buddhists.
The Save the Lyme Tick Foundation.

Gay Republicans for Self-Flagellation.
The Militant Vegetarian Terrorist Strike Force.
Jerry Falwell's Voter Registration Drive
For Christian Fetuses.
The Recovering Alcoholics' Islamic Study Group.
Madd Mothers Against Practically Everything.
Or my own personal special interest group:
The Vampyre Mike Committee
Against Self-Righteous Pompous Pinheads
Who Waste My Time.
Would you care to make a contribution?
We're doing very important work.

Maura O'Connor   b.1967

We (Babarians) first saw Maura reading at a Shattuck bakery reading and got her to come to the Babar. She has almost a religious cadence, reflecting a deep sort of existential fare, with directness of statement, and precision of imagery. Her voice is very precise and musical – kind of a big sweep. She's a perfectionist; a young poet with a mature voice, who grew up in a family with alcoholism. She has several chapbooks, including, *Mercy Hates His Job,* Cyborg Press, 1991, and *The Hummingbird Graveyard,* Zeitgeist, 1992. *Hummingbird Graveyard* backcover notes: Maura O'Connor attended Orange Coast College, where she won a scholarship for her poetry in 1988. Her poetry has appeared in *Bullhorn, Dangerous Stew,* and *The Women's Quarterly.*

Love Poem

Love is not
a long-legged
surgically perfected
bleached blonde
selling extra sensitive condoms
with a porcelain smile.

Love does not
wear contact lenses
to change the color of her eyes.

Love has been
wearing dark glasses
to hide the bruises
standing on street corners
trying to forget.

Love is not available
in shiny plastic packages.
Does not come in trial size.

Love has gotten lonely
sits up at night
studying the patterns
in the shadows
on the ceiling.

Love is not
the black haired
green eyed woman
in the blue silk dress
you took home.

She came twice
never called you again.
She said she was Love,
but she lied.

Love wears baggy clothes
sits in all-night coffee shops
reading pulp novels
smoking cigarettes.

Love spare changes
for cheap red wine.

Love has been 86'd
from the Golden Triangle bars

her weeping disturbed the customers.

Love watches
black leather boys
knife fight for five dollar crack bowls
remembers when they used to fight
for her.

Sometimes Love calls you on the phone
hangs up when you answer.

Love sat across from you on the bus
it had been so long
you didn't recognize her.

Love remembers how you wanted her,
and all the times you beat her
to make her understand.

Love is unemployed,
has stopped looking for work.

Love's skills are obsolete
in the computer age.

Love is tired
of talking about herself
at 12-step programs.

Love wants you to take her home again
feed her
make her a drink.

Love is covered with street grime
and wants a bath

Love is dying of AIDS.

Love is sleeping in your doorway
shaking in the cold

Love knows you aren't really looking for her.

Survival

I light a cigarette on the stove
tie my hair in a knot
fasten silver loops to my ears
make coffee
lace my feet into thick black boots

This is how I get through the day
reminding myself
a symphony is made of movements

This is the season of fires in the hills
fires that make breathing harder
and the sunsets more beautiful

Mornings I curl into my lover's stomach
let him coax me awake with kisses

When I feel brave
I imagine growing old with him
a lifetime of mornings being licked awake
like a kitten

When I'm scared
I see myself at nineteen
thin from Dexatrim and slimfast
in a blue nylon dress from St. Vincent de Paul's
lips waxed the color of eggplant skin

talking to cut carnations
and the dog
because they have the sense not to answer

I see myself in the hospital
a pale mummy wrapped in sheets that smell of bleach
leaning on the IV stand to get to the bathroom

I remember a friend
who swallowed blue pills with cheap whiskey
but wouldn't let her lover hold her

I finger a scar on my head
where hair won't grow
bite my nails
phone friends to make sure they're still there

I count food stamps
plan the soup
curse the small pains in the curve of my back
make a mask of hairspray and lipstick

Yesterday I counted five delicate orange flowers
growing from the gutter

I am still the child
who watched a family of black ants
march up the side of the new Sears refrigerator
when I could have been out with the other kids
beating the fence with a stick

Still the thick-legged fifteen year old girl
who carved her wrists with broken glass
who wore long-sleeved white Oxford shirts
buttoned
to hide the damage

The small creatures only have camouflage
for defense

I am still the girl who offered him a hand
that night at the poetry reading
because it was warmer than
his half-pint of Jack Daniel's

who thought love should be tidy as a bank statement
dates of deposits and withdrawals
in black ink

Now when he sleeps
I lie next to him
bury a hand in his thick brown beard
and think how he was learning to be alone
with his heart
in this apartment with photographs
pinned to the walls

while I chewed on the end of a black Bic Pen
in high school biology
learning about Darwin

They never taught me how the heart survives
whether it needs camouflage

determination
or teeth

Now as the coffee provides some courage
I imagine his beard gone gray
and the sixteen years he was alive
before I was born

The sixteen years between us
that part like the red velvet curtain
before the movie begins

I study my reflection
this strange mixture of thick hair
and thin skin
eyes the color of postcard oceans
but twice as deep

But I can't see myself in mirrors
that's why I write poems
to know myself
and the things I remember
in my belly

Gravity

Today I am fragile
pale
twitching
insane and full of purpose.

I'm thinking of my lover:
my soft hips pressing his coarse belly,
my tongue on a salmon nipple,
his hand buried in my thick orange hair
the telephone ringing.

I'm thinking we tend our illnesses
as if they are our children:
fevered
screaming

demanding attention and twenty dollar bills,
hours we could have spent
making love with the television on.

Faith is a series of calculations
made by an idiot savant.
I'm in love.
I'm alone
in this city of painted boxes
stacked like alphabet blocks
spelling nothing.

There are things I know:
trees don't sing
birds don't sprout leaves
the sky never turns to wine

roses bloom because that's what roses do,
whether we write poems for them
or not.

I concentrate on small things:
ivy threaded through chain link,
giveaway kittens huddled in a soggy cardboard box,
a fat man blowing harmonica
through a beard of rusty wires
brown birds chattering furiously on power lines.

I try not to think about
lung cancer, AIDS,
the chemicals in the rain;
things I can't imagine any more than
a color I've never seen

My heart is graffiti on the side of a subway train,
a shadow on the wall made by a child.
Nothing has been fair since my first skinned knee
I believe death
must be.

I cling to love as if it were an answer.
I go on buying eggs and bread,
boots and corsets,
knowing I'll burn out before the sun.

I'm thinking of
the days I tried to stay awake
while the billboards and T.V. ads
for condoms, microwave brownies, and dietetic jello
lulled me to sleep.

A brown-eyed girl once told me a secret
that should have blown this city
into a mass of unconnected atoms
Our sewage is piped to the sea.
Beggars in the street
are hated for having the nerve
to die in public.

Charity requires paperwork,
Relief requires medication

as if we were the afterthoughts of institutions
greater than our rage.

Gravity chains us to the asphalt with such grace
we think it is kind.

We all go on buying lottery tickets
Diet Coke and toothpaste
as if the sky over our heads
were the roof of a gilded cage.

We provided evidence that we were here:
initials cut into cracked vinyl bus seats,
into trees growing from squares
in concrete.
a name left on a stone, an office building,
a flower, a disease, a museum
a child.

Tonight the stars glitter like rhinestones
on a black suede glove.

In the coffin my room has become,
I talk to God
about the infrequency of rain
about people who can't see the current of gentleness
running under the pale crust of my skin.

I tell him under
the jackhammer crack, the diesel truck rumble,
even the clicking sound traffic lights make
switching from yellow to red,
there is a silence
swallowing
every song,
conversation,
every whisper made beside graves
or in the twisted white sheets of love.

I tell him I can't fill it
with dark wine, blue pills,
a pink candle lit at the altar
the lover
touching my hair.

God doesn't answer.
God doesn't know our names.

He's only the architect
designing the places we occupy
like high rise offices or ant hills

I know this
the way I know
sunrise and sunset
are caused by the endless turning
of the Earth.

The Wind

There is a clock in the center of the Earth
ticking out love affairs   wars   and Christmases

There's an alarm about to go off
but I'm certain that no one will hear it
There's a fury in my red hair
a fire that grows from my skull

At the welfare office we line up like schoolchildren

a skinny junkie a paralytic a woman without underwear
a brown-skinned pregnant girl with long braids

They leave the door locked until after eight

There should be a wind

We're snow on the rim of the volcano
a sugar angel given to a child

Only God is forever
and he doesn't love us enough
to be angry anymore
I see him sometimes in the round wet eyes of children

He looks sad and distant like
Napoleon in exile

As we pack him away like old birthday cards
put him on a shelf in the closet

In the two a.m. dark
I hear drunks whisper
I hear my neighbor sing in Spanish to the mirror
A soft voice on the radio says
"Call 976-LOVE I'm here to listen"

There should be a wind

There is a song in my throat like a peach pit
as I carry free bread away from the park

As a policeman makes a wino leave the bus stop
as a thin man checks his reflection in
the window of the Bank of America

They say the heart grows larger before it dies

I watch a fourteen-year-old girl
push her blond hair over her shoulder and
neaten her thick film of makeup
I see a wall of shatterproof glass

As the twentieth century runs out of gas
somewhere in the middle of the desert

as we draw up intricate blueprints of desire and
build lonely cathedrals of wishes

Where green-eyed stained glass window saints
raise empty hands to heaven
As the speeches of secular martyrs
crackle on the radio like bacon

As we talk about love and hope
and the wars that bring us together

There should be a wind

There is a song I have known since I was a child
a song of rage and survival

if survival makes me ugly
then I will be ugly and wear my hair down

I will sing until the wind comes
on a corner
my hat left out for dimes

For L.

Your long tan legs, muscled calves
your dark nipples against a white lace tank top
your eyes:
brown and still as a frozen doe's
your long fingers curved around
a filterless Camel
your house in San Jose:
blood-clot colored Persian rugs
caked with dog shit,
snowed with ashes
your sparrow thin arms spiraled with
homemade pine-green tattoos
your plastic juice cups full of
two-dollar-a-bottle apple wine
your stories about mexican migrant worker johns
who picked you up on the first and fifteenth

your favorites, you said, because
all you had to do was lie still
your green Doc Marten boots, black lipstick
licorice whip tongue
your job restocking Coke cans, tampons and
ham sandwiches at the 7-11
your acid flashback:
worms crawling through the jars
of beef jerky

The night you begged your husband to take you
to the two-star French restaurant with
real lace table cloths,
because you wanted to say you'd eaten snails

The night I sat on your front porch
swatting mosquitos
while you got drunk

Your confession that you didn't really feel much:
your husband could be just another john
and the only man you'd ever loved was your pimp

Your softness as you talked about your unborn baby:
"I want to give him a mohawk for
his first baby picture," you giggled,
"I want him to have anything he wants ... you know:
lots of clothes and a motorcycle – he can
play his music loud and bring his girlfriends home –
I won't care.
I'm going to be a good mother."

Your brief hug the night your husband threw me out

The way you said I shouldn't ever call you

I know you weren't really a friend,
but I loved you

I still have a photo of you on your porch
in San Jose,
smiling too hard
holding your pregnant belly
wine bottle set beside your feet

12 Days Of Rain

a cardboard city washes down
the old women tie plastic scarves
around their hair
the little boys in their raincoats
squeal and splash in the gutter

on the sidewalk everyone moves with
an urgency

after ten years of drought
the April fires
bricks in the toilet tank
this is a good rain

i've made payment on my walls
and a door with a good lock

inside my fingerprints are everywhere
on the mirror
on the wineglasses
on the keys of the typewriter

i can't leave fingerprints on skin

for valentine's day he gives me flowers
and a laundry basket
he tries to listen when i tell him
i'm afraid of umbrellas and
would rather get wet

i make him a thick steak and try
not to stare while he eats it
i ask him six times if he liked it
he goes in the other room

love has become learning which places
not to touch
in my garden the lily collapses,
her yellow tongue licking the concrete
i admired her for blooming out of season

the rain keeps falling

this is my time of learning to live inside
i take command of my closet
arrange the skirts by length
the blouses by color
i tell my secrets to the houseplants
they grow new leaves in return
i learn how much water to add to the coffee
which he always makes too strong

i learn to apply my makeup without
studying my face

i learn to lock the door behind
whether i'm coming in or
going out

i make lists of what makes sense to me:

we know what revolves around the earth
but we don't know what's at
the bottom of the ocean

even beneath the ground there is an order:
first, rock
then water
then oil
deepest of all is fire

the rain keeps falling

a family of black ants moves into our bathroom
and continues to work
forming lines, carrying away the dead

i try not to step on them as
i smooth my hair before work

the novelty of two bodies in
one set of rooms becomes routine
his sharp pile of whiskers in the sink
infuriates me
he complains about my clothes on the floor

we begin writing rules
for our country:

he does the dishes,
i cook the fish

we argue about the balance
in the bank
i throw a milk bottle
he throws the garbage can

rain keeps falling

on sunday we make peace in front of the television
remove our clothing while
Michael Jackson sings for the Pepsi generation

it was easier to learn what places to touch
this way
to know that he likes black garters
and loose hair
to remember the place behind his ear

after he falls asleep
i make a ritual of turning off each light
studying each new shadow

the valentines flowers die
a week after they open

i cry for them

the next morning there's sun

The Hummingbird Graveyard

These days
I cover my face with bottled skin
and scented creams
stain my lips the color of rose juice
wear black
my eyes deepen

The man who once called me
that girl in the white shirt

is my lover

He carried me home in a magician's casket
cut me in two
I came out whole

I'm a kindness to climb into
a Dresden doll found in the basement
of a burnt house

These days
I buy the book with the ugliest cover
comb the thick orange hair
of the innocent child
I never was

While my heroes are knocked down
like pinatas
while we wear surgical gloves
to the laying on of hands

I've folded suicide in four
laid it on a bare white shelf
someday it may gather dust
I might toss it away like an old dishrag

I'm young
green as bread mold

I'm seeking witness

I want the testimony of
Hitler
Stalin
the shadows on the bricks
of Nagasaki

These days
the newspapers serve a menu of clay pigeons
bring your own bullets

I want to ban the colors of the television
the perfect thighs
and plastic wishes

I want to put my next breath
in my lover's mouth
I want to burn Jesus leaflets
and wear his sandals

I'm taking it all off
in the bars of my ribcage

While the politicians find work
for each idle child
while two terminal patients
place bets on the existence of God

These days
I show the years when I didn't want to live
in the gray spokes of my iris
I'm coming apart like a ten-cent toy
I carry my head under my arm
like a rag doll

I want to sleep in the ruin
of last night's makeup
I want ancient recipes over instant rice

I want to find the hummingbird graveyard
I want to fill my mouth with black beetles
and walk the edge of Eden

I need a new commandment

I will collect single bars of old songs
I will weep a page of black ink
I will be an unprotected witness

My country serves three-day notice
to the starving
my country's hands are tattooed
on the belly of a battered child
my country sleeps in the snow of the television
after its anthem is played

Let's burn the country
and keep the flag

This night is falling in pieces
this moon is cream on a raisin sky

I will evolve thick skin and filter
I will plan my next breath

I will watch the four riders
foam their horses into glue

It isn't over yet

Ken DiMaggio   b.1960

DiMaggio is currently finishing a novel about suburban high school honor students who run amok when they find a dead baby and then go through a Keystone Kops routine in trying to sacrifice it to Satan. He is currently going to school to get certified as a high school English teacher. He is anthologized in: *Horsemen Of The Apocalypse*, Cyborg Press, 1991.

Slouching Towards The Great American Convalescent Home

I own no books! I barely read the newspaper! I die in the suburbs! and live to work in the bureaucracy! I snore to church every Sunday! and pop up like a piece of toast on Monday! I have responsibility divorce and kids! And I am programmed to burn out before the age of fifty! And so journey on down to the Great American Convalescent Home! Journey on down! With atrophied brain cells! A passive docile work force! Amusement-themed vacation spots! A careered and sexless brain-dead spouse! Journey on down! After a life of Teflon! Instant! Episco-urban and frigid! Journey on down! With your promotions your Kiwanis your twenty years at IBDumb your angina ulcers and fallen arches and journey on down!

by starting with a polyester business memo indentured career!

Journey on down!

with eight hours of office machines and eight hours of television every day for the next thirty years!

Journey on down!

with spectator living political indecision mortgage alienation and family self-destruction! Journey on down! to the wheelchair! the bingo! the electro-shock and the human warehouse that waits for you at the end of a great middle class and junkmail-literate career! But right now I'm a King! Right now I'm a supervisor a manager an executive an SS Officer right now I'm a Queen! Right now I'm an attorney a broker a reporter a right-wing Afrikaner but only when it comes to the beggars and the homeless mental patients who feed my delusions of power! Only when it comes to humiliating aged clerks idiot mailroom boys high school dropout messengers only when it comes to beating into submission my spouse my son my daughter but that's more than enough for the American who owns no books that's more than enough for the American who helps to produce pulp in order to live in the disposable suburbs! Because I have people working under me! I have beggars and clerks and wetbacks and death row prisoners! I have thousands of people that I can look down on and pretend to own! And I have a religion and a society that encourages me to think in dollars victims and social stereotypes! and that's why even though I'm twenty I already have one foot in the grave that's why even though I've been to college I already have rigor mortis settling in my brain and that's why even though I'm a professional I already have trouble remembering the names and the faces of the people who are married sired or work for me and that's why even though I have success social standing and a mortgage I already have a problem doing anything with my free time other than sitting in front of the TV and that's why long before I retire my education my social standing and my memory have already begun to atrophy! That's why before the age of thirty rigid patterns have been settling in making me think only of the boss's ass the amusement park-themed summer vacation and the sports-fascism hilarity of the television! And that's why long before I reach the top of my profession bureaucratic games Madison Avenue and suburbia already have me slouching metaphysically towards the convalescent home and so I'm slouching towards the human warehouse

I'm slouching towards that starchy Lestoiled bingo-playing dump

I'm slouching towards the end of the American Dream now

I'm slouching towards the perpetual elevator music the children I trained to be competitive and who never visit I'm slouching towards that illiterate arts and crafts therapy nightmare I'm slouching towards the end of the American Dream now I'm slouching to where it ends at

the convalescent home

where the clerks and messengers I once humiliated now have the
chance to show me their power yes the dropouts the hillbillies the mini-
mum wage earners I used to treat like beggars will now be my atten-
dants orderlies and caretakers yes the human beings I stepped on like
cockroaches the human beings I helped make stupid with subliminal
fascism will now become my manager supervisor and SS Officer and
gee I wonder how their cultural sense of the disposable will feel towards
my senile sick and elderly gee I wonder how their Hispanic Black or
White Trash-oppressed identity will feel about my never practiced but
always preached sense of equality gee but these dropouts shmucks and
lumpens are going to be my caretakers aides and wardens gee this hill-
billy with only an eighth-grade education and a love for slasher movies
at the drive-in is going to take care of me when I'm unfamilied broke
and eightysomething gee the person I can piss on gee the person I can
now fire humiliate and underemploy gee when I'm babbling wrinkled
bedridden gee that good old boy or brother is going to be my boss

and my great American son and daughter! My mannequinned-skinned
replicants practicing fascism or environmental disaster! Will just forget
about me! Will just dispose of any duty guilt or obligations just like cig-
arette lighters! Party Makers! And maimed-for-life veterans! My little
Kodaked dancer and Pee Wee leagued trophied pitcher! My Wonder
Bread offspring disasters! My spoiled and tyrannical little Eva Braun
and Adolf Hitler! Hope you're doing fine Mom and Dad! And just sign
away your life on the dotted line Mom and Dad! We won't be able to
visit you for this decade Mom and Dad! And the grandkids never ask
about you or send you their love Mom and Dad! Have fun with the
wheelchair the restraints and the bingo Mom and Dad! Besides it'll
soon be over or you'll slip into a coma and you should see the urn we
have for you and what can you do about the help when the state's pay-
ing the bills but just hang in there hang tough winning is the only thing
we love you its been good having you as parents but you're a burden on
our lives and that's just the way it goes

and so have fun Mom and Dad try not to irritate the orderly too much
try to hold your bladder for as long as you can because that's Capitalism
when you're eighty-something and no longer an eyeteeth stealing
supervisor that's Capitalism when you have no more Moloch-making
skills to offer and expect your ex-world to believe in human relations
that's Capitalism when you're wheelchaired social securities and a bur-
den to your lampshade-skin children that's Capitalism that's just the
free enterprise system that's Capitalism that's the more for me and the

fuck with you Christian American and God bless'em middle-class values we believe in

and so journey on down

with a Reader's Digest American career and by humiliating the lumpens under you

Journey on down!

with that winning is the only thing son and daughter and people are poor because they don't want to work philosophy

Journey on down!

eight hours of office machines eight hours of television every day wearing a mask every day your head up someone's ass I'm slouching towards the convalescent home I can barely read the newspaper I'm slouching towards the convalescent home but I know how to brownnose and get promotions I'm slouching towards the convalescent home even though I say it's never going to happen to me it doesn't matter

because that's where the American Dream ends

the bingo the wheelchaired the neglected the arts and crafts therapy nightmare that's where the great business career the Better Homes and Gardens Family and the Wall Street Journal meaning of life finally end

God bless the values we believe in

Winning isn't everything it's the only thing

At Shady Acres our highly skilled professional staff will tend to your every need

I hope I'm not around

Bucky Sinister b.1969

Bucky mc's at the Chameleon, a wild reading series in a bar; and works in distribution at Last Gasp Comics. Has several chapbooks, including *Twelve Bowls Of Glass,* and *Asphalt Rivers,* Manic D Press, 1990 & 1991.

Venice Beach Strays

Eleven-thirty at night
At a pay phone on the beach
I watched several stray dogs fight over something only dogs
   would understand
And only twenty feet away
   a stray human slept underneath a palm tree.
A police patrol car came by
   and the police said,
     "The beach is closed.
     No sleeping on the beach."
The beach did not look closed to me;
   no one had even turned off the waves.
An unmarked
   but obvious
   police car
with a "Dare To Keep Kids Off Drugs" bumper sticker
pulled up for assistance
As a cop got out of the first car,
   woke up the stray human,
   and made him leave;
But the dogs,
   who were watching from a cautious distance,
  got to stay,
   and they figured it was something
     only humans
     would understand.

Running The Gauntlet

2:30 a.m.
I was three blocks from home,
running the gauntlet
past the projects.

At the end of the first block,
a guy came up the street
and said,
"Ten shot? Weed? Anything you need?"
"No," I said.
Two blocks to go.

A van pulled up.
"Hey you got a smoke?" a man asked.
I gave him one, lit him up.
"You need a ride?" he asked.
"No," I said.
One block to go.

The van, going the other way,
did a U-turn
and pulled up slowly.
I've been paranoid of this scene
ever since that night in L.A.'s Hoover District
I was waiting for a near-mythical bus
when a low rider drove past,
backed up to where I was,
and stared at me with tinted-glass eyes.
I thought I was going to be shot
but it just drove away.

I started looking for cover when a voice
from the passenger side said,
"Hey, you got a cigarette for me, too?"
I gave her one with my matches.
I just wanted to be home.
"Are you sure you don't need a ride?
We're trying to get some gas money."
"I'm sure," I said.
They drove away.
I got home.
My roommate's bird was perched in the livingroom.
the cage is left open often
so she can fly around the apartment.
I went over to her,
she crawled onto my finger,
and I put her in the cage.
I closed the door
and covered the cage with a blanket.
She squawked.

"You're welcome, Percy," I said.
"Good night."

People have tried to sell me many things,
but most of the time,
all I want is a cage
and someone who will cover me like a blanket.

Charles Whitman Told Me I'd Have Days Like This

An ex-marine had had enough one day
shot his wife and his mother-in-law
climbed a belltower
and shot sixteen people
He was killed that same August day in Texas
and it wasn't the heat people complained about
as much as the humidity
and it wasn't the humidity people complained about
as much as the high velocity lead
that came down like the lightning bolts of Zeus.
Three old men sat around the general store
drinking coffee and watching tv
saw the news
and talked about World War II
they all agreed "sixteen was nuthin,"
in their day they could've done better.

No one knows why he did it.
He wanted to be a god.
he was an ill-trained dog,
or plain old fashioned fear.

But it takes more than a few holes
to be a messiah,
confusion is common as ticks,
and new fears come over the rooftops
like metallic-angel helicopters,
and asking why he did it
doesn't get me anywhere
when there are so many questions
crawling in my head
like cockroach SWAT teams:

I don't know the difference between

bleeding to death and
dying from chemotherapy.

I don't know the difference between
having nightmares
and being possessed by demons.

I don't know the difference between
being lonely and
being from another planet.

I don't know the difference between
being wrecked by love and
getting strung out on your drug of choice.

I don't know the difference between
being dependent on a philosophy and
being an insect in a biology project.

I don't know the difference between
picking a flower to smell
and holding a dead plant in my hands.

But I'm shooting down these old fears
from the top of the belltower of my mind;
Mr. Whitman taught me how.

Rotor blades thump percussion,
Bullhorns screech electric guitar solos,
squad cars give the light show,

I listen to the music.

I've got enough ammo to last all night.

The Bitterness I Taste Is Not From My Barley

I took a drink but all I got was ashes
the butts were your brand

didn't think you'd be seen in a place like this
didn't think you'd risk people like me
        drinking after you

if we are both here all night
we will not be in the same room

but watching each other
like looking in the neighbor's window

Is that me over there
        talking to you
Is that me over there
        fighting with you
Is that me over there
        having sex with you
Is that me over there
        or is it you

We will interact,
        simultaneously becoming voyeurs
        standing outside our bodies
                next to each other
                backs turned
As our corpses become congenial
        we become nauseus

I need a drink
        to keep talking to you
I need a drink
        to keep fighting with you
I need a drink
        to fornicate with you
I need a drink
        how about you

I look around this place.
I see no one to talk to.
No one else will understand the horror
        of being in love with you
No one else will understand the horror
        of being in love with me

so we're stuck with each other
incestuous Siamese twin Volkswagon Beetles
        in a lover's spat
using each other for spare parts.

The bitterness I taste is not from my barley
so could you buy me a beer
to wash it all down?

The Jesus Virus

If you were unfortunate enough
to be lonely or depressed in Boston in the mid eighties,
especially if you went to malls,
chances are
I came up to you and
offered to be your best friend.

My friends and I
were infecting the town the best we could
with the Jesus virus.
Our ultimate plan was for the world,
but right now
it was going to be the Natick Mall, or Quincy Market.

We'd meet up beforehand,
get our pep talks that resembled lines of speed,
and assigned our quotas,
and take off in pairs,
always a veteran with a rookie.

Such easy targets ...
like animals with bullseye fur patterns
from one shoe store away,
we could tell who wanted to be talked to,
who needed an answer,
and believe me
we had all the answers you'd ever need.

Give us a minute, we'd take an hour.
Give us an hour, we'd take a day.
give us a day, we'd take a weekend.
Give us a weekend, we'd take your whole damn life away,
and you would be out recruiting with us next week,
dangling carrots of bliss in front of faces.

The answers and the companionship was there,
but there was no time to really question them
because I was always a little bit behind quota
and late for a meeting,
and since I was in high school
and working twenty hours a week
while going to fifteen ours at least a week of church meetings
I was just a little too tired to give a damn

about whether or not I was right.

I just wanted to sleep
and was looking forward to tomorrow
when the forty-eight hour fast was going to end.
Just about that time something would pop up
like an all-night Friday prayer meeting.

I still catch myself
sizing up people in a crowd.
Finding targets,
people that would listen to me for five minutes
and come on a weekend retreat with me.
I leave them alone now,
try not to think about them,
but it pisses me off knowing how easily
they could walk right into it,
catch the Jesus virus,
or the Krishna plague,
or Moon disease,
like they were licking a bus station toilet seat
because it's that easy
and I only wish it were that obvious.

Nancy Depper b.1966

Regarded as one of the more-important voices on the scene, Nancy Depper's work has terrific surface tension, depth and passion. Nancy frequently performs in many Bay Area spoken-word venues; and represented San Francisco in the 1993 National Poetry Slam. Her work has appeared in *The Berkeley Poetry Review*, and *Disability Arts Magazine* in the U. K. Has two chapbooks: *Bodies of Work*, Manic D Press, 1992; and *Scrambled Arms And Eggs*, Blue Beetle Press, 1992.

Girl's-Eye

I began as a salesman's daughter, reckless
and stuttering with mysteries
and accidental rhyme
now I am she she she, spit out
in a lovers' spat
I crouch to lay that confession,
a yolk at my own heels
a yellow mouth of a baby
unmade like
my own bed in shambles,
in brutal parody of housekeeping;
Staring up at the ceiling
that girl's-eye view,
the glow-in-the-dark stars
I stuck there
remind me that night has
its sharp edges even
if all of mine are blunt
Hell, I burnt candles
and stared until even the hiss
of that light was doubled
I peeled away the skin of each day
but my naked hours are so
ugly and I am only modest
when alone
My wits have gone begging
and everyone is straining to see
eyes wide like the horribly curious
at Nana's funeral who
finally got to see
got to confirm it
and murmured

"she passed, she passed"
as if death was a test
But I was born wanting
like a short-sheeted bed, and
with that same posture, flat
and all wedges and spheres that
I was never happy with but
made do, even undressed
I wouldn't make the first move
and I hoped I looked frail
when sleeping,
I was more puppy than girl
5th grade, 4th string
reckless daughter with the
wind knocked out from a football
thrown straight to the gut;
Tonight I am still breathless
my left hand finishing
what was left undone
my left hand moving in the same
rhythm of his soft snores
But tomorrow music will stroke
back to me, too,
and getting my head up over
your knees
will be second
to getting it up over mine
my easy fist will recline
and swing me out to
my mini-Chinatown where
snap necked ducks glisten
tangy and orange, where
old women bent to impossible positions
scoop up their cowlicked young
and lead lives I cannot imagine
and do not care where I have been all
night, or with whom or
whose, so long as I have exact
change and do not stare;
I hang my thumbs in my pockets
like skinny nickel rolls, keep
my girls-eye trained to the sidewalk
and smelling of fish and ginger,
puffed up on all this clarity

I can hear everything
I can hear my pupils shrink
in sleepy daylight
I can hear my need for
a fistful of aspirin burn
like an Indian twist to the wrist
I can hear my sister snap her fingers
to a favorite song
while she fries an omelette
I can hear my hair knitting itself
into a sweater and my skin
crinkling like rice paper
I can hear the lovers' still fighting
but kissing now, stabbing each other
with my name on their tongues
I hear my stomach rumble
30 minutes after breakfast
I hear the things I didn't learn
in college laugh at me
I hear myself laugh
at the things I did learn
And I hear my head bubble
with fever from all this listening
I can tug on the rims of my ears
like horns but those flaps
are not nearly mute enough for
my own voice like a pizzeria soprano;
It's Saturday, I should be
having a picnic,
all my pots should be boiling!
And this morning on 12th Avenue
still not a genius
still uninspired and
still reckless
I climb up the stairs and back
into bed, I stare up
at the ceiling again
minus its glitter by sunlight
I shut my eyes, not
Against the day plainness
but to harvest something from it.

Phil Vincent

My son,
I enlarged you
until you could be seen under X-ray
bright and shiny
as a first tooth
white and jagged
you would not be softened
by my teething lullabies.

You are my test
my trial by sores
you pound my head and say:
"Look what you have grown!"
this little bead
my quiet clot,
I could roll you between my thumb
and finger, shoot you
like a pee-wee
the baby marbles I was always
in such danger of choking on;
now I am the human bomb and
this little ticker gives kisses

But if I have rewritten
my body with language
then I am guilty of you
You are disease
and I am a disjointed poetry;
I am the parasite
I formed around *you*
I live so that you might have
my life
to give for one of your own.

And I loathe this creation of mine
even as I take the credit
I am as proud as any mother
who sculpts a fine bullet
nourishes it, and finally
marvels at its perfection
as it enters her eye

Yes, and you are blooming
in my brain even now
as I sip the sick stalk
and picture you tasting my death
one finger at a time
But to die at 25
is a life in exile from
a place that does not exist
And if my body is a string of words
I make up as I go,
then let my life sentence sing
sometimes in sign language
a snapping ballet
for two strong hands,
and sometimes in tears,
that plague of drowning in the
tiny bedroom that now
is mother's den,
I cry at dinner to bleed out
Phil Vincent
my homemade affliction
my family member
and I write to ink you
out, damn spot
when you scream for nursery rhymes
that I must write
because there is no better metaphor
for a headful of poetry
than a tumor
in the brain.

Other Needles

Hamilton Fish short-circuited
the electric chair
with needles hidden in his skin
And you pierce your body to much
the same end, that delay,
that cheating thumb tugging
at a wet noose
fighting off the sleep horns

you feel beginning to sprout;
you would breathe through that extra hole
if you could
But I just fiddle with the hoops there
and listen to the tiny bell music
they make as you
grab me up in tight handfuls,
my soup stomach and blunt eye.
both dimpled and winking,
the me of make-pretend
that raises her breezy ass
when I'm not looking

I don't know how to explain
my own silver dangles except
that I hung them from my ears
to look pretty. That's all.
I didn't do it to fight anything
but I understand that if
you can punch a hole through something
even a piece of skin,
you've got yourself a hiding place
and not even I am brave enough
to explore that tunnel,
you are the Trojan Boy
and I'm afraid of who I'll find
when you open up.

Hopefully Not In Memory Of D.

He is biting
the hair off his arms.
I have seen it.
There is a cracking
That accompanies the snap of each follicle
the finality
of his teeth meeting
around that bastard blade
and the filth
it carries.

He is chewing his cheeks
and hanging his hair on

the lampshade
He is living in his head,
that terrible dogsuit,
he is plucking out his
eyeteeth and
injecting them into this palms,
stringing them together with yarn.
I have seen it.
I have seen her
rush to re-place a fallen
comb because if he suspected
someone had held it
he would never touch it again.

It is always at least
100 degrees in the apartment,
no windows and one locked door,
the whole life
is suffocating in stacks of
RC Cola bottles
and hat boxes,
in a bathroom sink that
requires a chisel,
in a man who is never clean
enough, and a woman
who would sell her collarbone
if it would help.

I know she
can only weep with
my eyes
and I have counseled her
to leave:
this man and the world
are mutually toxic
to each other,
I have no morbid fascination
with this man,
I want him gone
but there is not enough room
in her brain for the thought
of her life without him.

As if, with her presence
she could set
the broken bones in his mind
As if she could
bleed out the
10 little Satans
he finds hiding
in his fingernails
But he cannot be cured,
Dona, by you,
for all your love
and soft naked stretches
he is still a walking Holocaust
and if you are fishing
for an epitaph,
"I Loved Him"
is a poor excuse for one.

Hamlet Mouth

The web he spins
as white as aspirin
halfway down a throat that cannot decide
a strand of a skinny Hamlet mouth
spinning, teasing me,
he says:
Step into my pallor,
said the spider to the flighty one,
Step into the pale.

The A-B-C of him,
that language,
that fiery dictionary,
he is 21/25ths of me
and growing
now he is with me and silent
now he is gone.
He is still silent.
But he hums my torch song
When I am the siren singing
But he hums
his lips like the red menace
in that tight line

to hide a boyish grin that
could not have seen more violence
if each tooth was a fist.
He was *born* at the end of a rope
and he is still clinging
to that history of suicides;
The deaths he swallowed
and never spit out
now nothing escapes his mouth
myself included
he holds his breath, smirks,
says nothing.

I would not stand for it
if I could stand at all,
But I am falling
asleep with my hand over his heart
so any blade that finds him
will crucify me
to his rib.
And like his rib, he
stretches long and clean,
without one single secret,
all bones and no skeleton;
he was never aware
of how time passes for me
how I needed my legs held
like knitting needles,
stretching leggy yarn
Now I am a sweater
around his neck,
And when I wake up,
6 o'clock smells like fire,
a brilliant grey morning
slow-cooked by summer
and him,
with his throatfull of burden,
his swollen teeth, resting
his head on my lap,
my forgiving thighs,
his mouth in that "O";
and I looked inside
for his hiding places
I found only a miniature cocoon
and a caterpillar that was not sleepy yet.

A Season In Health

Don't call me brave
pin that on them
with less to lose.
I am not sharp or
bright enough to
illuminate it;
I break the way
I always break –
in a diagnosis that
puts a pistol in my mouth
or a green light
not long enough
for me to cross,
I break in the field
that is my breast, my
wide and white breast
that holds none
of its indigenous milk
There will be no child
for me to cripple genetically.
My life is a lesson
of losses –
I learn one at a time.
I break
until there are no
parts of me I recognize, until
I am the stranger
I shouldn't talk to
but who says
Nevertheless, Live
who says to Patrik
who put a piston in his mouth
held it in the rub
of his fingers
Patrik, Live
because the murderer
of my friend
is my enemy;
I break for him
and for me,
even if I'm not

the filth-eater
I see in my mouth
I've swallowed my share
of shit;
even if I'm not
the cripple walking
with a poem crutch
whole afternoons have
limped past while I
have yet to set foot
on my avenue.

And Jerry Lewis says
with a diagnosis of
neuromuscular disease
you might as well
put a pistol in your mouth
I break
under what I have seen –
the inside of that machine
the doctors use
to observe me
and my own hands
screaming black and
bruised rage at
the injections I allowed,
even if you know
firsthand the tragedy
I have bled dry
I haven't forgiven you
your two good legs
when I dream at night
I am flying
I dream I'm an angel
with feet too small
for earthly shoes
then wake to find only
my pistol kiss
And I break
Nevertheless, I live
in those mornings
waking in the arms
of the only one
whose arms are allowed;

I wish my cricket knees
up and around
the hips, the waist,
the double clutch of what
sometimes is the proudest
expression of love
and sometimes is just
the best sticky aspirin
for what ails me;
I break and he
holds my pieces together
without ever knowing me
whole: he has never
seen me dance or
use a knife and fork
he doesn't know the glory
of me on top
and grinding
or me before I learned
that grief and love are
not enough but will
have to do
because I will never
put a pistol
in my mouth.

Ashkenazi Venus

Absent as amputation
this is how
love affairs end.
but we wind down
into close friends,
a casual intimacy and
five nights a week
alone.

Somehow, my love
my pointless shepherd,
you will learn
to steer thyself
and I
will practice
emotional mathematics
to see how to add
me up
to see what I equal
and who equals me.

Tough as a thug
love dies like a pig
snorting blood and dirt
frothing with terror and foam,
a fat Russian pig
who reacts and reacts
stretches and snaps back
making scenes
about as private
as a bread line.

But this is subtle also,
no sharp lip
points kisses toward
me mouthwise, only cheek
that significant inch
too far left
or right;
And I've never
been one for subtlety –
vulgar silence offends me

I would just as soon
vanish under his chin
and ride that apple up
and down
on that accent
the words that he speaks
marchingly
but that halt
at the tiny guillotines
in my mouth;
And what's left
for me to chew
is the meat and potatos
of a broken heart
a real
sticks-to-the-ribs
main course
and I would pull up
to the table
if I had the arms,
your Venus,
if I had the arms.

q.r. hand, jr. b.1937

q.r.'s been in the west coast poetry scene since the Spaghetti Factory. He started the Babar poetry readings. qr can handle about five or six different vocabularies lyrically in a poem, like a Harlem James Joyce. q.r. performs some pieces with other poets and musicians behind them. q.r.'s voice is beautiful and full of cadence and melody. Four Takes appeared previously in *The Black Scholar,* October 1985. He has several poetry chapbooks out, including: *I Speak To The Poet In Man,* Jukebox Press, 1985. He works as a San Francisco community mental health worker.

four takes from a short and personal history of summer

that summer

i drank bottles of moon glow
took the sub way express to love in brooklyn
from harlem streets i loved so much

took the A train there and back
every evening when i knew she'd be there

one time we sizzled in to coney island
rode the cyclone twice
frenetic guts atwist

sweet dizzy awry and
hold on tight all night long

i hoped

looked under the board walk
and decided not to

spent a langorous train ride back
wishing we had

swollen lipped
hands slowly under clothes
hornier than bunnies at a gang bang

right up to her front door
and parents

i rode the sub way back to harlem alone
steaming sweetly

dreamily gave my self to the new morning sun
crotch still wet pants stained

couldn't wait to go back.

on a sweet summer day

love first came to me like this
hot shivers and wet chocolate

I chased her and caught her
chased her caught I now part chase

panting sweating swearing
we were wet with each others'
holding quick silver in the sun
as long as we could make for ever last

music played us through that night's supple magic

turned on dawn that day I swear we did
just like in black orpheus

still slippin an slidin
hands full of the penultimate spasms
we were determined to slop our selves in
to sleep
with

sun struck

this was

we walked home to harlem
in magic island of manhattan summer morning sun
after a night of parties

carousing in west village bars

dancing with dancers
looking with painters
talking shit with writers

trying to talk a hole in the head
like we used to say
of one lovely new woman after another
lotta sweet talk lotta sweet music

we would walk up seventh avenue
stop for coffee at a fifty seventh street all nighter
frequented by musicians
then walk to the central park zoo
to wonder on the sea lions splashing

wet and swivel slither
black and silver curving
smooth sun shatter undulations

at the carousel we stopped
laughed back at the antic freeze painted on the horses

in the hush
began the murmur of traffic
on central park west

we wished for a month of sun day mornings
just like this one

smoked the last hit of panama red and
got ready for the long haul up town

the land of easy living all around us

it was

during the summer
big city blood began to boil in me

steaming hot new york city nights
new gleam of sound and color
each street be bop and calypso

moon light boat rides on the hudson
wet canyon between palisades and sky scrapers
buddy walker and his band played all night long

we partied
this was our land we thought

went to the paladium and mamboed our asses off
played conga drums in central park
facing the plaza hotel just before the sun rising

til' the cops chased us out
and we followed our ways home

how sweet it is

the revolution tried to bludgeon me   with commitment
told me to be free   with each crack on the head

the revolution had no medical plan   for my aching skull
and the man's doctors prescribed 9 to 5 and
lots of greenbacks for my headache

the revolution told my old lady to be free
didn't tell her how to relate to me   nor me to her
except give up some head once in a while   for liberation

the revolution shot me and my friends up with media
hand in hand with the networks' contingency plans and
left me here with a spoonful of words

the revolution calls a squall   a typhoon
                a shopkeeper   a tycoon
                a poem   an anthem
turns rhythm into syncopation   and creation into proletarian news
trains cadets to sing the blues   in make believe ballroom time
and   gives the marshalls degrees in critical arts   and science

the revolution missed the people   in its zeal
poured caffeine into the finest crystal
made a killing in blue jeans
dungareed the social register in dingy splendor
charging their public accounts with the masses' ragged debts
and passed judgement in lynch mob terms
from university chairs reserved for the asses of the classes

the revolution turned the myth of the man into everyday truth
taking us out of we
made each difference a deep fault we fell into
with only the weak fibre of me   to pull ourselves up with
gave starry equations in splendid incantation
planting a collective maypole in the ruts of spring
polling universal need with the central committee's questionnaire

the revolution washed the brain out of my head   in the name of
our liberty
the revolution bought bentleys and cocaine
and private sets in the california hills
jamming all night with freedom now and the 6 coquettes
caviar on their nipples   gyrating on peppermint sticks
coming to tell the truth to the city   when tomorrow gets here
if they come to get us in the morning

the revolution sent strollers on a long march   without a map
mixed black and brown into a 3rd concoction anyone can handle
and not have to ask is this the real thing
and liberated space from everybody's closet
said come on out   the mace is fine
from poolside havens sipping black russians
with a publisher or two fawning and feignting   a jab of reverence
at each toast

the revolution stashed panama reds and acapulco golds
backyard greens in a natural crock   and
sent the brave into the jungle and the catacombs
to establish the territoriality of identity in the libraries of the cosmos
while workers jammed pension funds with rich pollution
and ate steaks sprinkled with ethnic jokes

the revolution made a hole in me
trying to make a whole of us
that only we can fill

the revolution is you and me listening to each other
filling holes with our guts and making wholes with our love

the revolution is that steamshovel lyricism
we are running back home to get
now that we've been had and been a hullabaloo
and everything else we thought we were missing

the revolution is our bloody love song
on nobody's hit parade but our own

CAPRICORN

in the basement of our old house in brooklyn
in the basement past the coal dust
in the basement past the old furnace
our father had converted to oil after or was it
during the second world war
past the furnace that one day
exploded
leaving a hole the size of a cannon ball
in the asbestos and piss poor plaster job
filling the whole house with smoke and
harsh sweet burnt oil fumes

the furnace the fire department decided wasn't
a fire hazard in spite of the hole in it

in the basement past the pile of
stakes and puptents
canvas and canteens

bandoleers and gas masks
mustard gas covering and helmets
knapsacks messkits insignia
theater of war ribbons
musty khaki mess mostly

past the pile of junk
where we used to create
each and every battle of
the second world war
right off the radio
hot out of the n y times

the pile of junk that our uncle
sent to us from hawaii
where he had gone
after the fbi explained to him the advantages
of officers candidate school over leavenworth

waheenies and administration beat forced labor any day he thought
he sent us pictures of flower bedecked sweethearts to prove it
him smiling like clark gable
gold bars gleaming
holstered .45 popping in our heads

past the pile of mush and pulp
my first collection of baseball record books
our mother had hid there
to keep my head in the right textbooks
that pile of mush made by a broken drain pipe
that flooded the whole cellar and put out the furnace

past that pile
stood an old wooden door planked like a cargo hatch
opening to a wine cellar
built when the neighborhood was white and respectable
the old wooden door creaked like inner sanctum mystery
room empty but for dust and dirt
and old steamer trunk
symptom of lying splendor
rusting in place

in the basement past this pile
past that pile of interesting irrelevance

in the wine cellar unlike our grandma's filled
with shiny new garbage cans of sugar and
shelves of canned delicacies
hoarded to beat the rationing
it was empty but for dust
the trunk and the echoing creaky door

past this emptiness
through the well constructed
stone by stone mortared wall
past the dust and dirt was
a beach i knew well
white sand triumphed by red sand bluffs
pink wild roses
blackberries blueberries and wild raspberries
we used to pick for grandma to make pies with

white sand leading you to a rushing into the bay creek
our parents and friends used to crab and eel in
before they settled down to their mysterious all
night nude drunken brash beach parties
we could never attend until
we were old enough

white sand getting wetter and wetter
softer and softer until you
could hear yourself crunching
and crackling fiddler crab holes
looking at your great size
even at eleven years old

emerald beach flies buzzed and bit
you slapping them away continuously
and it was no great trouble   fun in fact
you looking towards an interminable stretch of
tidelands march green that stretched you knew
all the way to the easthampton golf club
where stuart tripped into the mud one sweaty afternoon
collecting cattails to dry and burn
to keep away the mosquitoes or so we told ourselves
any excuse for an adventure

crossing the rushing into the bay creek
played into more white sand

only here in the basement
only here in the wine cellar
only here past the well constructed
stone by stone mortared wall
where there used to be a vast
to the eye and ear tidelands marsh
was an endless desert
that led me on and on

strangely trudging inexhaustible
both of us   me and the desert
the sun always bright scorching
daring my searching eyes
only horizon to see

white sand level as the base of a triangle
stretching in lazy intent
and it really didn't matter
i walked it   lord how i walked it
inexhaustible searching eyes
sun in searing yellow orange red white
always in the same spot

i walked it   lord i walked it
alone trudging gazing searching
listening to the silence of my feet on the sand
blistering bearable footage of quiet intent
and it really didn't matter that i
didn't know where i was or where i was going
because i was there and i was doing it
no questions asked

the sun looked at me and i looked at it
there was no room for agreement or disagreement
i was doing it no questions asked

the sand white hot sun sodden and silent
was doing it no questions asked

and that's what it was
no mirages   no temptations
just doing it drily   endlessly
for a long time in a day that lasted a lifetime
a millennium an epoch

doing it on the desert
in the sun that always burst
from the same spot in the sky
about the size of an onrushing
just about to collide planet

on the white sands
that told you nothing forever

until it occurred to me

it was uncanny

i didnt have to repeat it   in my head
nothing changed except my direction

i had not chosen it
nor had i not chosen it
it was not chosen

it was a change of direction
on this eerie desert
i watched myself come back from

the same way i had gone
no questions asked
the sun in the eyes of me looking at me
coming back to where i didn't know

i was looking at me doing it
only horizon to see
sun always bright scorching
daring my searching eyes

no mirage   no temptation
endless stretching white silent sands
level gritty perfect plane
inexhaustible   both of us

no room for emptiness or fullness
i was doing it endlessly
leading me on an on
looking at myself
strangely trudging

... and the creek whispered
and the creek whispered
and the creek whispered
i was doing it   crossing it
inexhaustible and quietly
glad i was doing it

swift bayward tug
at my knees calves ankles toes
and white sand of a beach i knew well

past the creaky door echoing
the statistical mush
the slumped puptent
the furnace with a hole in the side

past war games and coal dust
up creaky wooden always threatening to betray you
cellar stairs into the bright baby blue hallway
leading to the wrought iron gate i walked through

into the streets of brooklyn
to play another game of you
show me yours and i'll show you mine

inexhaustible

Joie Cook b.1951

Oh God, what can you say about Joie. *"It's a Joie."* Joie is like a moving freight train going through about sixteen skyscrapers without noticing. She's reads loud and frantically. Joie came on the scene all the way back to the Spaghetti Factory. When she first turned up – in performance there was nothing holding her up but skin, bones and rage. When the Spaghetti Factory (and their poetry readings) were closing, at the last reading she leaned out her arms to all of us (poets) and said, *"You are my family"*. Following that Joie mc'd many readings at bars, coffee houses and cafes. Joie is a performance poet par excellence. Joie admires Bukowski; she's a city poet. She's a *living legend* in the San Francisco poetry scene and draws and commands crowds wherever she reads. Biographical notes in *My Body Is A War Toy:* Since the age of three, Joie Cook has spent most of her life. She has held several positions as a college student, cocktail waitress, blues singer, rock musician, wife (several times) and mother (once). Joie has several chapbooks and books out including: *Cash For Color TV's,* Gorton Press, 1984; *My Body Is A War Toy,* Zeitgeist, 1990; *Acts Of Submission,* Manic D Press, 1990; *Lust For Life,* Mel Thompson Publishing, 1993; her work has appeared in *Bullhorn, Poetry: San Francisco, Poetry Quarterly* and other publications.

The Poet's Extinction

there's always a crowd to destroy yourself in
george told me: "they want you like that"
THEY WANT YOU LIKE THAT:

worn, drunk, depreciated,
mumbling to concrete
in search of a bottle
or one last hand out;

they want you like that!
breathing fire into someone else's lust
but always alone
put on remote control
by other peoples saviors

they want you like that!
bent over, vomiting into gutter winds,
loathing the person you've become

they want you like that!
hurting in napa with a tube up your ass,
jaundiced eyes and green teeth

they want you like that!

burned out at thirty, buried at forty,
crying tears that no one sees
until the pallbearers
put the final dust
in the dampness:

cold/flesh/ZERO.

Now That Marriage Is Back In

now that marriage is back in   i am on my way out
a product of too many martinis and trips to reno
where wed rhymes with dead
before pimps turned minister pimps inject words
of couple addiction:
i will   i do   i promise
the last time i thought of a bonding monogamous
wedding pact, i was stopped by a .44 smith and wesson
one last bullet in the chamber
before i blew my brains out i remembered
that marriage is back in
and thumbed through brides magazine
in search of the perfect garter belt
to wear on my fifth or was it?   sixth?   honeymoon.
once i was married in a presbyterian church
we were both tripping on mescaline
and my father was dying
something about church weddings
i got pregnant at the reception
shot speed for three months straight
i have a very mellow child
another time i was married on stage at the
crowded cafe babar to a boy who resembled the
bride of frankenstein ...
i believe i got *him* pregnant that night,
nonetheless, there is no longer a warrant out for
my arrest as a child molester!

but now that marriage is back in
i am not invited to any of these new age do it yourself
ceremonies, i only hear about them, discreetly
and watch my teenage daughter
decorate her face with dark cosmetics
becoming a toxic perfume of the night

like all those dead husbands
she is leaving too
she has been weaned
she will survive
hopefully without the lace & gold bands

a predictable addiction
she has seen me kick
in my rage
many times
insane or not
a product of too many.

That Day At Laguna Honda   – *for Robert*

all those times we came home late,
wallowing in sweat poured linings
of shoplifted daydreams ...
now you, on the rooftop of Laguna Honda –
a facility controlled by the state
to put aside the few with terminal everything,
a home for incurables!

i saw, see, seesaw entire weightlessness
in the dining room sitting
by a 93 year old man with the gold wedding band
embracing his weathered shaking hand.
J.W. was there too,
wearing a jesus-on-the-hudson cross
and you both ordered heroin for dessert.

i must say, the scar is looking better, honey,
THE EXTERNAL ONE.
here, top of the hill, nut house,
alzheimer's land, occupational therapy,
wheelchair ramma lamma ding dong!!
reciting kaufman, corso,
how they crashed at your places
and how messy the fuckers really are.

i climb the wall on the roof
no cause for panic, I Won't Jump,
i'm afraid of heights.
it's just that i appreciate GOOD VIEWS!
good views perched above this nesting place,
fare removed from otherness,
the other that brought you here,
rain-coated, bleeding in a white orange orange ambulance.

i'm observing, that's all.
they actually let me LEAVE this place,
even though i really want to stay!
but their theory is that i am not qualified to stay because
i can distinguish a nurse from a bedpan.

here, on the roof, Laguna Honda,
once a military installation,
i volunteer to entertain you
entertain you in this fortress
of sick poor poets painters
prophets
                    whose landscapes never change
                    until release papers are signed
                    by doctors who maybe care
                    while the planet outside these thick walls
                    turns counterclockwise
                    beneath firmly tucked blankets

exhaling love's last breath.

Explanation No. 937

maybe we didn't try everything.
our temperatures were always too high to be
          serious travelers.
you were always hard to reach on the telephone.
I was always hard to reach in person.
     roll the video tape.
     someone's got answers.
we polished off a bottle of codeine cough syrup
one night after the liquid morphine ran out.
     i knew, then, we were,
     only then, friends.
your demons were easy to approach.
mine surfaced after entertaining too many
          unwanted visitors.
i always hated that saying "familiarity breeds
contempt"
          until we got too close.

you lost your style.
i lost my appetite.
we moved away from each other.
   i'm drunk with laughter now,
   reviewing the past.
there is always a terrible chord
at the end of each unwritten symphony.
         we didn't fit in.
         never would, could.
you died.
i stopped shooting heroin.
the world was good to us for awhile.

Everybody's Darling   (a true story)

she was a simple girl.
washed the dishes every night.
took out the garbage.
never shoplifted.

the easy-going type.
never bit her nails
or wrote a bad check.

she was voted "most popular" in her high
school yearbook
"miss congeniality" in the miss georgia pageant
did summer stock in THE MUSIC MAN

kind of girl most people want next door.

she said she was happy.
never read an anne sexton poem.
only drank white wine, and only with dinner

got a job anchoring the 6:00 news in a small
florida town
married a trial attorney
had 2 well-formed children, a dog, cat.

one night she announced on her news broadcast
that a special bulletin had just come in
held a revolver to her head

and blew off half her skull.
some people said she did it for attention.
others claimed she needed the ratings.

I used to know tons of girls like her
in high school.
only problem is,
most of them are still alive.

Writing From The Spoken Word

so everyone will have a shot
at the brass ring
of late twentieth century poetics,
we open the arena
to anyone bold enough
to face rejection

we open the door of publication
to anyone who ever satisfied a publisher
or who might keep a secret

for everyone who enjoys the acceptance
of applause,
we print your poem on milk cartons,
distributed through chinatown

we hang your favorite trousers
above phone lines
at grant and green

we photograph your teeth
after an intense evening of gnashing

for everyone who enjoys the sound
of one hand clapping,
we reserve a table for you and a guest
at the poetry awards (coming soon)
and a space in the Paris Review
for your obituary

Remissions Of Grandeur

I've been injected with thought.
it takes a large dose to get me started,
a large fucking dose. blank walls usually
appear in the morning, right before noon.
this is when i get up and look out the
window, not for any other reason than to
see the same view that i saw the day
before. i'm always hoping i'll look out
one morning to fire and brimstone.
all of the predictions will come true.
i'm convinced that everyone will get
their wish. jean dixon and jesus, too.

i want to sleep for days.
unplug the phone.
kill the cat.
it sounds easy enough.
i also want a twenty-four hour nurse
on call in the next room
who is silent and feeds me
from a bedtray.
after the days of sleep and nourishment,
i want to rob the bank of amerika
SLA style and never get caught.

when i no longer thirst for the frivolities of youth,
when i no longer walk with a brisk air
about me,
when sexual contact entails numerous
electrical devices,
i will go to my window.

the view will be the same as before.
except for the flames
covering everything.

850 Bryant

the best poetry
i heard this year
was in cell number F3
850 bryant
sixth floor
yeah, i'd say
they've found their voices
all seven of my cellmates
hollering, bartering,
for cigarettes, slim jims,
milky ways
with the television off at 10:00
nothing left to do
but tell stories
trade secrets
compare tattoos
jerk off
rival one another for the title:
"BADDEST BITCH ON THE PLANET"

those voices never stopped
until the jangle of the guard's keys
toned the cellblock down
to a hush
a sacred laugh between us:
the jailed ones
whose medication had run out
batteries juiced on legends
food served up like dog shit
through an iron grid
13 hours in the holding tank
16 hours in the cell
collect calls to everyone
straight to hell you'll go they said
just one more felony
don't plea bargain with the devil
unless you can stand the sound of seizures
two bunkers down
or brave
the jaundiced sun.

My Body Is A War Toy

I used to play combat with my brothers
rolling down greasy slopes of eastern america
harnessing imaginary weapons
dreaming plastic rifles could somehow transform
into guns with true bullets,
hard, thick.

but instead we settled for water pistols
to hose the enemy down,
ramming rival gangs to submit to us,
once and for all.

then came the winter
when the dog ate the rabbits,
still moist from birth;
the family cat lay frozen on steps to my father's
music studio.

time had come to carve out my name
on a maple tree
with a soldier's son
who wore a black cape
and painted over gargoyles and monuments with tar.
one day after school we were fixing amongst the
spring change of leaves.

he told me my body was a weapon.

we dropped out of school and put down our squirt guns
for more practical cylinders and pistons;
shooting off venom, we played,
in humidity of summers anxious sound:
together our bodies were war toys.

the cars we drove had fins in front
and back seats like couches in lingerie shops;
my brothers would tease us about diseases we got,
cured by men in white uniforms who said we are accidents,
all of us, accidents,
begging for lessons on anything.

the boy i quit school with died of AIDS last month.
i'm sure that our names are still carved on that tree.
and they're still selling capguns down at the toy store.
and all your lethal weapons must be registered with the state.
and there is a list of all your ex-lovers and their
ex-lovers posted in the lobby of harrah's in reno.

and we've all frozen still on the way to the battlefield,
symphony or morgue.

Jack Micheline   b.1929

Performance has always been a key part of Micheline's poetry. He's a sophisticated poet who has chosen a direct appeal to the affections of average people. Born in the Bronx Jack Micheline began writing poetry and participated in the poetry renaissance in Greenwich Village in the '50s. He's been widely anthologized, often in the company of Beat poets. Jack has 14 books of poetry and prose. His poems often represent people from downtrodden segments of society who might otherwise go unnoticed: prostitutes, alcoholics, immigrants; his appeal reflects his genuine love and appreciation for the beauty of these individuals. When Jack Micheline performs and he's got all his lights on, belly button into the wind, roaring, he's like a big ship under full sail. Jack received the award for the Most Valuable Performance at the Kerouac Conference in Boulder, 1982.

Hiding Places

There are hiding places in my room
where beautiful poems are hidden
Poems hidden away in boxes
on sheets of brown paper
Poems of spirit and magic
workers hands hidden in boxes
beautiful thighs
there are blue skies hidden in my room
dolphins and seagulls .
the heaving of breasts and oceans
there are skies in my room
there are flies in my room
there are streets in my room
there are a thousand nights hidden in boxes
there are drunks in my poems

there are a million stars on the roof of my room
all hidden away in boxes
there are steps down side streets
there is a crazed eye of a poet in my room
there is the sunlit morning
there are dancers dancing in my room
there are old Arabs exploring the desert near Escalon
there are sparrows and bluebirds and wildcats in my room
there are elephants and tigers
there are skinny Italian girls in my room
there are letters from Peru and England
and Germany and Russia in my room
There are the steps of Odessa in my room
the Volga river in my room
there are dreams in the night of my room
there are flowers
there is the dance of affirmation in my room
the steps of young poets carrying knapsacks full of poems
there are the Pictures of an Exhibition in my room
Moussorgsky and Shostakovitch and Charlie Mingus in my room
Composers and painters all singing in my room
all hidden away in boxes
one night when the moon is full
they will come out and do a dance.

Grant & Green

Keep your head high chappie
it's a cold night out there
there's Tommy the hook
his magician's hat and conjurer's trade

For lonely sailors
guys with dreams
long lost loves and adding machines

Keep the whiskey flowing
Keep the juice alive
keep your head high chappie
it's a cold night out there
Love is gone out the window
Let's go to fantasyland

Willy is there
Tony is there
Gino with his sad eyes and expressive hands

The juke box is playing
the endless booze
all the girls look beautiful
liquid is flowing like a waterfall
the Indian girl Joie keeps walking through the door
the old guy on the bar stool
he's been there since '64

A round for everybody
the poor bloke says
he wants to go home
and paint on his wall
he's gone crazy on the endless street
where people too sensitive and lovers meet

The crazy Russian Jew Jack
with them wild crazy tales
of redheaded chicks
and girls in the slam
and vagabonds and Chicanos
tough guys and the blonds

Keep it flowing chappie
on a merry-go-round
see that guy on the street
he took out his cock
and let flow a log leak
right on my floor
I'll kill that bastard someday
he's not coming in here no more

Your looking for a buddy
You know he's in the bar
He's got the same seat for years since 1964
So keep your head high buddy
there'll always be a war
and all the girls are beautiful
and the liquid flows like a waterfall

There's Specs with the old jokes
postcards from the working class

his museum on the wall
Bobby Miller jokes were classic in 1954
Bob Kaufman humming symphonies
Big Jim still dreaming looking for the girls
Foxy's laughing like a maniac
Gini he hit Keno $554
Bustop Whitey cleaned out Ruggles
right on Carlo's floor

Sam and John and Sally
Barbara, Alice, Blue
Big Jim, Gene and Jerry
Big Black, Red and Blue

The stage is always open
on the corner of Grant and Green
the hook standing there smiling
his big hat in his hand
keep your head high chappie
there'll always be a war

It's open house day and night
on the corner of Grant and Green
Willy is there
Tony is there
Gino the conductor
the Indian girl Joie she's walking through the door
and the tall guy on the bar stool
he's been there since '64

The liquid keeps flowing
just like a waterfall
it's a cruel world Buddy
it's an adding machine
it's a carousel
it's a merry-go-round
it's an open house in the afternoon
On the corner of Grant and Green

There's Russian Jack the madman
he's laughing on his flying machine
put the magicians on the airplane
put the conjurers against the wall
put the politicians in the madhouse
and the poets on the floor

And the Indian girl Joie
Keeps walking in the door
and that guy's still walking the street
for twenty years or more
and the tall guy on the bar stool
he's been here since '64

It's a cruel world Buddy
it's an adding machine
everything flows so easy
on the corner of Grant and Green
Foxy's laughing like a maniac

Russian Jack on his flying machine
put the magicians on an airplane
put the conjurers against the wall
put the politicians in a mad house
and the poets on the floor

Keep your head high chappie
there's a cold night out there
there's that guy on the bar stool
he's been here since '64
three feet from reality
three feet from the door
Keep your head high chappie
your just three feet from the door.

Zero Is Nothing

31 Fish in the pond
30 gold
and one white
in the Oaklawn Sanitarium
in Hollywood
the original mind
keeps score
and fresh air
Executive 100
Power 100
except for blackouts
Bullshit 75
Alcohol even money

Cosmetics and toys 88
Ass kissing 80
Poverty zero
Sensitivity zero
Lorca not listed
Hemingway 47
Mailer 32
Bukowski 27
Norse 12
Martin 3 1/2
Blacks even money
Poor whites 5
Poetry 11
Dollar bill 100
Lawyers 96
Waitresses Even Money
Swindlers 91
John martin 90
Rat Packs and Cliques 82 1/2
Beggar 2 1/8
A.T.&T. 183 4/5
Freaks 4 1/2
Horses 74
Flowers 91
Finks 87
Genius 1000 - 1
American Zero
Russian Zero
China Zero
graveyards 88
Thieves 71
Mutation 1 1/2
Sunshine 7
Pussy 69
Dreams 0
31 fish in a pond
30 gold
and one white
in the Oaklawn Sanitarium
in Hollywood
The original mind
keeps score
and fresh air

Bana Witt   b.1954

Bana came on the scene mid Babar. Bana is a performance poet and has performed in cafes and nightclubs in New York, Los Angeles and San Francisco Bay Area. Her voice is *Modern,* almost *Chrome.* Bana was born in Fresno, California, She moved to San Francisco in 1974, where she made a few short pornographic films for the Mitchell Brothers and later was one of the first fifty employees at Apple Computer. She began singing and writing rock music in 1983. Her last band, *The Kage,* was a collaborative effort with the guitarist from *The Dead Kennedys.* Bana has several books: *Compass In An Armored Car,* Zeitgeist, 1988; *Mobius Stripper,* (autobiographical short stories) Manic D Press, 1993; *Eclipse Of Reason,* Roadkill Press, 1994.

I Cannot Find You Annie In San Francisco

I hear your bird calls in the fog
and Annie I become you
I made bird calls in Antioch on New Year's
they did not get answered

> Now you're hot on the street
> treading the edge like it was the sidewalk
> and I cry for you Annie
> on the cracked pavement
> watching you hitchhike alone in the eucalyptus berries
> bundling your coat against the cold
> wearing transparent dresses
> and moving too fast for anyone

I've lost you Annie in the artichokes
your first instinct
always to run
it was right

> The people who clung to you like pilot fish
> they followed you Annie
> the compass in an armored car
> but I
> I kept losing you

Annie your morning cough comes through to me
in the bushes I hear your sobs
they keep telling me
you've just been here
the wet madrone saw you go
and I keep kissing you after an accident

Annie in my dreams I find you
the blatant maniac
too beautiful to cause offense
with that look you're always handing out
don't show it to me Annie
your screams are coming from my mouth now

Wake Me Up

Last night I dreamt too hard
        it took me hours to wake up

My mother
        dead now for eight years
wanted to take me to Africa
        she gave me just four hours to prepare
        I was working in the rice fields
someone from Rolling Stone
        was trying to find me

                You weren't supposed to walk
                across the young rice
                but I had to get to a phone
                I had to pack for Africa

                        But what do they wear in Mauritania?

The mud sucked at my ankles
        I got to a phone at a nearby store
        I was counting
        the cost of calling Rolling Stone

        And a woman stole my wallet

The field boss was yelling at me
        my mother was waiting at the airport
        and I couldn't find anything sleeveless to pack

                The man from Rolling Stone
                finally called again
                I dropped my suitcase
                and grabbed the phone

        He said he wanted to sleep with me
        I started crying
        I thought he wanted to make me a star

Thorazine And Sunglasses

In the seventies I learned
    urban survival
        when I loved twisted drag queens and linear drugs
            before the realities of cellulite and AIDS
                when insanity was chic
    Well before
        the ugliness of crazy and old
            pressed its mangled face
            against the window of my car at stop signs

    I leaned how to tell when its time
        to strip away the fat
            and get a naked toehold on the ledge

        When the time is ripe
            for Thorazine and sunglasses

It's about understanding
    spectral physics
        and the cellular dynamics of
            pointless rage

    When the noises inside
        are louder than the noises outside

    When the squeak of the crepe souled nurse
    moving briskly across the polished linoleum floor
            feels louder than her voice
            or the chattering of your teeth

    And the faster you rub your hand
        on the cool steel guardrail of the bed
            the slower your thoughts become

This is the time for chemical Bandaids
    and optical pacifiers
    and a resolution to stay
        away from open windows
    and the single edged utility blades
        in the red toolbox under the sink

Thorazine and sunglasses:
    one filters the acerbic sounds
        of teeth and a civilization in decay
    and one filters the ambient light

And one does what one can
    to avoid autopsies and taxes
        and one can only hope
            that the rest
                will take care of itself

Shrimping

We are fishing for shrimp in Alaska
I am with a man
who is the local poet and
a couple who have lived the myth

The woman is dying of cancer
she weighs just 89 pounds
but her acidic wit still
cuts through the cold
as great chunks of an iceberg float by

She tells me
she will not let the doctors poison her any longer
as her husband uncurls yards of net
out into the dark water behind the boat

She yells to him on deck
something about the engine

She says, "It's not the cigarettes, you know,"
as she pulls a long drag into her
irradiated throat
an eagle flies overhead

"It's not the cigarettes,
it's all these years of yelling at him
over the noise of the boat"

The nets bring up
gruesome bottom fish
called Irish Lords

Someone's crab pots
filled with sideways movement
an old battery
and a rubber bucket
covered on one side with
an anemone that looks like
throbbing gristle

The Canadian Rockies
silently explode to the East

I listen to the woman talk
in the cabin of the boat where it's warm
I think how elegant she looks at 89 pounds
her body like pick-up sticks
under layers of wool

My great aunt waits for me at home
on the island
at 83 she has swapped stories
with death at 30 below on the Kushaquim
and she remembers everything

She is kind to the gifted
and retarded alike

As I drive back from the docks to her house
it is snowing

It is three in the afternoon
and she will be napping

She has found a pleasure in routine
not a prison

And I realize it is not death that scares me
it is life that murders my sleep

Sacrificial Blonde

I want to be beautiful
            so you will want me
    what's inside is too complex

                I want to be helpless
                            so you will help me
                I want to be doe-eyed and crippled
                            so you can feel strong

        I want the bones of my spirit
                    crushed like an accident victim
            so the men in the emotional ambulance
                    will tell me
                            everything's going to be just fine

        I want to be beautiful and mute
                so I cannot scare you
                        with the viciousness of my voice

    I want to be beautiful and sexy
                and pimp the illusion
                        that I can be caught

        I want to be a fluffy smooth
                milk-fed sacrificial blonde
                        with painted toenails and perfect teeth
                with her hungry young pussy
                        spread open on expensive sheets

    I want to be beautiful and sexy and feel nothing

                            I want my memory erased
                so I don't have
            this tremendous backlog of case histories
            that calls itself a past

    I want to stop crying

            I want the fog outside to come in
                and cover my bed at night

I want the abandoned
    articles of clothing in the bushes
    to all be mine

I want to be bury my rage and anger and loneliness
    on the beach
        like the afterbirth of love
            during an eclipse of reason

I want to be beautiful and sexy
    and feel
        absolutely
            nothing

Crow   – *for Artie Mitchell*

I will kill a crow and drink its blood for you
I will wear the hair shirt you left on the floor
like it was Cashmere

I will leave your vodka in the freezer
because part of me has become you
and part of me has died

Was I spared
or was I just uninvited

Let me try one more
of those little white pills

Melting them under the tongue
makes them work faster
though they will never work fast enough
or hard or long enough

I would eviscerate myself
on the spot where you died
but I always hated that house

I will never know
why the sand
does not hold the shape of our bodies
after we leave

I will avoid those who thought they knew you
I will not try to figure out what we had
or why you pulled the stakes just now

I have nothing that smells like you

Thank god we never made it all the way to mundanity
but I'm hoping for safety there now

I will see things that would suit you
and wear them myself

Picking up the phone will no longer be
emotional roulette

Knowing that art and anarchy are sisters
who were once joined at the hip
now they lie on different sides of town

Sisters who wanted to fuck your chaos
thinking you had real estate in paradise
when it was just a plot in the valley

Something big was brewing
and you already knew its taste

Your mouth was the only home I wanted

I watched the young ones fall for you
looking for an epiphany

I watched your chest hair turn to grey
and your head grew naked of its own accord
as wives and girlfriends came and went
time and children sweetened you

I will make turtle soup
and feed it to strangers
I will forgive everyone
who got more of you than I did

Those who bought your underwear
and cooked your food
who nursed you through your fugues

Or all the women who cared for you

I could only write you poems
and visit your arms as a foreigner

I will feel widowed for years
stuffing pain through the strainer in the sink
when wisdom tries to visit

I will ignore people with vision
they increase my desperation

I will ferret away
everything you said
in the banks of a river

I will watch the barometer
and learn the tides
hoping for omens and signs

I will learn to forgive
and I will start with you

I am the last of your hostages to come home
and I don't want to be here.

Tell Me

Tell me you'll never betray me

Tell me you'll never betray me
     by being successful
     by reproducing
     by giving up drugs
       or joining AA

Tell me you'll never betray me
     by growing old or dying

(That seems to be the general trend)

Tell me you'll never
     see my face on the pillow
       and wish it wasn't

Tell me you'll never criticize me
     or correct my grammar in bed

Tell me you'll never hold me responsible
     tell me you'll never hold back

Tell me you'll never betray me
     by wacking off
     and please
          never tell me to trust you
             just slap me instead

Never betray me with the truth

You'll never betray me
     by watching the sunset
          too intently
     by becoming mellow

By sleeping in my presence

By forgetting to cross yourself
     when you leave my bed

Don't betray me
     with fine lines and liver spots
     with painful self awareness
          and annoying insights
          into what made me this way

With a warm night in September
     with horchata and street noises
     with the dying saxophone
          in the apartment next door

By trying to open the valves
     of my autistic heart
     by hearing the sound of
          gurgling infants
             in the drainpipes in alleyways

Don't betray me by being uncool
     by being kind
     I couldn't handle all that
Don't betray me by sharing
     the warmth of your skin with the sun

Don't betray me in little ways
        or big
                in flagrante delicto
                in the Hall of Justice
                in the hell of pretense

Tell me you won't betray me
until you absolutely have to

Mel Thompson   b.1959

Mel Thompson is a superb performance poet. Melvin is the publisher of Cyborg, Blue Beetle, & Mel
Thompson imprints. Has put out many little saddle-stitched poetry chapbooks and published perfect-
bound poetry books too, enriching the scene tremendously. Publishes an annual little magazine: *City Voice*.

The Ambulance

It started out as a visit
To the doctor's office,
But now the ambulance is coming.
It is occupied by Mr. Craft and Mr. Jones.
Mr. Craft is a tall and lean man
Capable of driving seventy miles an hour
in a traffic jam.
Mr. Jones is a stalky and muscular man,
Ready for any contingency,
Up to, and including, paramilitary situations.

You should never fall to the ground screaming,
Unless you want the ambulance to come.

Because you told the doctor
Your life was over,
The ambulance is coming.
Because you can no longer be trusted
Out on the streets alone,
The ambulance is coming.
Because adding water
To a can of Tomato Soup
And eating it with a spoon
Is beyond your capacity,
The ambulance is coming.

The ambulance is coming
Because it will probably be three days
Before you are able
To select items from a menu
Without crying over your indecision.
The ambulance is coming
Because you honestly believe
You are dying
When your worst physical symptoms
Are heart palpitations and sleeplessness.
The ambulance is coming
Because you have to be under observation
When you're on the stuff
They're going to have to give you
Just to shut you up for five minutes.

Mr. Craft and Mr. Jones will be polite
So long as you cooperate,
So long as you are not violent.
No one has ever won an argument with them.
Ambulance rides are strictly on their terms.

They are in the lobby now
To take you away
Because you haven't seen your mother
In twenty four years.
They are in the lobby now
To take you away
Because you can't work at the same place
Or date the same woman
For more than two months
Without running away.
They are in the lobby now
To take you away
Because you can't stop fantasizing
That you are a secret agent
Or a rock star
Or the President of some third world country
Or the greatest philosopher that ever lived
Or some incarnation of God in the flesh.
They are in the lobby now
To take you away
Because you're getting way too old
To be making $10,000.00 a year,

To still be living alone,
To still be calling your friends from high school
Because no one new
Would tolerate you for ten minutes.

You messed up
When you climbed the high voltage power lines
And the police had to take you home.
You messed up
When you got caught stealing things
And they called your parents.
You messed up
When you almost failed out of high school
And got put on suspension.
You messed up
When you asked a woman you didn't even like
To marry you.
You messed up
When you moved to the East Coast
To live with a girl
You'd only slept with four times.
But now you've really gone and done it.
You've crossed that fine line
Into the big leagues of Weird.
And now,
After all these years,
Finally,
The ambulance is coming.

Daniel Higgs b.1964

Daniel Higgs is the closest we've got to a Babarian religious poet – writing a kind of a love poem to everything. He's a tattoo artist and a musician with a touring rock band. Daniel writes epics attempting to go past the human voice. *In The Mouth Of Union*, Cyborg Press 1990.

The Exploding Parable (excerpts from a long poem)

"This is the evening of two-fisted prayer." – Kenneth Patchen

I courted poetry
I questioned my function
I purged my function
Now I serve no function
You must be careful what you wish for
She propped her ankle stumps up on the kitchen table
As a sort of interrogative proposition
Fresh pink toes had poked through the callous stump flesh
She said there is a naked beast in the guest room
O you angels
O you proud oracular flesh
O you infinite quilt
Cast before my conscienceless eyes
There are things I wish I had never seen
Visions which contaminate every subsequent vision
Profanity oozing under the door of every idea
There are impostors in me that are bred for violence
So sick of being sick of being sick of it all

Fall upon me
PANTHER FACE
PANTHER FIST
PANTHER LOIN
VIOLET NIPPLE FLANGE
RODEO FLOWER SUCK FORCE
We've reached the wall of the container
The seams are sealed with a brittle law
Let's burst the container
Let's blow death
With wet hot logic
Let's flog the airplane
Let's blow death
TRUTH OBSCURED BY THE SYMBOLS OF TRUTH

I burn a bridge every day of my life
Not by choice
By nature
Let's blow death
•
It's all wilderness
This city hall this marketplace
This grid of boulevards
In desperation we attempt to extend our family
Hoping someday to breathe easy
It's all wilderness
It's all the vicious void
It's all crawling and stalking
It's all a random measure of an exploded reality
That I am the edge of
I'm cutting through you
I'm seeking shelter
This whole world is touched
This whole world supports a single wooden gallows
A marble library
A spring mattress
A cotton field
A hornet nest
I'm waiting for my orders
I'm waiting to face
My twin-assassin-mate
We're sucking fingers
Twitching from caffeine
•
I know when I'm being cheated
I know when I'm being transferred
My stature is noncommittal
We slop in her holiness
The topography of her tongue
The midriff of Jesus on the body of a farm girl
A feast of dove and sheep flesh
We are the intersection
We all lead home
We will outlast this absurd journey
Until it is no longer absurd
Until it is no longer a journey
Let's sleep in a pile of family
Let's reel in a fish full of answers
Shellfish and multicolored livers
Gentle bones and whistling skulls

It's all wilderness
This rented room
The garden in the backyard
The weightless cobwebs
I have not seen a human yet
That I did not recognize
Not a grain of sand
That I did not recognize
Not a reflex
Not an execution
Not an utterance
Not a wish
That I did not recognize
It's familiarity that keeps me brave enough
To walk out my front door
Realizing that you are as insecure as I am
As horrified
As silly and euphoric
As reckless with your schedule
I'm coming home to a new hopeful sisterhood
We're engineering a filthy (stainless) code
I'll step into a second hand skin
And glorify all that is flawed.
•
A long bitter winter of joy and happiness
A brick rising in the gentle oven
There's clay on our hands
Honey and locusts
Lips smeared together
Where does the vision begin and end?
The confines blur into ruthless passages
Down up and away
When does the message begin and end?
We feed our ignorant eyes
We hang ourselves from the steeples of hope
Swaying in the breeze that conceived us
Oil from the sides of our noses rubbed into leather holsters
Define your nation if you can
DEFINE YOUR NATION IF YOU CAN
When everything says I AM at once
It's all speaking at once
And I regress into the darkest auditorium in my brain
And deliver a violent selfish sermon
Of suffocating sabotage

A spreading epidemic of individuation
eyes blink open everywhere for the first time every second
Crouched naked in steel box sunk in the mud
Near the muddy road
Beyond the muddy pond
The archaic nozzle blasting water at my genitals and hers
She was crouched there too
Fully crouched
In the honest puke box
Fully operable and fully circumcised
Fully confounded
I can not afford a retreat
I can not accept your definition of religion
You must not accept my definition of religion
I went to sleep a wise father
I woke up desperate and paranoid
A member of a paranoid species
I've got a headache from wrestling with myself
My own blemished face challenges me
I feel so fungal
I met a police officer once
He had been shot in the head 8 times
•
I got religion
I got a bag of bones
I got a rainshower
The elation of a primary awkwardness
When joints won't lock
Double fisted triumph in a dilapidated arena
Captive gases escape and burn off
At the point where the spirit breaks
And that sure is a pretty universe
I have many siblings
There are mushrooms growing on a bible in the basement
yesterday I was foolish
Today I am a fool
Tomorrow I will fly
It's a mundane resurrection
A predictable healing glory
A gash in our memory that issues a rich fluid
To preserve and nourish the memory

Unnatural son of the natural
Trampling on moral ground

Tuning into holy ghost transmission
Carved lenses charred ribs paper buckets plastic knives
Portrait of a violated campsite
All the mottos and slogans end to end
It has always been the last days
It is always the final hour
This instant is the end of life as we know it
In the Endtime we uncover any urgency to support any passion
We round up the flood
And wind up in a radio chamber as big as the sun
Each crystal instant of fear
Arranged in an honest biography

Natural son of the unnatural
Subnatural son of the supernatural
The idiot rope in the idiot well full of cold idiot water
Idiot shoes on the idiot road in the idiot procession
Idiot pangs for the familiar idiot town
Gone and done
The very last dodo breast mashed between molars
Absolutely extinct
It happens like that sometimes
Perhaps our own children will simply vanish in the action
In the burgeoning history
In the ripple and the thud
In the dumb blessed oblivion
In the tireless merciless gristmill
In a holiday weekend
I'm not sure if I am ever sincere
I don't know what I mean
I don't know why I want what I want
I'm not sure if I'm telling the truth
Son of the daughter
Progressively splitting every seam
Done and gone
I want to shut up

I'm waggling my wings in mourning
The hand has perished but its grip remains
Every human song sung in memoriam
Take your knife to the christening
Take your wrench to the wedding
Take your feather to the funeral
Absolute musical absolution
Shaking the hand of every manifestation

Nuzzling and groping and stroking
With complete martyr conviction
Every motion so deliberate
Sweeping past ruins and cliff faces
heaps of flattened automobiles
Herds of cannibalized railroad cars
The algae thick as a blanket
The clay as orange as a barricade
Fingers swathed with ivory fat
There's a cemetery in my mouth
I am ligamented and jointed
I am collapsing toward you
I have delivered my skeleton to you
I devoured my ideals to survive
They drew the shortest straw

•

I woke up this morning
Everything had been scoured beyond recognition
Everything held back its dead hair to spit forward
Every foot pumped every brake pedal
Everyone was so close to a fiery launch date
Everyone was so close
What was chambered swelled itself to open air

The clouds descended as dense fog
Slab and timber and iron and canvas falling down
Landlocked and broken masted
We got lost in the cold
When the fog lifted
There were a couple of fat lips and bloody noses
I went home and wound up my clock

At my worst I assume the worst of people
At my best I assume little
All I'm trying to do
      Every yank
      Every transgression
      Every handshake
All I'm trying to do
I put myself in a space
Deliberately
Of my own conception
And determination.

I will guzzle and kick and contemplate

Beneath broad domes
Over bedrock
Between gases
I will roll and fuck and confess
I will wrinkle apart
In all my grandparents' sky and sun

I work for the city
•
O silly deathride
I am here
I AM HERE
I approach you coming to me
I don't know whether to cough or grin
My body is virginal in the morning
My body is a rebel faction
My body is a bloody revolution
My body puts poems where they can be heard
So many apathies
Perhaps apathy is bold acceptance
A dire discipline of steady sobbing
Perhaps beneath all apathetic exteriors
Churn furious engines of give-a-damn and resolve
And concentrated wishing efforts
A silence akin to the stoic womb
I know that you know what I know
How good it can be to urinate
To swim in public fountains
To sleep in a tree
To kiss until fucking doesn't matter anymore
It's so easy to slip and write a love poem

What I dream
Revolves around
What I know of Love's corruption
I sought a new identity
And I was assassinated into a false agency
I'll never say what I saw
For fear of what I say becoming what I saw
It's been thousands of days now
The shifting truth is rarely acknowledged
Never respected
Needs no tempering
A pig swinging in the smoke house
There is only one thing I have been trying to say

It's something dead and daily
If we truly understood what poetry was
We wouldn't use it as an excuse to share
The repellent magnets of us
Mother's whiskers and coffee too strong to drink
The moon is bleeding
The moon is bleeding
Rocks and buildings and trees are bowing
I'm gonna meet my mother
And she will be my brother
I have known two hats on one head
High impact under low domes
There's a concept I want to shirk
It's something dead and daily
My whole wounded outlook
Sprouting from imagined wounds
My blushing head and my nervous mouth
All about to jump
All involuntary and that's no consolation
That warrants no invasion
I'm speaking the english nothing more
A universe crammed in an ambulance
You got your government inside
Go punch the ocean
Hatred makes us go too fast
Love makes us go too fast
Jumping to inconclusive nets of burning safety
I have never known combat
I have never known the devil
What little truth I have held has stained me
A toucher and a feeler
I would share a tree with your invisible voice
The crown of a human skin suitcase
The eye in the pyramid on the dollar bill
Marks it as a note for beggars
I'm talking out of my pores
Any and every opening
The grimace engenders the flat face that bears it
Men and women purloin and placate
Every word an unstable explosive
A flyweight necksnap kissing the chinbone
It's something dead and it's something daily
It's all one poem
We tend it together

Rolling the torch in tar
You can call it god
You can call it the street
The mountain
The truck
Americaninium
A book a cannon
A foot skin converter
Who are the farmers?
So many worlds at once
Who are the jet pilots
So many worlds at once
Who are the killers and midwives?
So many worlds at once
Some pounding inside
Some echoing outside
Some are dead
Some are daily
Some asleep at the detonator
Panting in headlights
The grim skull of the supermodel posing in the tender mud
There is life here
Pivoting on a risk
A life-wish fueled by a death-wish
A pattern of deviation
Nose to the knuckles
Outbound time burn with an inbound posture
We harvest what every road shares
One long necklace
Heavy as a spoonful of sun
Heavy as africa
To choose to lick another
To choose to suck another
To choose to revolt in a single burst
The seminal squeeze the tool grips at hand
I have stopped saying the word HEAVEN

Kim Nicolini b.1962

Kim Nicolini is an artist (painter) as well as a poet, with a brutal and delicate voice. She has several self-published chapbooks out, including: *In My Mouth*, 1993; *Bad*, 1992, *Dirt*, 1992 and *Black Drum*, 1991.

Fall Of The '70s, Or Sloe Gin Fizz

1. Primed

Sow belly girl of
fifteen. Red eyed
virgin. KOOL smoking
and oh so cool.
Bell bottom Levi's
and platform shoes

she really believes
every inch
adds a year.

Bleached blonde to a
yellow glare.
Eyeliner thick as melted
streets under her eyes

she is oh so
ever so
grown up.

But when the bald faced
Navy boy/man
says he really wants to
fuck her
says she looks like
the hottest lay
he's ever seen

she doesn't
understand.
She truly is
offended.

Because pancake
face or no
she is a virgin.
True blue
cherry full bitch.

2. Done

White jeans, black
panties and sloe gin.
It was a set up.
Yeah, she set it up.

Led Zeppelin, red
lipstick and her parents'
empty bed. Everything

planned. You can do that.
I mean map your own cunt.

Pimpled and bone stricken
sixteen year old
boy/man. With so many
pills to offer he must
know how to do it

right.   Like in Penthouse
or the Happy Hooker.
I mean he has his
own car. He shot up
twice. He has the marks
to prove it.

But it is a sloe
Gin Fizz. And then
another one. Red.
So red they're
purple. The color of fresh
blood clots and just as
sticky. After the third

she starts to
drool. Her spit
spattering her white
jeans with pink.
The room is a

turntable – the music
white noise. she is
pulling her skinny
boy to the bedroom.

Rubber walled
hall. She rolls
off the walls
in waves.

Jeans pulled
to her ankles. He is
on top of her
whimpering.
She didn't know
they whimper.
Sick puppy sound.

There is a fumbling
a grunting
something stiff in the black
elastic. A squirting
a groaning and a
snoring.

Standing on the
bathroom tile
there is something
running down her leg.
No one told her
about this.
That you don't
feel anything
but you do
get real dirty.

It drips onto the
floor. She touches it.
It's sticky
like a Sloe
Gin Fizz.

Hotel

It moves into me –
the *Sam Wong,* 1977 and all
its luggage moves in with it.
Night is a sob
a dog run over
legs dragging behind.
Blue mascara
puddled on my face.
Wet rabbit fur
stuck to my back.

The halls are endless.

A shadow stumbles
out of 310, lunges
disappears, looms
up behind me.
Hand on my shoulder
in a fleshy fingered grip.
Voice a dry whisper.

We'll make it
better. Promise
we will.
We know how
to make you
disappear, everything
washed away in smoldering
brown. And now

the vampire
kiss. Needle
kiss. Mix of blood
and water kiss.
Dilute.
Disappear.
Silent black
fist kiss.

And all that exists
is the green
rug, coffee
stains, piss old

dog stench, a
bobby pin, yellow
blink outside
the window.

The *Sam Wong* still stands
on Broadway. Still stands
in my bedroom
30 miles away
13 years later
still stands
in my skull –
granite – the street –
the floor. Always
the floor.

The *Sam Wong*, 1977
Rudy says wanna
shot. 4 a.m., his wife's
asleep in bed next
to me. I crawl
out, say yeah
I wanna shot.
Get it. Go
black. Brown
wash. Tumble

gut. Only the floor
is left. Green
rug and Rudy
on top of me
pumpin, his lips
moving in, swallowing
my face. I never knew
it could be so
cheap. Dottie stirs

on the bed. sheets
rustle like dry
leaves, old
paper. Rudy covers
my mouth with his
hand. Plunges.
And only the floor
the rug, flesh, black
kiss is left.

True Story

They found her room as empty
as her face, iron framed
bed, drawer of
condoms and the cold thing
swinging from the ceiling –
blue rag gone limp
and hanging – a purple
ring around her neck
as if she's wedded to the
knotted sheet in which she's
caught. Last night she had a

story to tell, her plucked
and drawn face pulled tight
as she lifted her dress and showed
me a jagged mouth
cut deep into her right
ass cheek, said
a trick caught her
in the back with an
ax, said she kicked
his mother fuckin'
ass down the stairs,
said he was a
freak, was mad 'cause
she wouldn't let him
tie her to the iron

bed. She's been an open
sore ever since – sleep
beyond reach, hospitals too
curious. She turns
to the familiar – the bed,
the sheets, the tightening
of the throat. And now
as they wheel her body
away – a series
of lumps, leveled
mountain under a white
sheet – her two
bare feet bob
in the sun.

Psychosynopsis

I am addicted to talk shows
'specially Sunday night Rockin'
Sex talk. I have seen a midget
die. I have caused a suicide.
My favorite chips have always been
Cheetohs – the puffy kind. I have
fucked a Chinaman, have danced
in circles with mascara running.
This I thought was the definition
of fun. I have lusted for fourteen
year old boys. I have fucked the Italian
mafia, took speed and wrote
all night. I have no veins in my left
arm – not speed this time but
heroin. I have shot
Dilaudids and puked off a roof,
puked in my grandmother's
beauty parlor, puked in my
own shirt. I love to cook –
pasta my specialty. I got fat
at 23. I am too young for all
this weight and dead lust. I
never feel in love but think
I've loved many times. I fucked
freaks for cocaine. Limping wooden
legged dealers. I don't think I'll
do it again. I had orgasms while
hooking. Yes, I broke this law and
came under an Argentinian's tongue.
He was a surgeon at Mary's Help.
He liked my leather jacket. I have
lived in hotels for years. I gave
myself my first orgasm after fucking
so many men I lost count. I took
my own virginity. Sometimes I paint
things I can't look at. My brother
died of heroin and it's killing me.
My mother gives me
a stomach ache, makes me cringe.
I am constantly embarrassed by
my own words. I have seen transvestites

pee and tuck their pricks between
their legs. I have slept with women
and made them cum. I don't want you
to touch me. I run 7 miles a
day. I am 28. I have a degree. I
was married at 16, kicked down the
stairs at 17, in the Air Force and back
on the streets at 17. I have
very few friends. My vagina
has always been on display.
I had a homosexual relationship
at eight. I have stripped for
neighborhood boys. My brothers
sold tickets. I have been called
a lying whore and slut many
many times. I like to read
a lot. I put my used gum
on my bed post. I sucked my
thumb until I was thirteen. I
sleep with a teddy bear. My
father is dead. I never
knew him. I am a drunk
at times an addict.
I have overdosed on pills.
Yes it was intentional.
You may not believe this
but there are things
I never talk about.

Deborah Lee Pagan   b.1960

She writes: Deborah Lee Pagan is a pseudonym for Deborah Lynn Fruchey, who got tired of having her name mispronounced. Author of an award-winning novel, *The Unwilling Heiress,* Walker Publishing, and three poetry books under her own label, Last Laugh Productions. Ms. Pagan keeps two cats and several chocolate companies in business. Her history consists of an ungodly number of years spent in churches, mental hospitals, and 12-step programs (in that order).

The Next Voice You Hear

Sometimes, when I have nothing better to do,
I have delusions.
At least
I have been *told* they are
delusions – Yeah,
OK, You guys have
all the pills.
So you win. They're delusions.
But, let to myself, I'd rather say
that I hear voices,
and that oftentimes they're ... pushy.

It's not so strange:
Most of us hear
our mothers and fathers
and recent exlovers,
and people like that.
But you hear them one at a time,
so you're lucky.
Most days,
my head is a cocktail party.

I can live with that.
What I mean is the raised and anxious voice
the wild outrageous Right-Now voice
the one that says I AM DYING IN TWO MINUTES
LISTEN TO ME.

You've heard it too, but you think it came
from that crazy guy on the Oceanside bus,
the Religionist over on Telegraph,
the kid getting beat up next door.

I, on the other hand,
suffering formerly character deformation,
and having attended
far too many 12-step meetings,
tend to call it God
(I knew a man
who called it Howard,
but I call it God).

I don't tell that to the cops, of course,
who tend to get upset about this sort of thing
and give you these trashy punk bracelets
and take you to Highland;
I tell social lies,
like a good girl does.
    'I have to go now, I don't feel well.
    'I have this disease. I take these pills.
    'Here is my number. Call me tomorrow and see
    if I'm still alive.'

They're more comfortable with disease than God.
But I know God when I hear him,
and I say, "Sorry
about that interruption, Howard –
– what were you saying?"

And I nod and lock all the doors and windows
and listen to all the things he thinks
I ought to do
He's not a bad story teller
He knows a good joke or two

But some days God's mixed up and angry and yells a lot
and some days he's sad or he's drunk
and he gives me
advice that would bury me ten foot deep
if I ever tried it.
I don't introduce him to my friends but
I accept God the way he is
protect him from hostile strangers,
pay his parking tickets
and listen.
That's mostly all he wants.

Alan Kaufman b.1952

One of San Francisco's most-publicized poets, Alan Kaufman came on the scene late-Babar from New York, and is politically active in the poetry scene. He regularly leads tours of poets to Europe, where he also receives lots of press. He has been quoted about the poetry scene and/or his work has appeared in *Time, Der Spiegel, Modern Maturity, Village Voice, L.A. Times, San Francisco Examiner, San Francisco Chronicle, San Francisco Bay Guardian, San Francisco Weekly* and *SOMA*. He recently performed with Allen Ginsberg and Kathy Acker in Berlin. He has helped bring national and international attention to the San Francisco cafe poetry scene. His books include *American Cruiser*, Zeitgeist Press, 1990; *The New Generation,* Double Day, 1990; and *Before I Wake,* Cyborg Productions, 1991. His work is included in *Aloud! – Voices From The Nuyorican Poets Cafe,* New York, Henry Holt & Co., 1994.

Who Are We?

Into the past
I go like a stranger
to discover why at night
I lay alone as a child
waiting for the front door
to slam, my father gone
to night-shift work,
and my mother, Marie, to enter,
unable to sleep, and tell me

tales of childhood
war, pursued by those
who, as she spoke,
seemed to enter the room,
Gestapo men in leather coats
who ordered me to pack
and descend to a waiting truck,
for I am still going to Auschwitz
though a grown man in 1990
I am still boarding the freight,
crushed against numbed, frightened
Jews and Gypsies and Russian
soldiers and homosexuals,
crossing frontiers to be gassed

I am her, in my heart,
though I am six feet two
and two hundred and ten pounds
and have played college football
and served as a soldier
and have scars from fights
with knives and jagged
bottles smashed on bars

I am still her, little girl,
hiding in chicken coops
and forests, asleep on dynamite
among partisans

I am still her, brushing teeth
with ashes
from the ruins of nations
gutted in war

I am still her brown eyes
and black hair of persecution
foraging scraps for thistle soup,
a star-shaped patch
sewn to my shirt

I am still my mother
every day in the streets
of New York or San Francisco,
the chimney skies glow and swirl
with soot like night above
a crematorium, or the Bronx

incinerator chute where I
threw out trash in a brick
darkness shooting sparks

I am still her in the streets
of Berkeley, walking among
sparechangers, dyed-hair punkers,
gays in stud leather, Blacks,
Mexicans and Asians

I am still her rounded up
among poets and thieves
and politically incorrect
social deviants
on sun-drenched sidewalks
in the Mission and the Haight,
Greenwich Village, the Lower
East Side, or anywhere the weird
congregate in tolerance

And every day in the age
of Reagan and Bush,
in a mental ghetto
affirmed by the homeless
I pass the dying
with the loud ring of my boots,
ashamed to think that perhaps
my heels are the last thing they heard
Every day I am a survivor of AIDS and poverty
Every day I sit in cafes
watching tattoos turn to numbers
and I grow angry
I want America back
I want America to be
the home I never had

And you, who are you
if you hear my voice?
Who are you, stranger
if you read these words?
Who are we
who stand threatened
in these times of darkness?
Who are we, condemned to die,
who do not know ourselves
at all?

The Time I Drew Angels

I once drew angels ...
during my second marriage ...
No, actually after the marriage was over,
when it was all in ruins.
After I had run off with Rose
(My wife's best friend, and my best friend's wife)
and ruined that, as the war dragged into
its third year – The Lebanon War in '82; this was
in Israel and all us men were in the army. I was close to nervous
breakdown. My betrayed wife called, invited me to her place;
when I last saw her she broke a radio over my head. I had since
heard that she was threatening murder, had friends in the Israeli
underworld; for a time feared that she would have me hit – but I
went to her home anyway. Why not? She had moved into a dingy
tenement neighborhood, a bleak slumlike project building, but she
was putting her life back together and looked better than she had
when I was shuttling back and forth between Rose's bed and the
army, and would spot her from a distance on a street, wearing dark
sunglasses and dragging home fishnet shopping bags filled with
bottles of cheap brandy – there were bottles
out on the table now when I came in. She cooked a lousy diner,
bologna and eggs, some such crap. And the booze was out. With
her, dinner was just an excuse to drink, that's all, and we drank
now, as always. We were the ideal drinking mates. I had not even
minded very much – such good mates we were – when she
betrayed me with that cab driver one night; fucked him right in the
back seat while I sat upstairs in the house, pouring myself
tumblers of brandy and I even brought them down two helpings –
but found them busy clasping white in a confusion of black lace
and tense thrusting buttocks, so I took the glasses back upstairs
and drank them both down – she unscrewed the cap
and poured me a glass now.
I was in bad shape. "You look terrible," she said.
"I'm full of remorse," I said, "I'm sick with what I've done."
She poured. She was silent. We sat and drank.
(And O.K. I'll own up. I was having a nervous breakdown then.
Period. I was even having paranoid delusions in my army unit: imag-
ined that my fellow soldiers, the best friends possible on
earth, the bravest kindest guys really, that they wanted to kill me
with a secret bullet to the base of the brain – crazy stuff like that)
"It's bad,' I told her, "I'm having delusions."

She nodded. "Why don't you draw," she suggested, "draw how
you feel. My shrink strongly recommends it."
"O.K." I said.
She rose, returned with watercolors, set out paper.
I began to draw, and sipped from time to time from my glass.
She drew from the bottle straight. It was gold-colored
in the room and felt safe.
The pain between us actually formed a kind of embryonic womb,
enfolding and protecting us. We each had already hurt the other
too savagely to fear pain anymore. So, I drew. I drew
people with wings on their backs. I drew an angel. He had on a
news vendor's cap, and a poor man's sports jacket. He stared
toughly from the frame of the portrait. He looked gentle but tough
as nails. He was full of the heartbreak of his
love betrayals, full of the mercy that he felt for others. And it was
beautiful, it was located in a kind of nighttime Brooklyn with a
starry Van Gogh sky, and the angel's eyes were like both Bambi's
and Sylvester Stallone's, and they seemed to say that never again
on this earth for as long as the angel lives will the good or the
gentle people of this earth be murdered or shamed
or betrayed ... And she liked my angels very much, she said.
It was the first and only time that I have ever drawn angels. It was
the last time that I was ever to see her too, because soon after, at
the height of the khamsin winds, she threw herself from a sixth
floor window
and was buried near Tel Aviv.

House Of Strangers

Her face,
cut from patient
ebony, looked ill

A trash bag
of belongings
rode her lap

I guess her
life had been
a suicide of kindness
repaid in grief

And somewhere in Cheyenne
I asked where she was going

and she said that she
was going to the
House of Strangers
in Reno, Nevada

where God sits in a
clapboard casino
playing the one-armed
bandit

"Heaven is a hotel,"
she smiled, "and if you meet
His price, the Big Guy
will let you sit

and listen to the wind
blow: *Whoooooooo!*"
And I knew she was crazy

"My daughter-in-law
swore I'd die, but
it's good exercise
for me to ride. Look

at me, am I dead?"
And I knew
that she was

I laughed. "You look,"
I said "like morning
in Atlanta"

She grinned and
wrapped my hand
in a glove of bone

"Is it a way still?"
"Not far. We're
getting there"
"Good," she sighed,
"I'm ready"

She showed me a bag
big with silver dollars:
"Ten years of my life
there," she laughed

And later, while she slept,
I stole a few
to feed myself

Kuwait

I feel good.
Do you feel good?
This morning, jets zapped me too fast to
    catch their model and make
    I'm all shot up
Tonight, tanks broke my neck
The dunes shriek and moan
to cum in dying boys with rolling eyes
    and impact sucks off Scuds with spewing heads
    in streets of cringing kids
but I go on, joyous – George and Saddam
    to liberate the holy shrines
    of Exxon and Islam

I am enraged afraid in my trench of jackals
    baring grins at searchlight moons
I had never seen in Kansas
    tracers stitch the night's black coat
    or so many bellies split like dropped
        shopping bags
    so many thoughts blown
        like sand from the mind
    so many footprints tracked like ants
        to the nuclear picnic
    so many smiling chests, bullet-
        kissed with blood

I feel good.
Do you feel good?
It's good to die in war, to lie spitting
    guts and gazing down at ankle-
        severed boots
Remember me when you pay the gas pump
You'll think, counting your change:
    Why, that cost ten cents less than last week
and as you pull away
you'll see my phantom wave friendly
    in camouflage fatigues and hear

the register sing Semper Fi
that I enabled you to take
    your mistress out
and drop your wife off
    at church
and ferry your son to
    his football game
all without walking
I gave you gas to cruise the Tenderloin
    on your night out, bargain with whores,
    a percentage of whose fee I paid for
    in blood

Don't cry for me
I lived. I saw T.V.
Had my tonsils and appendix pulled
Cracked the books and passed my tests
Saw all the *Honeymooner* reruns
    a hundred times
Broke my jaw canoeing on Lake Tahoe
Jerked off in bathroom stalls at school
There were just so many visits to MacDonald's
    left in me
I could never have afforded that Honda
    anyway
I did my skateboarding
I got under bras
I fingered holes
I had never been abroad
They cut your head off here
    for drinking booze
and by the time we took the streets back
all the veiled girls were gone

But don't mourn for me
Look at the nice frame they put my picture in,
    posed in parade dress
        behind a nailed-up flag
and my mother presses lips
    to my Kodak Color cheeks
and my sister makes
such a legend of me
that her dates dump her
    for chicks who worship sex
    more than ghosts

and Pensacola is the same
Trenton flows on unchanged
Chicago is still Chicago
Minnesota is still fucking cold
   Soon the World Series
   Soon the Superbowl
   Soon the NBA play-offs
   Soon, new elections
I'm glad we repelled the invader
The invader is glad he repelled us
Goodbye flotilla of international destroyers
   The tankers roll once more
   The refineries are belching
   The oil is gushing
   Onward flow black crude
   Onward vital stuff of speedometers
Onward mad angelic nectar of hidden radar,
   breath tests and hit-and-run.
Onward, go, go, go manic adrenaline
   of Neal Cassady roads
   restored to billboard health
   for motel saints
   with nukes and bazooks
   and copters and *Stealths*

Long will Kuwait live in the annals
   of our oil-heated stoves
You will sing of our sacrifice
   at the Indy Five Hundred
   and when 16 cylinder monster roadsters
   spew flames at National Speedway
You will place caps over your hearts
   to think of us in Chevrolet dealerships
      and used car lots

Our courage will purr in your
   Meineke mufflers
You'll bless us in Montana wastes
   when your plugs spark
When cavalcades of limos bear to graves
your well-fed hearts
   for heavenly registration
      on wings of license plates

Kathleen Wood   b.1964

Kathleen has a wild simplicity in her prose and poetry. Her work tells the story of urban life amidst decay and beauty. Kathleen's ability to reveal her true feelings, ambient aura of sexuality, and intellect have made her a poetic muse to many San Francisco poets. Growing up in Kansas the daughter of a university professor, her home life was abusive and from the age of 15 she repeatedly ran away to San Francisco, working as a stripper and dominatrix. She was part of the punk scene around bands such as The Dead Kennedys and M.D.C. Kathleen has several chapbooks, including *Tenderloin Rose* and *The Wino, The Junkie, And The Lord,* Zeitgeist Press, 1988 & 1989; and self-published four chapbooks of early work, including: *Black Roses And Wounded Tigers,* and *Signals From The Pit,* and *Sex, Drugs And Just A Little Politics;* and also published *The Anti-Zine.* Her work has appeared in *Poetry San Francisco, Bullhorn,* and *Worc's.*

Gregory

Gregory stumbled into the saloon.
He ordered a screwdriver.
I ordered a Beck's.
We introduced ourselves.
He said he liked my hair.
He wanted to buy me dinner
At Baby Joe's on Broadway.
We left the bar.
As we walked, he told me
All about his experiences
Fucking boys with Allen in Tangiers.
In the restaurant, we drank beer
And he told me he was
An ex-junkie and
An alcoholic and proud!
So very proud of it all.
He said everyone here gave him
a bad rap, but
Everyone loved him
In New York and
He would take me with him and
We'd stay at the Chelsea
Where Edie and Sid and Nancy stayed
And he would introduce me
To the most wonderful people.
And after we finished our pasta,
He asked me if we could go
To my place.
I said okay, but I lived
In a residential hotel and
He had to leave by ten p.m.
We took a bus to Fourth and Mission
And traipsed through the ritzy lobby
Past the disapproving glare
Of the desk clerk.
Halfway up the stairs
Gregory decided we needed
Vodka. We turned around
And went next door to Merrill's
Where we purchased a pint
Of vodka and a quart
Of orange juice.

As we paraded through the lobby
Gregory was swigging
From the vodka bottle.
Upstairs, we drank screwdrivers
From the complimentary plastic cups.
He said he wanted to fuck me
I said he had to use a rubber.
I handed him a package.
He said the grillwork
on my pseudo-Victorian bed
Would be perfect for bondage.
I gave him a few of my scarves.
I removed his shirt
I asked him why there were scars
All over his arms and chest.
He told me he'd been attacked
By an ocelot.
I stripped and he tied
My arms and legs
To the bedposts. Then
He fucked me.
We went and got more vodka
When we returned, he asked me
If I'd ever read his poetry.
I said no, but I would
Read it later. He said
I really should because
It was very good.
I told him I wrote poetry too.
I showed him my book
Of poems about punk rockers,
Junkies and coke fiends.
He told me it was good.
Then he said that he
Was a better poet than I was
Because he was a traditionalist.
I said I'd be sure
To read his books.
At five of ten, I told him
That he would have to go.
He said he was broke
And demanded ten dollars
For cab fare.
All I had was a twenty.

He told me he would take that.
His voice was getting
Louder by the second, so
I gave it to him.
He left. I was afraid he'd call me.
He never did. A week later,
A friend of his told me
That Gregory was in New York
At the Chelsea where Edie lived.
I discovered he'd left
His watch in my room.
I took the watch to a pawnbroker,
But the guy told me
He could only give me
A couple bucks for it.

Enlightenment

So they told me if I
kissed the asses of
enough dead kings,
I could come home,
but that's what all
the gurus say, right?
I never could grasp the concept.
People with models of
torture scenes around their necks,
statues of fat men
beaming at me from souvenir stores.
And Krishna, Krishna, Krishna.
I can't sit still
long enough to meditate.
Brown rice terrifies me.
I prefer my kings alive.
For three years
Mark lived with me
and figured out endless
unwise ways to spend
what little money we had.
He kept telling me
the material plane was illusion.
He played songs by the Beatles
and Donovan and Sandy Bull.

He was a terrible lay,
so I didn't bother.
He didn't seem to notice
as he babbled on
about Gurdjieff and Meher Baba.
He couldn't understand
why I didn't want to meditate.
After I finally left him
he started hanging out
with cafe paranoids
who convinced him Jim Morrison
was killed by Johnny Carson.
Somebody was giving him
coke. Hey, it's San Francisco,
what do you expect?
Then he disappeared.
maybe he's in some Tibetan monastery
but he's probably in New Jersey.
I guess it doesn't matter
if it's all an illusion anyway.
Besides, I never could
kiss ass to dead kings
or even to Mark.
But I wonder, Mark,
wherever you are,
are you enlightened yet?
And can your angels explain to me
why we spent four years of our lives
drawing a picture
in disappearing ink?

Dan

He said he was a Scorpio but he wasn't sure what day
He'd been adopted by Jesus freaks in Michigan and raised in a glass bell
which he shattered at 16 when he ran away to Hollywood
He grew his hair to his waist and turned tricks on Sunset Blvd.
In the early 70s he served as a houseboy for an actor who played a
    sergeant on a well-known 50s sit-com.
"He threw really kinky parties," Dan told me. "Did you know Bob Hope
    is bi?"
When the actor died he had to leave

He married a prostitute who took him to Sonoma
    where he found her a gig at a massage parlor
They had a son
For three years he raised the child while she worked the circuit of
    massage parlors and live-sex shows
She finally left him because he beat her
Somehow he wound up in San Francisco managing a welfare hotel on
    Turk Street
He made money on the side by selling acid to his tenants and lending
    money at very high interest rates
One day one of his elderly tenants died
Dan was notified that the old man had been wealthy and had left Dan
    all his money
The man's relatives were angry and took legal action to get the
    money away from Dan
Dan hired a lawyer and won
He bought himself a Mercedes and some musical equipment.
Then he drove around picking up hookers, giving them plenty of
    cocaine, and taking them to Vegas for 3 or 4 days at a time
On the rare occasions when he returned to the hotel elderly and
    speed-freak tenants would crowd around his door, screaming
    insults, threatening to rent-strike, and demanding toilet paper. One
day the owner came around and told him he was fired
He rented a cheap hotel room and went on a two month coke binge
He was running out of money
He hocked his guitars and amplifiers for rent and party money
Soon he was sleeping in his Mercedes
Complaining of a bad back he applied for disability.
The workers sneered at him but he was persistent
He got on G.A. and found another hotel room
He sold his car and bought a used Mustang
He found a sympathetic shrink, and began the first of a series of SSI appeals.
He stayed in his room for days listening to Pink Floyd and reading
    science magazines
He developed a theory on a new form of energy
He began to work on an invention that involved a bicycle wheel and a
    light bulb
I came over to visit him
"I don't need sex," he told me, "I'm going to change the way America
    sees energy."
After two years of appeals SSI gave in
Dan received a huge retroactive check
He spent the money on a farm house in Mendocino County, took his

bicycle wheel and his light bulb, and went away
He left me his phone number, but I left the notebook I wrote it in on
the 14 Mission bus.

Bob The Dead Poet

The week he died,
Two drunken beat poets
Invited me to Bob's wake.
"It'll be the poetry event of the year!"
Said they. "We will play jazz music
And drink rivers of red wine
And read all the poems
We wrote for the occasion
Like 'Bob, you owed me money
But now you're dead.'"
"But I didn't know Bob Kaufman,"
I told them.
"Oh, that's okay," they said.
"Just pretend you did."
A week later, my lover
Was reading a book by Bob.
"Bob was God!" he proclaimed.
This refrain quickly caught on
In the poetry community
As one poet after another
Took the stage
To dance his two cents' worth
On Bob's dead junkie bones.
"Yo, Bob didn't shoot dope, man,"
One beat old dude insisted.
"He injected sunlight into his veins."
One year later, Mayor Fineswine
Proclaimed Bob Kaufman Day.
She failed to attend the ceremony
Because she was busy
Sweeping undesirables off the streets.
Last week, a guy told me
He saw Bob's ghost nodding
In the bathroom at Specs.
He asked him for an autograph
But Bob only wanted spare change.

The Wino, The Junkie, And The Lord

I was on a bench at 18th and Val
Talking to a wino who said he believed in the Lord.
He said he needed money for dinner at McDonald's.
He said he wasn't asking for much.
I gave him a dollar.
He said he'd protect me whenever I was in the neighborhood.
Because he always looked out
For the people who helped him.
He said he had good reasons
    for being an alcoholic.
I told him I used to have good reasons for being an addict.
He asked me where I was going.
I said to an NA meeting on Eureka Street.
He said his daughters lived on Eureka Street.
And he hoped they turned out okay.
He want to know which drug I was addicted to.
I said several.
He said he wanted to know where the meeting was
Because the streets were dangerous at night.
He asked God to protect me
From the crazies in the dark.
He turned to a yuppie who stood nearby.
"I've got good reasons to be an alcoholic!"
The yuppie smiled at me and shook his head.
The bum asked the Lord to keep us all.
Then he stumbled off down Valencia.
The yuppie muttered something about crazies.
Our bus arrived.

Mission Street Peach

Wanna experience the taste
Of that peach, wanna
Feel the juice run
Down my chin like
Rivers so cold it'll
Take you days to stop
Shivering. Don't care if
It's old, wormy, moldy,
Rotting away at the
Core, I'll just eat
Around the cancer, I'll just
Eat around the cancer
And feel the flavor
Explode
In my mouth.
Fuck it all, man.
I don't care.

Tenderloin Rose

There was something I
didn't like in my eyes that morning.

So I covered it up
with about a ton of a makeup till I
couldn't see it anymore.

Now, I was just another Tenderloin Rose
on a plastic stem
in a grease-specked vase
sitting on a table in a hooker cafe
where everything was cooked with lard.

I could relax
I belonged.

David Gollub b.1951

David Gollub booked Babar readings for several years. He has a B.A. from Harvard, and a PhD from Stanford, and publishes *Bullhorn* – the monthly Babarian poetry rag – and is a great help to the scene. He has several chapbooks including *Special Effects,* and *As For Us,* Zeitgeist, 1992 & 1993.

God Comes Cheap In East Palo Alto

By six a.m. I'd realized
two things: I couldn't stay in the apartment
when the housekeeper's vacuum stirred the dust, and
I couldn't get myself to the emergency room
driving. I'd sit at the wheel
in the plush seat,
drive about ten feet before I'd have to
switch the ignition off,
engage the brake,
unbelt, unbolt the door,
spring out
like I was tormented by an itching
on the inside surface of my skin, get out,
stand up,
doubled over
the low soot-grimed roof of my subcompact
on the shoulder,
the right front window crushed up against
a tall hedge of dark glossy leaves.
Had gasped a whole can of albuterol
down my bronchials. No use.
They only burned
like they'd been sandpapered.
Now I was out of the stuff.
Thirty, forty, fifty,
sixty shakes of the inhaler
till my arm was sore:
no matter. All out.
Had to go it alone. Got about
half a block from home.
Couldn't think past getting
the next breath in.

Then the next. I sweated though the November
had been born deformed by drought
and the creek the road followed
had dried out to a bed
of sludge and brown weed stalks
in the shadows
behind the street lamp there.
Later I'll figure out
how I'm going to get out of this,
later.
        I hear a voice.
"Hey, man, you all right?"
What the hell,
I'm beat. I gasp,
"Asthma attack." He called the cops,
they called an ambulance.
Doors open. A light.
A woman paramedic's gentle hand pressed me
down onto the bench. They hooked my nose up
to a life support,
they hooked my mouth up. They started pumping
oxygen into my nostrils,
mist into my lungs.
We rolled off over the bridge
through gentrified shopping streets
into the dawn.   The season and I
both breathed easier
four months later. It occurred to me:
I could have died.
there was *no* reason for that guy to have happened by.
No reason for him to stop
and save me then
or even see me,
except the notice you'd give,
the concern you'd spend
on a total stranger
in passing. Such a momentary thing, and it was
as close to God as I will ever come, I suppose,
whatever God is.

Or maybe there was a reason.
Before he walked off he asked me, "By the way,

could you possibly spare about three dollars?
I fumbled for my wallet,
dumped quarters out of the coin pouch.
I'd hit a change machine
with a five at lunch
so I could buy a sandwich. Yes.
About three dollars. Only fair.

My Heart When It's A Whale, And At Other Times

My heart is awake twenty-four hours daily
but finds it painful to keep its eyes open
some of those hours. My heart is
a unique muscle in the packed parlor
of my body. Lonely heart
is a redundancy,
believe my heart, by which I mean, of course,
believe me. My heart aches
for good conversation.
My heart doesn't like
to talk about itself, but loves to sing
a gibberish it devoutly hopes
is the language that says
what my heart means, though maybe a language
no one knows.
If my heart happened to beach itself it would,
according to its mood, either
lie still and scratch its sides
till a full day's light
baking it had mummified it like a frog, or
bellow at the top of its lungs,
half in a dream,
rolling over and over
like the planet to keep all of itself
half in shade.
My heart deserves to wallow in an ocean
of disinfectant balms,
bellow its hale notes over the ocean floor
halfway around the world
to two or three companions. Four, maybe.
It's a small world for my heart
when it's a whale.
Small, and full of songs

Dominique Lowell   b.1960

Dominique is a performance poet whose voice is demanding a rebellion against the everyday. Backcover notes from her chapbook *Pile:* Dominique Lowell was born and raised in Detroit, Michigan and has traveled and performed extensively in major cities across the United States. Drawing on her theatrical background and her experiences in the contemporary urban wasteland she performs these works with fury and finesse leaving audiences ecstatic and exhilarated. Dominique often wins the *San Francisco Poetry Slam* open-reading competition. Recently she toured in Germany and Eastern Europe performing her work on radio; (she was thrown-out of Austria for sticking her tongue out at a plain-clothed policeman). She works as a bike messenger. Dominique has several chapbooks out, including: *Pile,* and *Bitch,* Grace Street Press, 1991 and 1993, respectively; *Noise,* Cyborg Productions, 1991. Her work has appeared in *Bullhorn.*

Women Are Hungry

women are hungry
they be hoes
they be sittin on your stoop waitin to drink your beer
eat your food
suck your dick
women are hungry

they need your favorite shirt your leather jacket
a house and a car
they just neeeeeed
they wanna tell you things, pretty little things about
the light in your eyes and the feel of your thighs
they wanna shave your balls
have you tell them about every clit you ever licked every ass
you ever eyed so they can
slice them all to ribbons
they're insatiable
it's biological

they just want and want and stretch their yearning arms at you
their craving lusting insatiable envelopes gawking open mouthed
must have must have must have it
you
now

whore mother goddess priestess convict jailer
needy neeedy needy needy
need your sperm need your job need space need more impossible paint
for another impossible face
crimson lips and concrete sharpened nails
blackened purple eyes
the beaten look, that's it
already been hit

feed me
feed me beer and cigarettes and dead idols who make me feel like
I might have a reason to die too
give me War and Coca-Cola and the promise of another American
chance
give me another good song to dance to
tell me I'm not fat
tell my my tits are jewels, my nipples gumdrops

tell me we can pay the rent tomorrow
tell me we are just like John and Yoko only I get to die first
O.K.? I get to be the one they light the candles for in Central
Park, O.K.?

Fuck Women.
They are such sluttish catfight evile bitches
every one of them
Beware. Beware.
They know what they are doing.
Does that scare you, are you scared

women are hungry
hungry for balance
I been called a whore so many times I almost became one
and it's not you personally I want anything out of
It's the world
the World owes me BigTime
The World leaves me hungry

When The Bitch Puts On Aretha You Know There's Trouble Ahead

(a menstrual poem)

It's getting dark again and I wish I had some hate to hang onto
some guts to cling on besides my own which seem to be sliding
out all greasy and tainted smelling of dead protein and the sea
of unwanted womanhood
It is too thick this smell it stinks
It is sickeningly strong how unfit this body is how it is not a
woman's body it has no
purpose it is not a man's body it has no
strength all it has is
endurance
It just lives and lives and bleeds and bleeds month after month
for no reason no procreative purpose just a sick joke
Why do barren women bleed?
What makes a woman barren?
Is it her personality?
If I had had just one abortion I would feel more like a woman
If I wasn't such a nice white girl when I need to be I would be

in jail
If I wasn't angry who would I be?
I'm a lousy cook
But I know all the moves
the Supremes did to "Stop In The Name Of Love"
I know all the voices, falsetto to basso,
to the Temptations "Cloud Nine"
And on a good day
I can hit all the notes in any Aretha song
"Dr. Feelgood", "Never Loved a Man"
All those damn Aretha man songs
And you can come after me
Accuse me of childless bad behavior
Pour hot boiling wax and old Rolling Stones lyrics on me
And I won't care
"I'll Be There"
with muthafuckin bells on
I'll whip a lawyer with thigh high vinyl boots on and never
charge him a dime
I'll spank a dyke for Christ
And I do not feel unworthy
No I do not feel unworthy
I dance on graves because that's all I've been given
And because I know
where the bodies are buried

An Oliver Stone Movie

Jim Morrison never had to be a busboy or a maid
work at Carl's Jr. or go on G.A.
he just took some acid
in the desert one day
and woke up a rock star
of course he was tortured
he was an artist and a poet and shit
he's supposed to be tortured
and he'd have these visions
of naked indians & medicine men
big ol bad Jim Morrison
he really thought he was a lizard

poor ol tortured guy
and these journalists
would drink his blood in weird ass satanic rituals
but he sure could party
damn that Jim could drink
and he had a really fine bitchin girlfriend
he showed everyone his prick
and got arrested and got all fat
but he didn't give a fuck
he smacked his girlfriend around but it was cool
she could take it
and she understood
when she found him dead in the bathtub

Sugar Daddy

there is something that exists between
what you want and what you get
and there ain't no use arguing about it

it was Father's Day
he bought me a beer
we get into his big ol car
Ford LTD way before they downsized em
and I got this new rule about who I sleep with
so I ask him
"Do you have a job and a place to live?"
he chortles
"I am a doctor of philosophy. I teach. I make videos about
young women artists. I am independently wealthy don't ask how"
oh no I'm thinking omigod how do these assholes find me
"I have this very interesting designer drug on hand would you
like to try some?"
he tries to take my picture I hide my face in my hands
he tries to tape our conversation I say turn that fucking thing off
he tries to tell me about this video of his
young women artists
he coerces me into doing a poem for him and I succumb
I dance for Grandpa
"You're tortured you're a poet," he screams
"I must tape you I must buy you clothes"
I say there's plenty of tape of me around and

I don't like it one bit
turn off that fucking machine
screw your silly ass video
just spank me good and fuck me from behind
that's what this is really all about isn't it
we'll talk about the clothes later

what is it
about ragged girls with stains on their crinolines
holes
scabby knees
stringy hair and dirty fingernails
that makes men with tan shoes say
"lemme take you outta this bus station baby"
while they're fucking you against the back of their couch
and your bra is around your neck
and they got their hands around your throat in mocking threat
because you made the mistake of telling them about the guy
who strangled you until your nose bled and you barely got away
and they're grunting and mewling in a t-shirt and bathrobe
so provocative
I mean he even left his socks on

I'm just trying to concentrate on what a cool thing this
weird designer drug is
morphic and psychoactive at the same time
I like it
there's still some left on the mirror
he'll let out the big groan soon and pass out
then I'll really have some fun

the next morning he takes me to breakfast
I'm pretending that he's my father and just
in town for the weekend
but this is San Francisco the waitress knows better
and really doesn't give a shit anyway
he gives me a ride home
says, "here I want to give you this hope you don't mind"
it's 40 bucks
of course I don't mind I say
thank you very much i say
but what I'm really thinking is
what a cheap fuck

Not Doing My Laundry Or Cleaning My Room

Not doing my laundry or cleaning my room I
survey my quarters
a hidden masterpiece
has to be
I am The Kid
plotting quiet mayhem in the corner
Shit into Art, Beauty into Shit
sorry sir I got my orders
straight from Iggy
the Guitar Army
search and destroy

alchemy
worship of the alchemist
changing shit into sugar and sugar into shit
I pop another budweiser and contemplate the
changing face of megalopolis
the cockroach starstrutting across my TV screen
beer dribbles out my mouth and down my front
ahh, Art

scuze me turn up the volume pleez I can't hear you
now were we speaking of matters of the spirit
of the flesh or the marrow
did we connect play ball footsie teeter totter throb
squish
he jests at scars
that asshole who never even felt a wound
that bunghole parading across my TV screen
that miserable insect
I am frothing at the mouth from dehydration and
lack of sleep
nothing but budweiser in my veins for days
cheap and soapy
I pretend I'm Gregory Corso
"Hey baby, wanna see my tracks . . ."

she jests at scars
that video slut
that cunt who never even felt a fucking wound
that's Shakespeare by the way

now now baby now baby now baby now
people are assholes let's just face it
now baby now
love just sucks so forget all about it
let's just ride the night
grease the stars
for every cockroach there's a star and they're all
twinklin at you
so just nod your head and dream baby
possess the night

A Poem I Swore I'd Never Write

moving day again
I get to play Anne Frank
next to Jane Eyre and Elizabeth I
its my favorite role
I get to smuggle my clothes out
wearing three outfits at a time
damn good strategy
the Hindus will never know the difference
throw my belongings out the window in garbage bags
and go
no longer doomed to another week's interment
at the Europa Hotel
with the guy in the shower screaming at himself
"YOU'RE A SLUT AND YOU'RE GAY
YOU'RE A SLUT AND YOU'RE GAY"
at the top of his lungs to no one
and the woman who wanders the halls
stopping to growl unintelligible messages
right outside my door
moving day
kinda makes you wanna reminisce

Another Job Bites The Dust

I still have legs
I still have a Black Sabbath tape
I can still dance

I still have my bicycle
I still have pubic hair that grows
long and red
I still got my hat
I find clothes on the street when I need em
like magic
I like the smell of my farts
even when they're nasty
I still have a place to live
for another two weeks

everybody whines
"oh the system sucks you dry"
but the system is too lame to
manage even that
the system can't even lick properly
I submerge from time to time
bob up to the surface
quit my job
and I still got all this juice

nobody's even bothered to try to
suck me dry

I dare you
I still got a cigarette
I still got enough money for another beer
I still go the MC5
I got my clitoris
even when the money's gone

I got trees and dirt and ocean
I got eyes and throat and teeth
I got tongue and breath and death
the night is mine

and I got work to do

Alan Allen   b.1947

He writes: Alan Allen writes spoken-tradition journalism books. *Storytellin' Muni Drivers* was reviewed for six weeks in the front pages & columns of the *S.F. Chronicle, S.F. Examiner, S.F. Chron/Exam & S.F. Recorder* in '89 – (vol 2 is scheduled for summer '95); *Old Rails' Tales* reviewed by *N.Y. Times* as "the creme of the crop, bold, buoyant, energetic, compassionate, extraordinary" in '91. Director, Activist News Network (ANN), & IntelligenceNet-newsWire; Publisher, The Press Of San Francisco. Invited to produce & host a monthly radio program of his own device on a national radio network (summer '95); & broadcast production & distribution of activist (& other public affairs) special 8-hr curriculums on radio to 1,400 college- & 1,400 community radio stations (winter '95-'96).

Telephone Call During TV With Last Wednesday's Lover

night is my refrigerator
what the hell
is my answer

and everyone on easy street
with a thin dime for a third eye
is drunk on the steps of the church

because the shadows
where old gutters meet
past the butcher shops and fish markets on chinatown streets
were twist-off tops for kisses

and the ketchup beating in the fleshy veins of night
is where the lost boats go and
the early cabs stuck in the traffic-lighted paper panels
of comic books

day is my freezer and
all the hunks of meat
packaged in their pretty clothes and manners
the fish heads wrapped in newspapers
the frost-bitten hands and
hungry silhouettes are
stuck in morning
like a bayonet

all the empty cans of beans
and shopping bags full of dreams
all washed up
in the watery coffee and familiar faces of strangers

I'm permanently on hold
the dial tone has stopped,
all the wrong numbers
are having a revolution
in the streets of a persian carpet and
a ticker tape new year's day parade
beneath the stars

They Say Beauty Is Something Everyone Has But No One Gets

that mars is red at night but never closer
than a coke machine at noon
in summertime
when you're 5¢ short 5 feet tall and 5 years old
that christmas comes and goes like clockwork
but never stays around too long
and jesus was a martian anyway
with a round-trip ticket to nowhere
but he's still hitch-hiking and begging nickels and dimes
because he'll be president someday

they say nickels and dimes pressed thru the eyes
end up in the wallet of a fat man
that lies cost more than truth
that dawn is tired of her job

and money slaves drugs and guns
make a billfold happy
with the smoking end of a .38
pressed firmly against the head
– into the galaxy –
but the record's skipping
and the street doesn't care

that the scratch of a cat's claws
stings more than a woman's kiss
that life was our lottery prize
hunger our reward
death our prayer,
but on my way to the bank that lie blew up
and scattered my teeth like stars

that we are hunted like animals
haunted by mad spirits,
and the best things in life are not free.

that we are pressed like flowers in books
dried butterflies under glass
caught like fish in schools
skinned like veal and
guillotined like chickens.

but karma lost her music license
and the bar's closed down tight
the wind is blowing dirt and
diesel smoke into a flattened streetlight's glare,
and the darkened alley brake squeal
and the moan of a old jalopy crashing into
parked cars scattering garbage cans
and drunken bums against the tall brick walls
disappears
when the light turns green
and the cassette music starts
you pass me a beer
and you're beautiful
as hell

Free For The Taking

I could speak of my friend Joy's death
but instead I will tell the death of sorrow
bound in ashes in an urn
& scattered over the landscape in a silhouette like falling snow
that began like lovers' eyelashes brushing against my cheek
& ended with a packed suitcase & a shallow grin

it was a day
unlike any other day
fueled by an inner voice
I began to take my dulcimer with me & my writing
– things with almost no life but mine –
to feel at home with myself where ever I was
so I always happened to be found by my own doing

My hand was so tired & old
& it was all coming in my head
& I could not read my own handwriting
(that was the sound of his voice)

all the graceful arches and swoops of the letters were spilled topsy-turvy
like dice
& each face of the die was high grade pharmaceuticals
ugly little gelatin caps filled with granules
each granule was snarling freeway traffic
& another waiting room crowd in the no-bed no-ticket county
mental county health, ward, 5 macdonalds hamburgers, I'm tired of sit-
ting in this chair, what's your story, I want to get out of here
(Joy was the man in the relationship. I told Joy's death after all.)

Her voice – Sorrow's voice, when she died – we sat around the bed
watching for her own death vomited out of this world like a new-born
child

Her voice came from beneath my fingers like
the sounds from the strings of the dulcimer
or heartbeats
that caught in my throat
& morning finally came

The candlelight bounced off sorrow's face
except there was no candles lit

Sorrow died a glamorous face like she was born,
free
for the taking

I Have Become A Country At War With The Sky & Trees & Water

friends strangling themselves with their own hands
glasses and plates crying out for sanctuary
not a tree
not a blade of grass
not a bird
not a soul
not one

a kiss like kites
a voice like song
a laugh like breezes and stars

I have run to the end of the alley
and wildeyed turn to fight
myself
I am trapped in a dirty mirror
filled with longing past how far I can see
I reach out through the bars jailing my heart to touch empty air

my soul looking back over my shoulder sassy and flip
to curse where I've been and my own beginnings

I fly ahead of myself to drink the blood of the moon

I bear no witness.

Damien Pickering b.1964

Damien plays blues guitar; works as a Pass Plan co-ordinator and rights advocate helping physically-, emo-
tionally- and/or mentally handicapped people develop business plans for self-employment grants from
Social Security.

Threshold – *Stanford Hospital, Sept. 1969*

Hospital bed goes bump, bump
across the crack
between the hall
and elevator floor.
Shutters shut the elevator doors.

In the basement,
surgery,
nurses white,
doctors dressed in pale green.
The corridor is harsh, and clean;
terribly clean.

Stop before two vast
electric doors.
Here – friendship ends,
and fear begins.
Brown Doctor Winter
who you love,
your wooly friend
with pebbles in his voice,
rides on his back,
care and laughter,
arms about his neck.

Brown Doctor Winter who you love
changes into
green Doctor Winter,
who you hate.
You want to shoot him with a gun
for all that he had done,
prying, and peering in your eyes.
You hate him – and you feel
he must hate you.
The doors jerk back,
the bed rolls through.
Inside, the lights are monsters from a dream,
Giant eyes
gaping white mouths,
a singing in your ears.

In the dream
they stare into your face
whichever way you turn.
They burn.
They will hurt you.
You cannot get away.
On the table
antiseptic paper cracks,
and this is not a dream.
Someone screams.

It is me.
I am three.

A white nurse grips my head
and clamps a mask around my face.
A hose leads from the mask.
The hose moves gas.
The gas is rubber, and onion in my mouth.
Her white face is turned aside,
no expression in the eyes.
I have been here before,
behind these doors
only this time
I understand
this cold face
is the last thing I will ever see.
Actually it is the lights
as they lay me back
for that hour's cold
unfeeling sleep.

And now, my bed rolls back
across the crack
between the hall and elevator floor;
bump
bump.

Waking I hear
drifting sounds.
I do not know if anyone is near.
There is a blank wall before my eyes.

Slowly, slowly
I will piece the world together
with a child's hands.

Michelle Tea b.1971

Michelle Tea is originally from Chelsea, Massachusetts. Her voice is strong and inquisitive. She writes: Michelle Tea is a restless lessie poet who spends most of her time sitting in San Francisco cafes drinking buckets of coffee. Her three collections of poetry are: *Oppress Me Before I Kill Again; Tripping On Labia,* Mass Extinction Press, 1994; & *Heartbreak Cigarettes.*

Go Kiss Go

i've got a two day old kiss and
i'm afraid it's getting stale, i'm
trying to keep it covered, keep it
fresh, don't know when the next batch
is coming. got an ache in my heart
from this two day old kiss, it's pretty
heavy for something that isn't even
there, it likes to jump from my ribs
like a high dive and go swimming in
my stomach, it likes to slide deep
down there, yeah there, you know where
and do a little tap dance, it likes to
catch a ride on my bloodstream up to
my ears, make them burn, make me sweat
a little, gets a little bossy, a little
greedy, kicks my brain out like it owns
the place, making my head swell full
with this two day old kiss which isn't
even anything, making me fuck up a lot
in work sayin' sorry, sorry, sorry, i forgot
to do that, sorry i did that wrong, sorry
i just forgot i was here, i just went
somewhere else for a minute. i just
got kissed two days ago and you know
that clock is ticking.

For My Nana

i liked this boy adam
with long hair and black eyeliner
and he was all i could think about
when i took my grandmother to boston
for radiation treatments.
they were zapping her lungs nuclear
and i was sitting in the waiting room
with gingerale and national geographic
and hidden hickeys, and you could hear
the machine buzz and hum as it
spit out nuclear stripes and isn't
cancer caused by radiation in the first place?
all that atomic 1950's air they were making
out in nevada worked its way to boston and
into my nana's lungs and now they've got her
drinking these uranium cocktails so that
her sink is full of wet hairs and later,
in the hospital cafeteria over rubbery hot dogs
and coffee she says *let's have a cigarette together,*
this will be your last one, ok? you inhale?
don't inhale, i never inhale.
this woman
whose judas cells are killing her
she tells me not to sit on the toilet
cause i might get aids and not to
put my lips to the drinking fountain
cause i could get hepatitis.
my grandmother died
with her eyebrows drawn perfect,
just as she'd requested. she died before
my boyfriends stopped looking like girls and
started being girls, before she could hate
me for being her queer aquarius granddaughter,
same zodiac sign as her, and did you know
that some cultures kill all the february babies
because their little bodies have so much bad magic?
she had psychic dreams, my grandmother, she knew
each symbol had a number and she'd play the
lottery and win a hundred bucks and she loved
my cousin brian, the connecticut hairdresser
with a joan crawford fixation, so who knows,

maybe she would have loved my hairy armpits
the way i loved how she pin-curled her hair tight
before it all fell out and she began hiding
her baldness with eva gabor wigs,
and i never visited her grave except that one time
my mother dragged me to the cemetery with a
poinsettia for christmas, there was nothing there
but a flat copper plaque, half covered with snow
and a group of groundskeepers
who sexually harrassed my mom on the
way back to the car, nana, if reincarnation
is true, you are a six year old child somewhere
on this planet. i hope your parents treat you good,
i hope you have enough to eat and a best friend
all your own, i hope you don't hate school too much
or maybe i hope you hate it a lot, i hope you
were born in february again, i hope you came back new.

Bruce Isaacson b.1956

Bruce turned-up on the scene at the Peter's Pub readings in 1985. He was one of the early mc's of the Babar reading. In those days the readings were dynamic, anarchistic and energetic events that defied leadership and control – the crowd responded to excellent work with silent awe and wild cheers. Bruce credits poetry at that time with keeping him alive. Bruce's voice is *Present Day*, very direct, accessible, and replete with popular culture references. His Russian poems are a personal take, not political – introducing today's Russian culture to us, and introducing the Russian people as Bruce met them when he spent six months in Russia with his wife Olga, trying to get immigration papers for her and his two stepsons. Bruce earned degrees in theater and economics from Claremont McKenna College and an MBA from Dartmouth's Tuck School. He was Chief Financial Officer of Wharton Econometric Forecasting Associates before leaving business in pursuit of poetry; going on to earn an MFA from Brooklyn College, studying poetry with Allen Ginsberg. He has since become well-known for poetry performances in contexts ranging from National Poetry Week, Helena's (Poetry in Motion readings) in Los Angeles, and San Francisco's Cafe Babar. Bruce has several books out, including *Cafe Death*, Opus II Press, 1988; *Bad Dog Blues*, Zeitgeist, 1988; *The New Romantics*, Apathy Press, 1989; *Error Is An Enlightened State*, Cyborg, 1990; and *Love Affairs With Barely Any People In Them*, Zeitgeist Press, 1990. Bruce is the publisher of Zeitgeist Press, (Zeitgeist produced many of the first books by Babar poets).

Single In My 30s

Some days I can't sit alone
writing at my desk
is too difficult, so I wander off

to wipe the table top
or fold the laundry
that lies round my room like oatmeal.

Anything to get some relief
from the monologue
of my life talking itself over

and over, like reruns of Bonanza.

My father had three sons:
Little Joe is a policeman in Walnut Creek
Hoss sells real estate in Malibu.

I am Adam, the eldest, dressed in black –
a poet in my teenage 30s
stuck in the backseat of a Chrysler

mind frozen on a family vacation
like some B movie terror that is
too hideous for the townspeople to discuss.

This is our Ponderosa!

Three single men in their 30s
a coincidence
which the viewers seemed willing to overlook.

Not me. I phone a lover to discuss it
but when I ask *How are you?*
a long silence takes the line.

She is single. And depressed.
Over something she doesn't know what
but she starts describing how her father died

how he turned crazy at the end, screaming
about how his children
would never be able to clean out his house.

I find myself agreeing with him.

With parents, children, or lovers
the failures between us –
these are the places we know each other best.

Are comfortable even. Without them
I don't now how to be myself anymore.
And then, too often, I can't help it.

The mirror climbs off the wall
and follows me around the apartment, nagging
in an annoying nasal tone. *Being alone is*

just a situation, a phase, a rationalization,
like some Ph.D at a big university
gets a grant for a thesis about
people in their 30s wanting true love. Not me.

To me, breeding is more like a game of tag
and today, I'm *It.*
Chasing the void around the couch

catching it, in a bar

at the end of Adler Alley
at the end of the Beat Era
at the end of a country's pride in itself

an age of self-destruction begins.
Here, the end of my bloodline *lives*
like a tapeworm. I feed it. With drugs, liquor,

love affairs with barely any people in them

as if love was the shading in a black & white
movie, as if
happiness were something you could look for.

On Father's Day

My father is showing me his house
The one he's built against old age

Now he's showing me the stonework
custom imported granite
and the bathrooms – designed black onyx modern
the counter tops in the kitchen
all done in high grade marble
Now he's showing me the outdoor hottub
ninety-two degrees rain or shine
the master bathtub also with jets
separate dressing room for both Mom and him
den for him – painting room for her
vaulted ceilings living room panoramic view
custom wood floors, twelve room intercom,
infrared motion sensitive alarm ...

My father is showing me his house
Six, count them, six televisions with cable
One on each side of the kitchen
My father is showing me his house
He's complaining about the work they did wrong
He's been here four months but none of the four showers work yet
Shower man's supposed to come next week
My father is pissed about
the placement of a screw on the blinds

Shhhh – he's trying to watch the ball game

The ball game is on in five rooms
It's bouncing off the 18ft ceilings
The batter steps up – *shhh!*
I'm trying to watch the ballgame
I'm trying to get some work done
Those people – those people – they don't know much –
Their expectations in life are modest – those people –
Shhhh – I'm trying to ...

> This is the man
> whose eyes got
> moist and sticky as
> a postage stamp

the day I told him
I had to leave
the family business

This is the man who said
OK –
this is my partner of four years
who looked forlorn as a cactus
when I told him I had to leave
This is the man who had
a stroke two days later

This is the man who had a stroke
Don't talk shit about him – he earned it –
Shhh. He's trying to watch the ballgame

this is my father
this is
this is me in my father's house
this is me in my father's body
this stomach is the thick trunk of grandma
this could be me
recovered from a stroke
losing twenty pounds
then midnight feasting on
new fat-free cholesterol-free Entenmann's
this is me saying
Betty you don't know anything
why talk when you don't know
we're trying to get some work done
could I get some coffee
christ no – no milk

this is my father
showing me
his house
this is me
showing you
my father
can love ever be in vain?

A Love Poem For The Others

I have seen so many faces
Blank ones, with the snout of the pig
Pretty ones, with my love in their eyes
Friendly faces, looking on sympathetically
at the random pains to the world.
And the truth of the matter is
that beneath the gold lamé panties
all of the faces are the same.
And I love them. Each of them.
See, a part of each demon wants confession
And the punishment for being a priest in hell
Is to be a priest in hell.
For this, I have poet eyes, and am glad.
Without them, all of the people I know
would be even more clearly
vague. Just faces
and weariness.
This is what I've learned about love.
That there are only two unforgivable sins.
One is ambivalence. And
I don't really care about the other
since I saw the best of my heart
trampled on by a drunk.
I was the drunk. And I am the numbness
you feel before your lover says goodbye.
I am all the the blank faces
residing safely where people could be.
I must feel nothing   to touch you.

Home For The Retarded

1. A Portrait

  With her two pair of pants and three tops
Her hair tangled and plain
Her calm eyes quiet at the reading
Her shy eyes while touching at my nipple
The salt taste behind her cheekbone after jogging

Her old apartment half a closet in the Tenderloin
Books and paper scraps around the room
The ex-roommate owes her for the phone
Her face turns pink as she mentions him
Her confession comes right after mounting me
Then her stories about her dead brother
Her patience in her job with the retarded
Her pay rate less than McDonald's
Her sweetness bumming change for beer
The sweetness of her phone talk with her Mom
Her sweetness
Her offer to heal me after surgery
Her description of the room where we'd live
Her awkward hands the night I arrive
She reaches to turn on the bath
Asks me to search her breast for lumps
Her smile as my lips find the nipple
Her eyes closing ...

2. Home For The Retarded

She couldn't keep an apartment. Or a job.
She was sexy. And a drunk. As in – *available*.
Bars, bosses, roommates – they'd fuck her a while
then out she'd go.
When I met her she'd just got this new job.
At 9 am the vans'd start arriving
in a big empty warehouse
and they'd bring them in –
autistic ones mumbling at the ground
retarded ones
dribbling out questions like ketchup
hairlipped children
barely held together inside overalls.

They'd bring in 60 or 70 or so
and 5 employees would watch them for the day
breaking up fights, giving out sandwiches,
trying to understand what they said.
She got paid $6 an hour – not really enough to live on –
but she could drink beers as long as she
kept it low.

We'd been shacking together three months
in a flat we shared
with six college-aged rock musicians.
I had this computer consulting gig – $100 an hour
I'd spend the days in our room
writing poems, smoking pot
until I was numb enough to program the computer.
She'd come home and we'd go for a burrito,
drink, read each others poems.

She was jealous – had to know every single
phone call, accused me daily of betraying her.
Our arguments got louder than
the roommates' rock rehearsals and we
scared the kids pretty good,
though just before it got violent
I'd head out to the
cool summer San Francisco air.

Back at the house, if I was lucky,
she'd be passed out by a couple
quart bottles of beer
and once when I wasn't so lucky we
fought and she fell and we
ended up at the hospital
her elbow purple as a plum
swollen big as a baseball
the doctor asking us sternly
about counseling.

The most important thing to me was
I never hit her.
After the 3rd or 4th comment about
who I fucked while she was gone
I'd scream *"Is this good enough for you!"*
and slap myself full in the cheek
or pound my head against the wall,
hard, three times
then scream *"Would you like some more?"*

As a man who watched Donahue, I needed to feel
the injuries were accidents
but looking back, if I didn't hit her

I wanted to – fantasized
splitting her head open like a pinata.
I loved her. At least
that's what the pathology feels like while
you're in it.

Once we fought because of some guy
phoning her. Turned out it's
a 300 lb. autistic kid named Brian who was
sexually fixated on her feet –
a head-butter, who was rumored
to have once killed a $6-per-hour employee
crushing the woman's ribs
using his skull as a battering ram.

One night when we argued she threw a punch
a good one, that caught me
in the back of the neck
and once I threw a Random House New World Dictionary
Second Unabridged Edition
that hit her shoulder blade but didn't leave a mark.
That day she got drunk gave some guy our
phone number and when he called her for a date
I threw her stuff out in the hall and as she
reached down to get it gave her
a big kick in the ass.

I think that's a complete record of the violence.
I still love her.
We can't even talk on the phone. We get
right back into it.

3. Here's What I'd Do

I'd move up close facing you
and reaching around
I'd squeeze your butt cheeks
like I was testing fruit
until you started grinning and squealed
"doooooonn't"
then I'd reach out my lips

to the smiling knob of your cheek
and place a kiss there
carefully
as if threading a needle
and then I'd just stand there
with my lips resting
like muslin on your cheek
and you, being a poet, would know
to just stand there
and if we knew what was good
we'd never have
moved from that position.

Marriage Poem

You come barreling over the Sierras
with the momentum of a boy leaving puberty,
tape player blasting, Dark Side of the Moon chattering
like a priest gone mad in a confessional.

You're getting older.
Haven't done anything so impetuous in years.
You make Donner Pass, with its cannibalist survival stories,
then drop down from the mountains into Reno.

The casino appears, jutting up from the plains, a monolith,
an architectural style created by German socialists.
As you're thinking how easy to appropriate symbols
the sun drops from behind a cloud and a rainbow, I swear,
a rainbow appears over the casino.

When the casino doors open, the gaming hits you
like a burst of electricity, buzzer bells, jackpot cash,
carpets that glow in the dark.

Inside, the people look strangely like cattle,
lumpy with steroid growth.
These are men who've raised families –
6'3", in a sportcoat and a cap that says *Peterbilt.*
Or standing in front of a slot machine

eyes lit up like a Christmas tree, sucking down
a filterless Pall Mall in 3 tokes.
Or 5'6", almost as wide as high, looking forlornly
at a five dollar bill dropped on the floor.
And their wives, too often, standing with the luggage
like they were part of it ...

These are not the woman you came with.

She is a young bull-headed Russian who speaks
almost no English.
Which seems to be an advantage.
You have to just assume the best, let the facts
work themselves out, and, you discover, love is
mostly in the assumptions anyway.

While writing this, you picture her in your mind
standing over a boiling chicken
tasting parts not even other chickens would touch.
You fantasize about marrying into the 3rd world.
And you know, like she says, that you're
a spoiled overfed American.
But she says it so sweetly,
eyes dancing like televisions, so alive,
that when the chicken bowels are placed to your lips
you swallow, and smile, and are glad.

As you walk across the casino
you see an older man win at least $700
and walk off looking stone-faced & sour.
Lucky in cards, unlucky in love, your lover says,
and you hope you never win at cards.
You don't.
The two of you walk past the roulette wheel,
past the slot machines, past the shopping boutique,
all the way to the end of the arcade.

You enter a small wedding chapel with
simulated wood pews, recorded wedding music,
a carefully non-denominational design.
Jews, Hindus, Muslims, anyone could be married here.
There is no image of God, and you're glad.
If there was a God, you'd be in big trouble
for getting married in a church in a casino.

But you are safe. Your lover likes your parents.
And standing at the altar your mind suddenly fills with
the halting 8th grade spanish you speak to one another,
and the picture of her pointing
at the strange neon six-colored letters
that spell out "Children's Fairyland"
on the lawn at Lake Merritt,
her laughing and pointing and
saying "muy simpaticos".
You realize, in your heart,
this was the moment you married her.
You are sure. This is right.

You know you'll have to spend
six months in Russia to get her out.
And her mother, a hero of the siege of Leningrad
will be losing a daughter.
And her brother, the communist army major, may be
less than pleased.
And the 2 stepchildren you haven't met yet
will come to America knowing no English
and start at Berkeley's Malcolm X Middle School.
And you know one of 2 marriages end in divorce.
Your first marriage was more like a chemical spill.
And as acquaintances joke obscenely at you about
second marriages being the triumph of hope over experience,
getting older, you feel, life's
just not worth living without love.

A Russian Mood

Arrived at the home of people who
obviously don't have enough to eat
They are forcing the best food down on me ...

This is the essence of Russian cuisine

As a health conscious American I'm accustomed to be picky
I don't eat pork
I don't eat fat
Or fried

I don't eat red meat

After a month eating here
After so many dinners of spaghetti butter and apologies
(no cheese)
After discovering that even though I hate cucumbers
I love eating cucumbers
After receiving the enlightenment of Spam
as treasured delicacy ...

Now when people thrust food on me here's what I do:
I eat.

I eat what's offered
I eat when I can
I eat fried potatoes and cabbage
I eat soup of garlic lentils and cabbage
Eggs canned ham and cabbage
Kasha and potatoes   Kasha and gravy   Kasha and warm milk
Add butter and it kind of has taste

Koo-shet! Koo-shet! Eat!
Pickled tomatoes   Pickled cucumbers   Pickled beans   Pickled
garlic   Some sort of pickled grass   Eat!
Stale bread that's been toasted – my favorite

One day last week we ate a chicken
It was small and old and stringy
and we ate every last goddamn organ
In short – it was excellent
I slept great

Kooshet! I eat canned beef with rice
I eat canned beef on a skewer
We took it to a cluster of trees by
a half-finished industrial building
lit a fire with twigs and cooked it
It got all mixed in with Russian soil

It was excellent and I ate it

The kids loved looking in the fire
The dog got a hold of the meat bag and ate a lot of ours
so there wasn't quite enough

That's why you hear lots of people making jokes about eating
cats and dogs
That's why so many cats and dogs
turned loose to make it on their own

We go to the private market
A room the size of a large high school gymnasium
Pigeons and sparrows live in the rafters and swoop down and
eat whatever they can

In the private market we find cherries dried apricots
two new varieties of pickled things
You bring your own bags cause there
ain't no Baggies in Russia
You save every one   Wash them out
Use them whenever you can
We walk up and down the aisles
A salami
A food-relief salami from Finland
It's priced too high   No says Olga way way overpriced

I throw a tantrum and we buy it

We also buy some kind of cheese
Olga knows I like cheese but this tastes strange
It's cheap and Olga says it'll be fine
Trying to maintain my vain western stomach standards
But Olga says she'll make blintzes ...

The blintzes are excellent
We put cherries on the blintzes and saccharin
I've been gone from America long enough I figure
I allow myself to imagine: it's Sunday morning
I've just ordered breakfast in Berkeley at The Med
It's excellent
Then ...
vomiting and diarrhea for three days

Not much refrigeration in the food distribution system
Not much you'd really call a system
There's the State Stores – low prices and grain
spilling from a hole in the bed of a state truck
we see on the road to Leningrad

There's the private market – bands of
tough Azerbaijanis and Gypsies looking to make a killing
They do – price for our one hour of shopping: 1500 rubles
More than your average Russian makes in a month

So what does your average Russian do?

I'm not sure, but I begin to see
how this makes every day a miracle
If you ate good today was blesséd
If not – you'd better do better tomorrow
This system's not so much a way to allocate goods
It's a way to allocate shortages

When people get hungry ...
we can maybe get a sausage through work maybe
a cousin has a boyfriend who works in a restaurant
maybe you'll get invited to the home of someone that eats good
maybe a foreigner with money for the private market
maybe ... maybe ... maybe not
It's hard for anyone who hasn't eaten native to understand:
how close the Russian people still are to serfdom

Hunger took Moscow from Napoleon
Hunger ate the Third Reich
A million died of hunger in Leningrad
Hunger – burning zen master of Russia
There are temporary triumphs but here
hunger is the playing field
A purpose   An imperative   A master plan

As Americans, we're usually only vaguely aware
how much food it takes to fuel the human body every day
And then, you develop habits here
of being careful food isn't bad
of not appearing to enjoy eating too much
of offering food first to others
These small graces keep you human

Today three times we ate rice with canned beef
Everyone's gone to bed
I'm sitting at the kitchen table and I'm telling you –
I'm hungry

I want to eat
I won't – That's okay – I *understand*
I remember an acquaintance   an American woman
a business executive   use to say
you can never be too rich or too thin

That's food enough to chew on tonight

I remember being with Olga in Denny's
and she kept stuffing her purse with those
little processed plastic foodlets –
mayonnaise, tartar sauce, Nutra Sweet
She wouldn't stop even after
I told her how weird it was

Well here we ate on them for a good two weeks
There's two mayonnaise packets left
but maybe they've gone bad cause when
babushka ate mayonnaise two days ago she got sick
but I'm not sure if it was *this* mayonnaise
cause she wouldn't talk too much about being sick
No one does   It goes with the lifestyle
The most important thing about this style of eating
is not to lose dignity
maintain civilities at all costs
raise doing without
to an art form.

I don't know how the average Russian does it
But then I'm not thinking about the average Russian
I'm thinking about two packets of American mayonnaise
I could eat one
With bread –   maybe find a slice of sausage
No – I'm thinking about the average Russian
The average Russian is thinking about eating
And I am thinking ... about literature
Yes – in this mood do you think we can
talk aesthetics?

Do we have any choice?

At A Major Russian Vacation Resort

Dark
Attractive
medium aged woman
Elegant – sheer formal skirt and high heels
standing at a muddy bus stop next to a large
brown & white
cow.

Flies buzzing.

So This Is It

In bed with her sleeping curled up into me.
Looking up to the ceiling – can't sleep – why? just can't.
A white June night glowing in through the open window ...

Six months tomorrow, six months, so this is being married.
She has such trouble sleeping, a terror without sleep,
don't want to move too fast and wake her.
She needs sleep, Atlas girl, carrying the weight
of disciplining the boys, all those dreams, housework, Lenfilm,
me ...

We argue enough.
She's stubborn, I'm impossible.
Fighting, okay, but like Mom says,
learning to fight fair –
that's being married.

She rolls a little to the left.
Damn narrow Russian bed.
Got to roll a little right to balance
warm head now on my shoulder.
I've actually found someone who can live with me.
Healthy now. Feel good. Wish we had the visa solved. And
what to do about money, have to find work,
new life back home, two, no three years.
School, poems, publishing. Now supporting a family.

Family, that's love, that's got to help with poems.
but how many friends I knew got married, lost interest,
dried up.
What to do, no one knows our work, must learn Russian,
work more, and what to do about medical insurance,
dental, three people all needing teeth, a fortune,
this is marriage, I'm thinking at the two a.m. ceiling
her feet rubbing lightly on my toes.

Strange eternity, the way her body continues to
twitch and move in sleep, and my own, ceiling eyes
narrow bed, problems, a soft face turning on my shoulder.
Trying to turn along with it.

How Are You Doing?

She'd been working the salad bar about two weeks
when he caught her a moment without anything in her hands
came up and just blurted it out:

How are you doing?

He was a wiry guy with brown hair and black glasses, fortyish,
large birthmark on his cheek.
He was the boss, and she just stood there and stared
cause she didn't know what to say.
Maybe he was trying to make a point
like she wasn't working hard enough
but she'd been cleaning all around the salad bar
picking up lettuce that'd fallen in the macaroni salad
wiping up cottage cheese spilled on the floor
but everything was clean so what did he want
she didn't understand cause her english wasn't too good
and she'd try to explain she was just learning english
and they'd say *seems like you're doing great*
and then go back to talking like computer chips.

So this time she just stood there
staring at the mole on his face
a large brown spot with one, two, two-and-a-half hairs
growing like geraniums from a pot.

Are you happy? he said
and twitched off a small smile that revealed his teeth
to let her know this wasn't supposed to make her nervous.

Are you happy. This she understood.
Understood what to feel, how to say.
In Rushshshsa I am taking two degrees
I am stagemaker, the Leningrad University
and also I am oceanograph.
I work on film making script documental theatre six years.
They are ready to give me my film now
but in Rushshsha everything broken
I cannot work so I come to America and now
I make four fifty salad bar.
She stopped and stared at him.

Well I could move you to pouring drinks.

She knew the kid at the drink counter.
Job paid the same
he was trying to get his family from El Salvador.
No, she says, *it's not necessary.*

So, you are happy.

She paused long enough to think
then put on her most simple-minded peasant grin.

"*Yes, I am happy.*"

A Different Kind Of Love Poem

It starts when you meet a woman.
But it doesn't end there.
Love somehow never stays in bounds.

It's not just that first time you come together.
It's wondering how you'll feel
living with someone else's children.
It's also: a six inch needle & learning to be tough enough

to push it in her deep so it does the job the first time.
It's her in the hospital and you alone with the boys
who speak no English and think this is the time to
show the big guy who's in charge.

And how do you get through it?
Easy. You learn a language. You break a window.
You look at the monster you could become
in the eyes of a nine year old boy.
You learn to give a spanking and
keep the anger from your hand.

You remember. How scary father was.
The poems you wrote him as a monster.
You learn. How impossible to live up to love.
The testing that rocks us back and forth
like lumberjacks pulling on a saw.

And now, as your father begins to lose his grip,
his eyesight, his house, his power,
as he becomes so much simpler, "lovable",
even attends the fourth grade spring Pageant ...
He doesn't look at the boy and see
the way the kid left his room.

You sit down, stuck between
your father and your wife talking over you like a table
as a group of fourth graders sing
Take Me Out to the Ballgame ...

And two rows up, about halfway over,
one of them sees you looking
and his face lights up,
trying to suppress a small fourth grade grin
as he mouths the lyrics in
a language he barely understands.

And suddenly he's
a Michelangelo in a garden of mannikins.
You can't take your eyes off him, love jumps bounds, and
you have a child of your own.

Whitman McGowan   b.1950

Whitman started the open reading series at *Farley's* and ran it for several years. He is a performance poet who often reads with musicians or tapes behind him. Including other Babarian performance poets Whitman produced a touring group act called The Naked Language. He enjoys actively involving the audience in performance. His chapbooks include: *Contents May Have Shifted,* Viridiana Publishing, 1994; *Smokin' Words,* Blue Beetle, 1992; *Big Petits Fours,* Viridiana Publishing, 1988.

Poetry In The 9th

Your attention please
Here are the changes for the 9th race
Mosquito Bite has been scratched
Poetry two pounds overweight
It's Academic will be wearing blinkers.

If I really thought Poetry was a winner
Do you think I'd tip you?
Well, maybe I might tell you
How Clocker Bob timed the predawn works
Poetry does 47.5 for three furlongs
Breezing on a sloppy track
"And the boy's holding her back, see ..."
Yeah, picture yourself with a big win ticket,
Just us and the playback people cashing in
I can see it now ...

It's anybody's race
They're into deep stretch
Romantic End on the rail
Here comes Litigation
Between horses it's Take A Breath
Electric Performer now getting the lead
It's A Funny Feeling on the inside
Followed by Video Offer
Personality Cult by a nose running easily,
Holding in there it's Straight Job by a head
From out of nowhere it's Mink Coat
And Canyouhearme coming on in a rush

Poetry also starting to move up through the pack
Then It's Academic and Your Penthouse is the trailer
Mink Coat showing her class goes out in front
Canyouhearme now battling for second
And on the outside Poetry being asked for more
Mink Coat by a full length
Canyouhearme beginning to fade
As here comes Poetry
Poetry now really turning it loose
Poetry and Mink Coat leaving the others behind
They're neck and neck
Poetry and Mink Coat, Mink Coat and Poetry
Then it's Romantic End closing fast and the field
Mink Coat and Poetry, those two going at it
Poetry and Mink Coat, Mink Coat and Poetry
At the wire Poetry wins it by a whisper ...
And you said Poetry was a dog

REPRINT RIGHTS have been granted by the publishers listed below for the poems of the following poets: ELI COPPOLA: ◊ To My Child Who Is 52 Days Old ◊ A Couple ◊ Jury Duty ◊ *As Luck Would Have It,* Zeitgeist, 1993; Casual Hands, Brutal Stars, Past Things ◊ Flying ◊ Enlightenment And Muscular Dystrophy ◊ Cross Walk ◊ What A Significant Amount Of Objectivity Can Do ◊ *The Animals We Keep In City,* Zeitgeist, 1989; (Some of the poems appeared previously in Longshot and Worc's). ◊ Worknights ◊ Black Water ◊ April Fool's Day ◊ Mississippi Street ◊ *no straight lines between no two straight points,* Apathy Press, 1993. DAVID WEST: ◊ For Jane, Wherever She Is ◊ *Evil spirits & Their Secretaries,* Zeitgeist, 1989. Elegy For The Old Stud ◊ The Cleanest House In Delaware County ◊ *Elegy For The Old Stud,* Manic D Press, 1993. ◊ The Show Goes On ◊ *Signs Of Life,* Manic D Press, 1994. ◊ You Only Get This Lucky Once ◊ How Was Your Day Dear ◊ The Night Before The Art Went On ◊ You're Not Alone ◊ Let's Get Some Guns ◊ Diseases ◊ *You Only Get This Lucky Once,* Apathy Press, 1993. LAURA CONWAY: ◊ The Cities Of Madame Curie ◊ *The Cities Of Madam Curie,* Zeitgeist, 1989. ◊ The House Itself ◊ Two Who Fell Off ◊ Don't Let Me Come Home A Stranger ◊ Blues For Daddy ◊ *Bullhorn.* SPARROW 13 LAUGHINGWAND: ◊ The Queen of Shade ◊ Sixpack ◊ Trollbusters ◊ Grannybones ◊ On The Downtown Bus ◊ *The Queen Of Shade,* Zeitgeist, 1993. ◊ And Fuck The Bad Karma ◊ Larry Said ◊ *Seven Dollar Shoes,* Manic D Press, 1991. ◊ Cocaine Pantoum ◊ Bums Eat Shit ◊ *Bums Eat Shit,* Manic D Press, 1990. JULIA VINOGRAD: ◊ The Berkeley Inn ◊ *Blues For The Berkeley Inn,* Zeitgeist, 1991. ◊ Listening To The Radio ◊ *The Blind Man's Peep Show,* Zeitgeist, 1990. ◊ Kaddish For Martin Horowitz ◊ *Cannibal Consciousness,* Zeitgeist, 1983. ◊

Childhood ◊ *Blind Man's Peep Show,* Zeitgeist, 1990. ◊ In The Bookstore ◊ *Poetry S.F.,* Summer, 1988. ◊ For My Tree In Israel ◊ *Graffitti,* Zeitgeist, 1988. ◊ The Sparechangers Came From Outer Space ◊ *Horn Of Empty,* Zeitgeist, 1988. ◊ For The Young Men Who Died Of Aids ◊ *Street Samurai,* Zeitgeist, 1989. ◊ Ginsberg ◊ Scarecrow ◊ *Lonely Machines,* Zeitgeist, 1992. ◊ My Own Epitaph ◊ *Paper Television,* Zeitgeist, 1993. ◊ In The Bookstore ◊ *Poetry S.F.,* Summer, 1988. ◊ Halloween Poem For My Mother ◊ *Street Scenes,* Cal-Syl, 1987. ZOE ROSENFELD: ◊ Scapegoat ◊ The Red Dress Story ◊ Motel ◊ Fortune Teller ◊ The End ◊ *Swarm Of Flies,* Blue Beetle, 1993. DANIELLE WILLIS: ◊ I'm No Good At Getting Rid Of People ◊ Pigbaby ◊ The Killer ◊ Breakfast In The Flesh District ◊ The Methedrine Dollhouse ◊ Job Hunting ◊ Kicking Omewenne ◊ The Awful Truth ◊ *Dogs In Lingerie,* Zeitgeist, 1990. (Zeitgeist credits some of her work as appearing in *Taste Of Latés, Tantrum, Screw, On Our Backs, My Comrade/Sister, Long Shot, IAO Core,* and *Bullhorn.*) Pigbaby, I'm No Good At Getting Rid Of People, and Breakfast In The Flesh District were originally published in Hydraulic Press chapbooks. DAVID LERNER: ◊ The Crucifixion of Johnny Carson ◊ Mein Kampf ◊ The Heart ◊ *I Want A New Gun,* Zeitgeist, 1988. ◊ Five Dildos, Not Six ◊ Hold On Tight ◊ For C.B. ◊ *Pray Like The Hunted,* Zeitgeist, 1990. ◊ America Is ◊ 18th & Broadway ◊ *Why Rimbaud Went To Africa,* Zeitgeist, 1989. ◊ The Long Walk ◊ *Bullhorn.* VAMPYRE MIKE KASSEL: ◊ Going For The Low Blow ◊ Blues Walking Like A Man ◊ Dead Girl ◊ *Going For The Low Blow,* Zeitgeist, 1989. ◊ I Was A Teenage Godzilla ◊ Why I Don't Buy *Hustler* ◊ Death Warmed Over ◊ *Wild Kingdom,* Zeitgeist, 1992. ◊ Death Warmed Over ◊ Fuck The Homeless ◊ Cable From The Bunker Of The Last Unrepentant Rocker To The Ghost Of Jim Morrison ◊ Poetically Incorrect ◊ *I Want To Kill Everything,* Zeitgeist, 1990. (Some of the poems appeared in *Bullhorn*). MAURA O'CONNOR: ◊ Survival ◊ Gravity ◊ The Wind ◊ The Hummingbird Graveyard ◊ *The Hummingbird Graveyard,* Zeitgeist, 1992. ◊ Love Poem ◊ *Mercy Hates His Job,* Mel Thompson, 1990. ◊ For L. ◊ 12 Days Of Rain ◊ *Bullhorn,* v5 #1, 1992. KEN DIMAGGIO: ◊ Slouching Towards The Great American Convalescent Home ◊ *Horsemen Of The Apocalypse,* Cyborg, 1991. BUCKY SINISTER: ◊ Venice Beach Strays ◊ *Twelve Bowls Of Glass,* Manic D Press, 1990. ◊ Running The Gauntlet ◊ *Asphalt Rivers,* Manic D Press, 1991. NANCY DEPPER: ◊ Phil Vincent ◊ Hamlet Mouth ◊ *Bodies Of Work,* Manic D Press, 1990. ◊ Girl's-Eye ◊ Other Needles ◊ Hopefully Not In Memory Of D. ◊ *Bullhorn.* Q.R. HAND: ◊ Four Takes From A Short And Personal History Of Summer ◊ *The Black Scholar,* Sept/Oct 1985. ◊ How Sweet It Is ◊ Capricorn ◊ *I Speak To The Poet In Man,* Jukebox Press, 1985. JOIE COOK: ◊ Now That Marriage Is Back ◊ That Day At Laguna Honda ◊ 850 Bryant ◊ My Body Is A War Toy ◊ *My Body Is A War Toy,* Zeitgeist Press, 1990. ◊ The Poet's Extinction ◊ *Acts Of Submission,* Manic D Press, 1990; & *Signs Of Life,* Manic D Press, 1994; & *No Cash For Color TV's,* Gorton Press, 1984. ◊ Explanation No. 937 ◊ *Bullhorn.* ◊ Everybody's Darling ◊ Writing From The Spoken Word ◊ *Lust For Life,* Mel Thompson Publishing, 1993. ◊ Remissions Of Grandeur ◊ *Poetry Quarterly,* Summer, 1988. JACK MICHELINE: ◊ Hiding Places ◊ Grant & Green ◊ Zero Is Nothing ◊ *Outlaw Of The Lowest Planet,* Zeitgeist, 1993 BANA WITT: ◊ I Cannot Find You Annie ◊ *Compass In An Armored Car,* Zeitgeist, 1988. ◊ Wake Me Up ◊ Thorazine And Sunglasses ◊ Shrimping ◊ *Eclipse Of Reason,* Roadkill Press, 1994. ◊ Sacrificial Blonde ◊ Crow ◊ Tell Me ◊ *Bullhorn.* MEL THOMPSON: ◊ The Ambulance ◊ Cyborg Productions, 1991. DANIEL HIGGS: ◊ The Exploding Parable ◊ *The Mouth Of Union,* Cyborg, 1991. KIM NICOLINI: ◊ True Story ◊ Dirt, *Self-Published,* 1992 ◊ Fall Of The '70s, Or Sloe Gin Fizz ◊ Hotel Psychosynopsis ◊ *Bullhorn.* DEBORAH LEE PAGAN: ◊ The Next Voice You Hear ◊ *An Army Of One,* Blue Beetle, 1992 ALAN KAUFMAN: ◊ Who Are We? ◊ House Of Strangers ◊ Kuwait ◊ *American Cruiser,* Zeitgeist, 1990. KATHLEEN WOOD: ◊ Gregory ◊ Dan ◊ Bob The Dead Poet ◊ The Wino, The Junkie, And The Lord ◊ Mission Street Peach ◊ *Wino, Junkie, And The Lord,* Zeitgeist, 1990. ◊ Enlightenment ◊ Tenderloin Rose ◊ *Tenerloin Rose,* Zeitgeist, 1989. DAVID GOLLUB: ◊ God Comes Cheap In East Palo Alto ◊

My Heart When It's A Whale ◊ *Special Effects*, Zeitgeist, 1992. DOMINQUE LOWELL: ◊ Women Are Hungry ◊ Bitch ◊ When The Bitch Puts On Aretha ◊ Sugar Daddy ◊ *Bitch*, Grace St. Press, 1993. ◊ An Oliver Stone Movie ◊ A Poem I Swore I'd Never Write ◊ Another Job Bites The Dust ◊ *Noise*, Cyborg, 1991. ◊ Not Doing My Laundry Or Cleaning My Room ◊ *Pile*, Grace St. Press, 1991. ◊ Work has also appeared in *Bullhorn*. MICHELLE TEA: ◊ Go Kiss Go ◊ For My Nana ◊ *Tripping On Labia*, Mass Extinction Press, 1994. BRUCE ISAACSON: ◊ Single In My 30s ◊ *Love Affairs With Barely Anybody In Them*, Zeitgeist, 1990. ◊ Love Poem For The Others ◊ *Bad Dog Blues*, Zeitgeist, 1988. WHITMAN MCGOWAN: ◊ Poetry In The 9th ◊ *Fessenden Review, 3/88*.

COVER DESIGN: Joseph Abbati
PAGE DESIGN: Samuel Jennings
PHOTO CREDITS: Richard Gibson: rear cover (at Cafe Babar), & all group shots inside Cafe Babar, & portrait shots of Danielle , Vampire Mike, David Lerner, Bruce. Front cover- & related photos: Alan Allen, taken at Musee Mechanique, (below Cliff House in San Francisco). Dominique – Henry Diltz; Eli – Silke vom Bauer; q.r. hand – Marvin Lichtner; Bana – John Peques; Julia – A. Sienart; Maura – D. Vinograd; Alan Kaufman – Margaret Casey; Alan Allen – Ginger; Laura – J. Cook; Zoe – self-portrait in photo booth.

THANKS TO THE FOLLOWING:
Bruce Isaacson, publisher, Zeitgeist Press
Jennifer Joseph, publisher, Manic D Press
Melvin Thompson, publisher, Blue Beetle & Cyborg
Paul Crespeli, publisher, Mass Extinction Press
David Gollub, publisher, *Bullhorn*
Steven Parr, Grace St. Press
Tommy Divanti, Apathy Press

<>

DAVID LERNER & JULIA VINOGRAD & ALAN ALLEN – EDS; INTRO – RICHARD SILBERG

New American Underground Poetry

vol. 1: the babarians of san francisco — poets from hell

What the critics say

"[Poets] meeting at Cafe Babar are the 'Babarians'. [These] new San Francisco poets love to attack the established social order, [they] are the incursion of poetry into popular culture!"
– **Modern Maturity**

"Subversive!"
– **Der Speigel**

"They join the ranks of Ginsberg, Ferlinghetti, Corso!"
– **S.F. Chronicle**

"Best poets in America today! ... crucible of spoken-word! ... cradle of American avant-garde! ... keepers of the flame! – poets doing poetry before it caught the public eye!"
– **Bay Guardian**

Dominique is very popular in S.F. & Bonn

POETRY FLASH – Eli Coppola – *"Tender; Fierce honesty; Intimate."* Laura Conway – *"Prophetic."* Bana Witt – *"Flamboyant."* David Lerner – *"Clever-savage rap"* & **FACT SHEET 5** – *"Ezra Pound of the Babar scene."* **S.F. CHRONICLE** – Nancy Depper is *"a shoustopper."* **DER SPEIGEL** – His [Alan Kaufman's] work is like mixing echoes of Angela Davis with subversive pop music." **S.F. WEEKLY** – Maura O'Connor – *"The fragile spirit of William Butler Yeats with an ability to finesse great emotional rawness; impressive."* Bruce Isaacson – *"Blends intellectual precision with intuitive grasp and the mysteries of emotion."* Mel C. Thompson – *"Skeus our fears and ruthlessly scrapes away at them to expose a layer of stark horror & keeps scraping."* Bucky Sinister – *"Punkish ... mischief & unpretentiousness."* **S.F. BAY GUARDIAN** – Julia Vinograd – *"Embodies the spirit & constancy of the poetic heart; contemplative & consistent, a solid spiritual conscience."* Daniel Higgs – *"Drives language to the cliff of pure song – other-worldly lines that defy linguistic gravity."* Vampyre Mike Kassell – *"Heavy metal magick & punk style; enormously entertaining."* Dominique Lowell – *"The Janis Joplin of spoken-word."* Alan Kaufman – *"Avatar of Lenny Bruce, Walt Whitman & Jackie Gleason."* **S.F. EXAMINER** – Danielle Willis – *"... as normal as the kid next door – if your neighbor happens to be a vampire-identified dominatrix lesbian Satanist stripper who loves transvestite men –[she] drips with venom."*

A NEW KIND OF ANTHOLOGY SERIES ◇ (Major poets have 15-20 pgs of poetry)

ISBN 1-41205270-X